Healing Trauma

The Power of Group Treatment
for People With Intellectual Disabilities

Nancy J. Razza and Daniel J. Tomasulo

AMERICAN PSYCHOLOGICAL ASSOCIATION
WASHINGTON, DC

KH

Published by
American Psychological Association
750 First Street, NE
Washington, DC 20002
www.apa.org

To order
APA Order Department
P.O. Box 92984
Washington, DC 20090-2984
Tel: (800) 374-2721
Direct: (202) 336-5510
Fax: (202) 336-5502
TDD/TTY: (202) 336-6123
Online: www.apa.org/books/
E-mail: order@apa.org

In the U.K., Europe, Africa, and the Middle East, copies may be ordered from
American Psychological Association
3 Henrietta Street
Covent Garden, London
WC2E 8LU England

Typeset in Goudy by World Composition Services, Inc., Sterling, VA

Printer: Sheridan Books, Ann Arbor, MI
Cover Designer: Berg Design, Albany, NY
Technical/Production Editor: Kristen S. Boye

The opinions and statements published are the responsibility of the authors, and such opinions and statements do not necessarily represent the policies of the American Psychological Association.

Library of Congress Cataloging-in-Publication Data

Razza, Nancy J.
    Healing trauma : the power of group treatment for people with intellectual disabilities / by Nancy J. Razza and Daniel J. Tomasulo.
        p. cm.
    Includes bibliographical references and index.
    ISBN 1-59147-160-5 (alk. paper)
    1. People with mental disabilities—Mental health services. 2. Group psychotherapy.
3. Post-traumatic stress disorder—Treatment. 4. Sex offenders—Mental health services.
5. Adult child sexual abuse victims—Rehabilitation. I. Tomasulo, Daniel J. II. Title.

RC451.4.M47R397   2005
616.89'152—dc22   2004003932

British Library Cataloguing-in-Publication Data
A CIP record is available from the British Library.

Printed in the United States of America
First Edition

12/30/04

To Jacqueline Siroka, ACSW, TEP, and Robert Siroka, PhD, TEP,
our mentors and friends, on whose tall shoulders we stand;
and to Devon, gift of His grace, for all the joy.

CONTENTS

ACKNOWLEDGMENTS

The interactive–behavioral therapy (IBT) model of group psycho-therapy has grown out of many years of work with people with intellectual disabilities. This work was conducted with the support of two key agencies: the YAI/National Institute for People With Disabilities (NIPD) in New York City, and the Arc of Monmouth in Tinton Falls, New Jersey.

YAI/NIPD was instrumental in bringing our group treatment approach to hundreds of people with intellectual disabilities through the creation of a professional training video in 1990, in addition to monthly staff training and supervision workshops on conducting IBT groups that have been on-going for more than 15 years. Additionally, YAI/NIPD has invited us to present on the IBT model at their annual international conference each year since its inception. We are indebted to Joel Levy, Philip Levy, Perry Samowitz, and Jerry Weinstock at YAI/NIPD for the foundation they pro-vided us and for their ongoing, unwavering support.

In 1990, with the help of a grant from the Robert Wood Johnson Foundation, the Arc of Monmouth created an Ambulatory Care Center for people with intellectual disabilities. Three years later the Robert Wood Johnson Foundation awarded the center a grant to provide mental health services to people with intellectual disabilities, with specific funding for services that would address sexual abuse issues in this clientele. Leone Murphy, director of the Ambulatory Care Center since its inception, and Deborah Trub Wherlen, then executive director of the Arc of Monmouth along with Mary Scott, the Arc's current director, were instrumental in securing these grants. The New Jersey Division of Developmental Disabilities has provided ongoing financial support to the program each successive year. Leone Murphy, a clinical nurse practitioner and dedicated advocate for people with intellectual disabilities, has maintained steadfast administrative support for our work and, in addition, has cofacilitated countless group sessions over the past 12 years.

In 2000, the New Jersey Psychological Association (NJPA) Foundation awarded a grant to the Arc of Monmouth's Ambulatory Care Center, funding a practicum placement for a doctoral student in clinical psychology. Through this funding we were able to provide a future psychologist with experiential training in the intricacies of treating people with intellectual disabilities. The commitment of monies to fund a practicum student at our site marked the first such effort on the part of the NJPA to address the needs of people with intellectual disabilities. As NJPA Foundation members became familiar with our work, their awareness of the needs of this underserved population grew. NJPA Foundation president, Jack Lagos, invited our practicum student, Christine Hudson, to address the luncheon meeting of NJPA's spring 2001 conference to speak to the NJPA membership about her experience. The Foundation has since awarded the Arc of Monmouth a second grant so that we would have another doctoral student for the school year beginning in August 2002.

There have been other important sources of support as well. In August 1998, we presented a continuing education workshop on the IBT model at the American Psychological Association (APA) annual convention. This workshop was the first continuing education workshop at APA's annual national convention devoted exclusively to providing psychotherapy to people with intellectual disabilities. It was very exciting for us to connect with psychologists from around the United States who shared our zeal for serving people with intellectual disabilities. We conducted a second continuing education workshop on the model at APA's annual convention in 1999 and a third at the 2002 convention.

Anne DesNoyers Hurley, editor-in-chief of *Mental Health Aspects of Developmental Disabilities*, the first and only journal exclusively devoted to the mental health treatment of people with intellectual disabilities, has championed the scientific development of treatment techniques for people with intellectual disabilities. The journal, now a peer-reviewed publication indexed in a range of abstracts, originated as *The Habilitative Mental Health-care Newsletter*. Dr. Hurley has invited our contribution of articles for many years and joined us in presenting our work at APA. She generously gave her time and expertise to read and edit drafts of this book. In addition, Al Pfadt, at the New York State Institute for Basic Research in Developmental Disabilities, and Ellen Keller, of YAI/NIPD, generated some of the first publications on the IBT model. We would also like to thank Rob Fletcher, founder and executive director of the NADD who has consistently supported our work.

Before closing this section, we would like to acknowledge Geraldo Rivera, whose adventurous journalism raised the consciousness of the American public to degrading and abusive institutional practices that had prevailed for decades. Without the legislative change and deinstitutionalization movement that followed, the evolution of treatment described in this book would not have been possible.

Finally, and with our deepest gratitude, we are indebted to the hundreds of people with intellectual disabilities who have opened their lives to us, trusted us, and ultimately taught us to be better therapists.

Healing Trauma

INTRODUCTION

This book is the product of many years of work with people who have intellectual disabilities. Our treatment methods have evolved from actual experience with people who have intellectual disabilities as much as from the growing literature in this area.

Our goal in creating this book is to present a clear way of understanding and working with people who have intellectual disabilities in addition to psychological disorders, and to share our hard-won lessons with other clinicians. Toward this end, we have used a number of case examples. The vast majority of these examples present an actual client with whom we have worked, not an amalgam of similar individuals nor a fantasized creation based on a prototype. Our thinking is that by using real cases, each with its own unique set of circumstances, symptoms, and reactions to treatment, we afford the reader the closest possible look at the workings of the therapeutic process.

We have changed the names of patients, along with details that might contribute to identifying them. Also, the terms *patient* and *client* are written interchangeably throughout the book. In our experience with professionals and paraprofessionals, we have found that both terms are regularly used. We avoid the terms *consumer* or *served individual* because we find them awkward. We use first names rather than initials or conventions such as "Mr. A." to convey a feeling for each person's individuality. Similarly, in our group sessions, members as well as group leaders generally address each

3

other using first names. (Some professionals may prefer to use their formal titles; we do not necessarily recommend against this.) When our writing references an indefinite individual, we alternate between the use of *he* and *she* to avoid the awkward *he/she* construct.

We use the term *people with intellectual disabilities* to refer to people who have diagnoses of mental retardation because this term seems to be gaining acceptance in the literature at this time, at least in the United States. The term *developmental disabilities* had been the standard for many years. But we feel the change from developmental to intellectual better clarifies and describes the nature of the condition, and so we have opted for its use throughout this book. In some cases, we use terms such as *people with mental retardation* or *people with cognitive intellectual disabilities* in reference to the same population. Often we use these terms when referencing literature that has that particular terminology.

We use the term *staff* to refer to direct support professionals, that is, human service employees who work in each of the many positions that exist for the support of individuals with intellectual disabilities. These include job coaches who place, train, and support individuals in community work sites as well as those who supervise them in sheltered work settings; day program personnel from the full range of vocational, prevocational, and mental health/mental retardation programs; and residential service providers from group homes and supervised apartment services. We do not use the term *staff* for sponsors. Sponsors are private families in the community who take in adults with intellectual disabilities and are paid by the state, a system similar to foster care for children.

Our choice of the word *staff* reflects the fact that this term is by far the most commonly used by our clients and ourselves in everyday conversation. Who the key staff people are, however, does vary by individual. For some, it may be their group home manager to whom they feel the most connected, for others it may be their vocational counselor at their sheltered workshop, for others, a job coach, and so on.

Finally, we would like to address the issue of gender in the cases we present. We most often refer to a survivor as *she*, and an offender as *he*. And while most survivors are female and most offenders are male, some of our female survivors have also committed offenses, and some of our male offenders are also survivors. As we began our work with this population, we decided to run separate groups for men and women, observing that, for many people, there is a greater comfort level in discussing sexual issues with same-sex peers. Our groups for women more frequently center on survivor issues, whereas our groups for men more often explore issues related to offense problems, but aspects of each inevitably arise in both. (We also maintain one "mixed" group, with both men and women, because of the benefits available with this degree of heterogeneity. Members of this group most often have referral problems not directly related to sexual abuse or offense, though later disclosures sometimes reveal issues of this type. We have been able to work effectively even with sexual issues in this group once the individuals have come to feel safe in the setting. In the broader field of group psychotherapy, there is much discussion regarding the pros and cons of this issue, far beyond what we can present here. Readers interested in further exploration of issues of group heterogeneity versus homogeneity are referred to Yalom, 1995).

ORGANIZATION OF THE BOOK

This book aims to equip the reader with a core set of therapeutic techniques that have demonstrated efficacy in treating people with intellectual disabilities and psychological disorders. To this end, we start with a historical review of related treatment issues and build to the theoretical rationale for a specialized model of group psychotherapy, the interactive–behavioral therapy (IBT) model. The mid-section of the book is dense with illustrations of actual group sessions and procedures. For readers intent on learning and implementing these skills, reading each of the chapters will enhance your competence. Do not be deterred by the target populations named in the titles. Each chapter will take you further into the workings of the group process. The model is carried out in the same way with offenders, trauma and sexual abuse survivors, and members with no (known) trauma history who display psychological symptoms. We have successfully treated many such members with symptoms of depression, agitation, anxiety, self-injurious behavior, and physically aggressive behavior. We break down the chapters by population because that is the way we conduct our groups. Moreover, experience has taught us that a very enriched group experience can occur with something of a range in the membership. That is, our groups for survivors generally include members with and without known sexual abuse and a range of diagnosable psychological disorders. Our groups for offenders typically contain members with aggressive and nonaggressive sexual offense behaviors, other aggressive behaviors, and, again, a range of diagnosable psychological disorders.

We would like also to offer encouragement to those clinicians who may feel some discomfort at the prospect of group as opposed to individual therapy. We discuss the unique value of group at length but would like to share with you our experience in conducting numerous training workshops over the years. Professionals who have gone on to implement group treatment have often reported back to us that they were surprised how productive and fulfilling they found their group experience to be. Their comfort level grew much more easily than they expected.

We round out the book with specific recommendations concerning the initial interview and with termination. We devote a chapter to individual treatment because of the unique needs it fills. Finally, we explore a number of typical problems and questions that frequently arise with new trainees.

Part I: Introduction to Psychotherapeutic Work With People With Intellectual Disabilities opens with a chapter about a young woman with cerebral palsy. She uses a wheelchair for ambulation and has mild mental retardation. The story of her experience in psychotherapy is presented, including her childhood sexual and emotional trauma, as well as key features of the therapeutic process with people who have significant impairments. Chapter 2 presents a summary of the relevant literature, with specific reference to the relationship between trauma and psychopathology. Sexual victimization, traumatization, and sexual offense behavior among people with intellectual disabilities are explored. Treatment methods proposed in the literature are discussed, along with current thinking regarding the prevention of sexual abuse among members of this population.

Part II: The Interactive–Behavioral Therapy Model and Its Applications begins with a chapter detailing the foundations of the IBT group model, including a brief presentation of its theoretical underpinnings. The unique contributions of the group psychotherapy process, in addition to the use of action methods, are highlighted with particular emphasis on the value of these techniques in treating people with intellectual disabilities. Chapter 4 presents the application of IBT group treatment with survivors of trauma and sexual abuse. The reader is taken through the group treatment process with the help of actual case examples of women with intellectual disabilities who have undergone this treatment approach. Strategies for determining patient eligibility and group composition are described. Specific details of the group process are presented, outlining the sequential stages of an actual group. Psychodramatic and group process techniques are detailed. In addition, group rules, such as safety and confidentiality, are discussed. Chapter 5 provides the opportunity to take a close look at the workings of a treatment group for men with intellectual disabilities who have committed sexual offenses. As in chapter 4, actual cases are presented along with specific how-to's for novice group leaders. Important issues in evaluating group candidates, establishing group rules, and planning terminations are discussed.

The IBT model is easily adapted for use as an abuse avoidance training vehicle. Chapter 6 is devoted to a presentation of this use of the model. A discussion of the distinction between therapy groups based on psychodrama and training groups based on sociodrama is given. Specific guidelines for use in establishing and running avoidance training groups are provided.

Part III: Treatment: Modalities, Processes, Initiation, and Termination begins with a chapter illustrating the initial interview process (chap. 7). Individuals with intellectual disabilities sometimes pose special problems for the interview process: Speech impairments, limited verbal comprehension, and poor attention span are just some of the conditions typically compounding the assessment. Furthermore, individuals with intellectual disabilities are rarely self-referred and may enter the interview feeling anxious or confused. This chapter guides the reader through an interviewing approach geared toward the special needs of people with intellectual disabilities. Consideration is given to such issues as obtaining background information, addressing the concerns of referring family members or staff, and involving caregivers in the treatment process. Chapter 8 reviews individual treatment techniques described in the literature and considers conditions in which individual treatment might be the method of choice either as an alternative or as a warm-up to group treatment. We also portray ways in which psychodramatic techniques can enhance individual psychotherapy. Chapter 9 addresses problems that invariably arise as the group process unfolds. For example, how does the facilitator respond to reported breaches of confidentiality that cannot be verified? How should monopolizing or disruptive behavior be managed? Frequently asked questions by trainees who have started their own groups are also addressed. These include such issues as coping with violence or physical aggression among members, as well as with nonviolent interpersonal conflict. In chapter 10 we explore the process of planning and preparing for termination, considering cases that involve risk of harmful behavior to others as well as possible self-harm. In addition, we address managing ill-timed and unplanned terminations. Finally, in chapter 11, we review data on the prevalence of mental retardation and common psychological disorders.

Many people have shared their stories so that otherwise abstract therapeutic techniques could be brought to life in these pages. You will get to know some of the individuals quite well. We, as therapists, have learned from them, and they from us. We are excited for you to join us and begin a discovery process of your own.

I

INTRODUCTION TO PSYCHOTHERAPEUTIC WORK WITH PEOPLE WITH INTELLECTUAL DISABILITIES

1

AN INTRODUCTORY TALE: THE CASE OF MARTINA

Life is either a daring adventure or nothing.

—Helen Keller

It has become commonplace to talk about marginalized groups: racial, ethnic, or economic factions cut off from the mainstream; the trivialized, underserved, or disempowered. But there are some fascinating things in the margins, stories untold, and perspectives unimaginable from center page. As philosopher and anthropologist Mary Catherine Bateson (1994) accurately noted, by looking at life from the sidelines of adjacent perspectives, we gain insights we could not have achieved from our singular view.

This is a story from the sidelines. It is the story of Martina, the story of a life lived almost entirely in the margins, so to speak, of human experience; the life of a woman with mental retardation. It is also the story of how a therapeutic group experience can straddle the boundary lines that otherwise keep some of us isolated and in pain. While the remainder of this book is devoted to teaching the reader *how* to conduct psychotherapy groups, the story of Martina reminds us *why* we must do so.

In many respects, Martina's case is not very different from that of many psychotherapy patients. Her childhood, replete with the abuse, neglect, and abandonment so familiar to clinicians' ears, led her into an adulthood in which her tortures played themselves out in waves of anger and depression, suicidality and rage. Martina had had two psychiatric hospitalizations prior to our first meeting, each brought about by suicidal threats. Following these hospitalizations, she was referred to the hospital's outpatient clinic for "medication maintenance," the only treatment considered "appropriate" for her at the time.

Among the numerous ways in which people with intellectual disabilities have been marginalized, sadly, is by the historic failure of the mental health profession to recognize and treat them. Until fairly recently, people with intellectual disabilities were routinely denied psychotherapy. Clinicians assumed people with mental retardation did not have the requisite abilities to engage in the therapeutic process. If this had merely been the misconception of a few individuals, things would not have been so bad. Unfortunately, however, it was the prevailing view of the mental health profession for decades.

When Martina and I (Nancy Razza) first met, she rolled herself into the room in her wheelchair and looked up at me shyly. She had cerebral palsy, which had left her with mild mental retardation as well as partial paralysis, necessitating the use of a wheelchair. She was reluctant to say much at first but gave the impression of being more uncertain than unwilling. She responded positively to my explanation of the voluntary nature of psychotherapy and the parameters of confidentiality.

In the earliest stage of her therapy, Martina could only talk with ease about immediate concerns involving her living situation. In part this was because of the fear of trusting others she brought to the therapy relationship. It also, however, allowed her to avoid focusing on overwhelmingly painful experiences from her past. At any rate, we began there. We explored her unhappiness with her present home, which consisted of a room in a "sponsor's" house, that is, the home of a private family who agrees to take in a person with intellectual disabilities in much the same way a foster family takes in a child. Many adults with intellectual disabilities live in the community in this way since the advent of deinstitutionalization and the decline of funding for alternatives such as group homes and supported apartments.

At the sponsor's home Martina felt very alone—a feeling, I later learned, made all the more intolerable by too many premature experiences with it. To Martina, being alone meant being abandoned, rejected, and unsafe. I did not begin to understand the power of these feelings until Martina was able to reveal her childhood experiences, much later in therapy. She described having a decent set of rooms in a remodeled basement, but, unable to negotiate the stairs, she could not join the rest of the household for meals or evening TV. She was brought her meals and ate alone. She rarely got out on weekends. She missed life in the group home, where meals were made and eaten together and weekend social activities were regularly organized by support staff.

Eventually she explained that she had graduated from the group home to a supported apartment, which had been her goal. There she lived in an apartment of her own, in a wheelchair-accessible building under the auspices of an agency serving individuals with both physical disabilities and mental retardation, such as herself. She had enjoyed the balance between independence and connection the arrangement afforded her, living as she did among neighbors who were also her peers. She had lost this apartment, for reasons that she could not seem to make clear in her early sessions. The pain around the loss of this apartment was enormous, however, and she would frequently break down in tears when discussing it. She eventually disclosed, amid wrenching sobs, that she had lost the apartment because her mother had repeatedly insisted Martina "help her out" financially. She would show up when Martina received her monthly SSI check and insist on cashing it and keeping a good portion for herself. Martina reported that she could not make her mother understand that her budget for this apartment was figured down to the penny. Her mother would point out all she had done in her life to help her, and though Martina's relationship with her mother was riddled with both very good and very bad exchanges, the fact that the good was in there at all made it a powerful contrast to her other family experiences. Martina was filled with guilt toward her mother, and horror at the same time that she would take from her what she knew she needed to live. Eventually she lost the apartment because the staff concluded she could not handle her finances, and she was "placed" with a sponsor who received and cashed her check for her. She had never told anyone of her mother's role.

The first round of Martina's therapy, then, became her finding the strength to bring this information to her case manager and to ask for another opportunity to live in a supported apartment. She eventually was able to do this, coming to terms with her feelings regarding her mother and the pain and shame she felt. Her sense of self improved considerably, and she ultimately succeeded in getting back into an apartment program.

It was clear that one of the factors that contributed to Martina's depression was a pattern of extremely inhibited self-expression. Martina had felt victimized by her mother for a long time but had been unable to speak, even when having done so might have saved her apartment. She had been locked in a pattern of secrecy that she had felt powerless to get herself out of. After having identified this pattern, and the dramatic improvement she made once she felt supported enough to speak, we urged Martina to become a member of a new therapy group we had begun for women with intellectual disabilities and psychiatric disorders. It was with considerable anxiety that Martina began the group. Although her participation tended to be limited to fairly circumscribed self-disclosures, she was readily engaged in the problems and pain others presented, and she grew increasingly vocal through efforts to give others support. As time went on, she became more and more assertive regarding her own needs and was able to assert herself at her work and with her residential staff. This fundamental change led to a greatly improved sense of self. Martina eventually decided to "graduate" from therapy, feeling fairly good about herself and understanding that she could request help again at any point should the need arise.

Unfortunately, her return to therapy was nowhere near so tidy. Approximately a year and a half after she ended treatment, a referral came to us through her apartment supervisor. Martina had been brought to the emergency room, severely depressed once again and voicing suicidal intent.

Martina reentered the group, connecting easily this time thanks to the safety she had found in her previous experience with us. She began to describe feeling disrespected by the apartment staff, a feeling that completely overwhelmed her. She felt trapped in her living situation. She saw the apartment staff as cruel, unfeeling jailers who did not have an ounce of compassion for the people living there. She felt she had been stripped of her rights, disregarded, and ridiculed. With Martina's permission we began some dialogue with the apartment staff manager, who appeared to be a caring human service professional. She very firmly believed, however, in a strict interpretation of agency policy and, as such, incurred Martina's wrath. In addition to this investigation, however, we felt we needed to help Martina pursue a deeper search into herself that might account for the dramatic reemergence of her depression. We worked persistently to prevent her from lapsing back into her previous pattern of guarded self-disclosure. With careful questioning we encouraged Martina to look again at her life experiences, to see if she could identify other experiences in which she felt disrespected and victimized. We already knew from her previous treatment that she had felt victimized by her mother and had cooperated in maintaining a long period of secrecy about that victimization. Perhaps she had been involved in other victimizations as well.

With tremendous effort, Martina was able to begin the work of connecting her reaction to these "abuses" with those abuses she had never before been able to put into words. She told us of the girl she used to be; a girl born into a poor home in a very rural area. The girl's mother was miserable and alone, except for her own angry mother with whom they lived. Her impoverished mother carried the girl around to doctors and hospitals, but no treatment or surgery could make her walk. The girl's father rarely visited. When he did, he hurried through the house, past the girl, and straight to her sister, whom he would take with him to visit his mother. The girl was silent, overcome with the horrifying knowledge that she would never be good enough to deserve his attention. A few other men came and went through the house, and a little brother was born. The girl's sister and brother got out a lot. The girl would watch them running with friends, dragging herself by her arms out to the front porch to watch until she could see them no longer. She cried to herself. Then, when the girl was age 10, her mother left for the city, a place where she promised to take the girl and her sister and brother some day, when she had made enough money.

Now Grandma was in charge. She would not tolerate the girl's "laziness." She set her to work, to "learn." She would be left alone in her room for hours, assigned the task of correctly braiding her hair or writing her name. She eventually managed the braiding, but never the writing. She tried very hard, though; she dreaded the "switch."

The girl hated her name most of all; it was long and tricky. She would try to copy the letters, but they never came out right. Her grandmother would rip up her papers in anger. She would berate her for her stupidity. "It's like this! What's the matter with you!" More papers would be slammed in front of her, followed by the slamming of the door. The girl would spend another day alone with the letters that wouldn't come out right.

But the day she hated most was Sunday, church day. The girl's grandmother always went to church, taking the girl's sister and brother with her. The girl begged to go with her. But the answer was always "no"—a "no" with annoyance: She should know better than to think her grandmother could still carry her around at her age. She would cry on the floor until she got sick. She hated her legs, and her life.

Then the worst part. Her cousin Edward at the window. Climbing in. Taking her clothes off. Pain and shame. Sometimes bleeding. Sometimes in her bedroom; sometimes in the bathroom, clutching at the sink. "Don't tell; you'll only get in trouble. You know what Grandma will do." She wanted with all her heart to tell, but Edward was right, of course. This would just be another thing to make Grandma mad at her.

Those years, ages 10 to 15, passed with a terrible slowness. But, to her amazement, her mother came back for her. She brought the girl and her siblings and grandmother to the city, where she had an apartment and a job. The girl reveled in her freedom from her abuser but never found herself able to tell her mother what she had experienced. She became angry, exploding into verbal tirades that surprised her family and even herself at times. She was especially angry with her mother but did not quite know why. Eventually, she got connected with a human service agency for people with intellectual disabilities and ended up in a group home.

Now we were back to where our journey with Martina had started. She had brought the girl to us; the girl she now carried around with her, not in any dissociated way, but in a very connected way, still powerfully feeling her pain. She presented her in detail over many sessions.

The group Martina was in consisted of a number of women with intellectual disabilities who had also experienced various forms of sexual abuse. The expansion in our program had resulted in many new patients, and many of these individuals had experienced some sort of sexual victimization. Martina's ability to disclose at this significantly deeper level was certainly aided by the presence of other members who were able to disclose their sexual abuses, along with the experience of observing that these disclosures were met with respect and compassion. In addition, there was the advantage of Martina's prior experience of success in the group, the presence of the same two group facilitators, and even some of the same members.

Martina's sense of safety in the group continued to grow. She came to group consistently, even fighting with her cab service to make sure she was brought in on time. As Martina continued to work on recovering from her abuse, she expressed a powerful sense of shame. This sense of shame was fueled by her belief, since childhood, that the abuse was her fault. This tendency to blame oneself, and thus feel ashamed, is common in abuse and incest survivors without disabilities as well. The developing child is easily led into thinking that somehow she has done something wrong to deserve the abuse, or even that she is innately bad, and therefore deserving of maltreatment. Martina's shame centered around her disability, because that was the most prominent feature of her existence. Because she was disabled, her father, who rarely visited anyway, ignored her when he did visit; her grandmother was regularly enraged at her for being a burden and being "stupid"; and ultimately her cousin raped her repeatedly, over a period of years, because she was too "feeble" to get away. As Martina evolved in group and discussed her experiences and her beliefs with the other women, she began to consider that perhaps she was not responsible for her own abuse. She saw, in fact, that many people had failed in their responsibilities toward her, and because of those failures the abuse was able to go on.

Moreover, like so many therapy patients, Martina was almost immediately able to see how wrong other women were to blame themselves for their own abuses. Seeing the same pattern in others' lives is a benefit unique to group therapy and can be an invaluable aid in getting an individual to challenge long-held self-concepts. Martina, through her compassion toward her fellow group members' victimizations, was able to understand her own in a new way. She could easily see, for example, that Jean's victimization by her sister's live-in boyfriend was no fault of her own, and that Sue Ellen, who had been gang-raped by a group of young men on her way home from work, could not be blamed for that horror. Martina readily supported these women. She consoled them, reasoned with them, and cried with them. Ultimately, she was changed by them. She could no longer believe her own abuse was her fault either.

Eventually, Martina felt a pressing need to tell her family about the abuse, after years of feeling she had to hide it from them. She longed for their support, yet still feared their judgment. After much discussion, she decided to tell her sister. Although Martina had spent most of her childhood in bitter envy of her healthy, able-bodied sister—the same one her father gave his brief minutes of attention to—that sister had since evolved into a compassionate listener. She was clearly the safest family member to broach the issue with. When she came in to group the following week to relate the exchange, she was awestruck. "Do you know what she said?" Martina began. "She said, 'Why, that bastard! He tried that with me, too!'" The group practically applauded. Martina went on to describe the love and validation she had gotten from her sister. In time she told her brother, and with some apprehension, her mother too. Martina had found some windows she could open, after a lifetime of closed doors.

Unfortunately, Martina's experience of abuse reflects a widespread phenomenon. Recent research into this area suggests that women with intellectual disabilities are many times more likely than women without intellectual disabilities to experience sexual abuse in their lifetimes. In a later chapter we examine the available data on abuse rates and factors that are thought to account for the greater vulnerability of women with intellectual disabilities.

As for Martina, she continues in therapy. After approximately five years she has not relapsed into any severe depressive episodes, though she still struggles with her reaction to certain interpersonal encounters, particularly those with staff she perceives as controlling and uncaring. She works hard to maintain a part-time job in the community, which means a great deal to her. In group, Martina encourages new members to "open up" as she has learned to do and is a very strong advocate of the rights of people with disabilities. Although her powerful, emotional reactions to the slights and injustices of the human service system have led her into important therapeutic work, they have also shed light on some critical issues in service delivery to people with disabilities, including fine lines concerning their ability to retain some personal decision-making capacity even when dependent on such systems. Her advocacy has led to hard-won changes with regard to how her apartment staff "allow" her to plan her time and her diet and to budget her money. And although Martina is still unhappy in many ways with the apartment program in which she resides, she has a much stronger sense of herself as a person who can effect changes when needed.

Martina's progress through therapy follows the path described by trauma expert Judith Herman (1992b) in her work with individuals who have suffered long-term, chronic trauma, and suggests that the recovery process for traumatized people who also have intellectual disabilities may not be appreciably different from the process nondisabled trauma survivors undergo. These individuals frequently exhibit protracted depressions as Martina did. Herman's observations concerning the stages of recovery such individuals move through fits well with observations of Martina's recovery process. In the final stage of recovery, the individual establishes a reconnection with others—peers, family, and social groups—in new, self-affirming ways. (Note: This should not be taken to mean that healing always involves disclosing the abuse to family members, as Martina did, or to abusers. The healing path is unique to each individual, and its direction is the individual's decision alone.)

Because of her group therapy experience, Martina was able to truly open and connect with others in a safe way. Herman (1992b) has observed that those trauma survivors who make good recoveries often become highly involved in social action of some form, taking on leadership roles as advocates and volunteers in programs for battered women, rape survivors, hate-crime victims, and so on. In her apartment program, as well as in our group, Martina has taken on the role of actively encouraging other individuals to speak up for themselves, and to keep pressing their point along the appropriate administrative chain of command until they are acknowledged. She has learned by her own experience to advocate for and bring about changes in the systems that affect her life, and she is committed to helping other individuals with disabilities to do the same. Through her recovery, she has developed a sense of pride rather than shame in herself, and she encourages others to take pride in themselves and their efforts, too. In fact, Martina agreed to tell her story of abuse and recovery for a publication titled *People With Disabilities* (Hunsberger, 1999), taking particular pride in the possibility that her story might give courage to others who need to speak up and tell theirs.

Martina's life, once marked by silence and shame, is now lived out loud, and in connection to a larger whole. It is no longer contained in the margins. And while we have detailed Martina's success in this chapter, she is but one of many people with intellectual disabilities who have demonstrated that mental retardation does not mean a person is incapable of finding the strength to change, or that a person's IQ score tells us anything about her ability to heal.

Perhaps what is so remarkable about Martina's case is that it is not remarkable at all. Many people who have both intellectual disabilities and psychiatric disorders are making similar gains in therapy. And, although in its infancy, current research is beginning to provide documentation of this fact. As you read through this book, you will learn more about research that is being done on the efficacy of psychotherapy with people who have intellectual disabilities. We will also look at additional real-life examples of people with intellectual disabilities who have worked in group therapy like Martina, and you will have the opportunity to evaluate their journeys as well. Martina's therapeutic passage will be revisited in later chapters also for what it illustrates about specific factors in the therapeutic process and what Martina's experience taught us about how to improve our group techniques for participants with intellectual disabilities.

Martina's life—rooted as it is in the margins—offers us the priceless insights Bateson (1994) described, insights that individuals bound up within the lines and spaces might otherwise never know. Martina, and the many like her, are our educators, teaching us to look past the artificial red line running down the page, the line that we thought separated people with retardation from "normal" people, "poor candidates" for psychotherapy from good ones. It is an invaluable education. And education, as Bateson reminded us, is not just something we do before an experience to prepare for it; it is the essence of experience itself, an ongoing moment-to-moment process. The page is completed by the margins, and some of our greatest teachers struggle to write their own names.

2

WHAT THE LITERATURE TELLS US

To say that a particular psychiatric condition is incurable or irreversible is to say more about the state of our ignorance than about the state of the patient.

—Milton Rokeach

It is generally recognized in the field of intellectual disabilities that the mental health needs of people with mental retardation have traditionally been neglected (Charlot, Doucette, & Mezzacappa, 1993; Hurley, Pfadt, Tomasulo, & Gardner, 1996; Reiss, Levitan, & McNally, 1982). In fact, this neglect is an apparent correlate of a wide-ranging neglect for the health care of people with mental retardation. A report by former U.S. Surgeon General David Satcher (Monday Morning, 2002) declares that health care in general, across the entire spectrum of medical needs, is still sorely lacking for people with mental retardation. Satcher concluded that the U.S. health care system has "failed to respond to changes in the lives of people with mental retardation," noting that, "Even a quick glimpse at the health status of persons with mental retardation, both children and adults, reveals glaring deficiencies that must be addressed" (p. 3).

Fortunately, however, the mental health needs of people with intellectual disabilities have been drawing concern over the past two decades. An evolution in our thinking about people with intellectual disabilities has led to a growth in treatment efforts and research studies on therapeutic advances with this population (Fletcher & Dosen, 1993; see also Hurley, 1989; Nezu & Nezu, 1994; Pfadt, 1991; Prout & Strohmer, 1995; Schneider, 1986).

In 1982 the first newsletter devoted exclusively to mental health issues in people with intellectual disabilities was founded. Initially called *Psychiatric Aspects of Mental Retardation*, the publication was originated by the pioneering efforts of now-deceased Robert Sovner, along with Anne Des-Noyers Hurley and Margaret Zwilling. This was replaced in 1998 by *Mental Health Aspects of Developmental Disabilities*, a peer-reviewed journal with an international subscription base. The year 1984 saw the establishment of the National Association for the Dually Diagnosed (NADD), the first association created to address the unique needs of people with intellectual disabilities and psychological disorders. NADD, recognized as the world's leading organization devoted to the mental health needs of people with intellectual disabilities, produces a news bulletin as well as a series of titles related to dual diagnosis. It sponsors numerous training materials, educational services, and conferences each year.

In 1992 Nezu, Nezu, and Gill-Weiss put forth an ambitious volume on the subject of psychopathology in people with intellectual disabilities, including a broad-scale literature review of the existing data on prevalence rates along an extensive spectrum of psychiatric disorders. These authors noted recent growth in studying the mental health problems of this underserved population and suggested that an important change was under way. A 1998 article by Hurley, Tomasulo, and Pfadt described early literature that reported successful use of psychotherapeutic techniques with people with intellectual disabilities, countering the prevailing assumption that such efforts would fail. Hurley et al. described modifications of standard therapeutic techniques found to be successful with people with intellectual disabilities. More recently, Butz, Bowling, and Bliss (2000) conducted an extensive review of the literature on psychotherapy with people who have intellectual disabilities. They concluded that there is a need for well-defined diagnostic distinctions so that subtle signs of psychological disorders are not missed simply because a person meets the criteria for mental retardation. Butz et al. stressed that psychologists in general need to be better informed about the possibility of conducting psychotherapy with people who have intellectual disabilities. Finally, they concluded that, although not widely known, there is a growing body of research on conducting psychotherapy with people who have intellectual disabilities. They described the existing literature as limited in that it tends to be "qualitative and descriptive" (Butz et al., 2000, p. 46) but acknowledged that this limitation is common to the literature on many other aspects of psychotherapy as well, not just to that pertaining to people with intellectual disabilities.

An effort to address the need for mental health treatment for people with intellectual disabilities was put forth by Strohmer and Prout (1994) in an edited volume that provides descriptions of various therapeutic approaches for this population. The book contains a chapter presenting an overview of psychopathology in people with intellectual disabilities that is particularly useful. A team of British psychologists (Emerson, Hatton, Bromley, & Caine, 1998) published an edited volume that attempted to address many of the issues related to the provision of psychological care to people with intellectual disabilities. Noting the absence of a "comprehensive" and "practical" text, Emerson et al., together with additional contributors, created a resource that provides information on the epidemiology and causes of mental retardation, as well as on the treatment of a number of clinical issues, including sexual abuse, mental health problems, parents with intellectual disabilities, and a range of challenging behaviors. It provides specific information on British legal, human service, and health care systems. Another group of British clinicians (Kroese, Dagnan, & Loumidis, 1997) contributed an edited volume entirely devoted to cognitive–behavioral treatment approaches for people with intellectual disabilities and various psychological disorders. The importance of accurate diagnosis and treatment of psychiatric disorders in adults with intellectual disabilities is the subject of a chapter by Moss (2001). A book by Hodges (2003), also published in England, is entirely devoted to the topic of counseling for people with intellectual disabilities (referred to as learning disabilities, the British government-recommended term). Hodges provided suggestions for helping people with intellectual disabilities to explore their internal worlds, as well as suggestions for working with the many social, governmental, and family systems that support the individual's functioning.

It is important to note that recent epidemiological research has demonstrated that the prevalence of psychiatric disorders is *higher* in the intellectually disabled population than it is in the general population. The extensive review of the literature in the volume by Nezu et al. (1992), referenced earlier, suggests that adults and children with intellectual disabilities may have up to three to four times the rate of psychiatric illness that nondisabled individuals have. Similarly, a review by Nugent (1997) concluded that at least one in five, and perhaps as many as one in three, individuals with intellectual disabilities also have a psychiatric disorder. In a review of the literature on prevalence rates of psychiatric disorders, Caine and Hatton (1998) reported that for people with intellectual disabilities, studies tend to find prevalence rates of 25% to 40%. They noted, however, that in studies in which psychiatric disorders are more broadly defined to include the range of "behavioral disturbance" commonly seen in people with intellectual disabilities, prevalence rates have been reported to be as high as 80%.

The variance in these prevalence rates is in no small way related to the complexities of discerning and defining psychiatric disorders in people who have intellectual disabilities (Day, 2001). Exactly what constitutes a psychiatric disorder in an individual with mental retardation is a subject of ongoing study (Day, 2001; Nezu et al., 1992). As early as 1982, Reiss, Levitan, and Szyszko reported that symptoms of psychiatric disorders have frequently gone undetected in people with mental retardation because of a tendency on the part of professionals to attribute symptomatology to the retardation itself. In other words, genuine, clinically significant psychological symptoms have been misunderstood as mere behavioral components of cognitive deficits. Reiss and his colleagues coined the term *diagnostic overshadowing* to describe this phenomenon. Even such severe symptoms as suicide attempts have been misconstrued merely as self-abusive behavior (Kaminer, Feinstein, & Barrett, 1987). Our sensitivity to the accurate assessment of the mental health of people with intellectual disabilities has benefited greatly from continuing research, yet even the recent literature review by Butz et al. (2000), noted earlier, suggests that diagnostic overshadowing still muddies clinical understanding in general practice.

Of equal importance is our understanding of the *nature* of the psychiatric disorders experienced by people with intellectual disabilities. Despite early misunderstandings and the unfounded assumptions of many mental health professionals, people with intellectual disabilities experience the same types of psychiatric illness as their nondisabled counterparts (Charlot, 1998; Nezu et al., 1992; Nugent, 1997). Charlot's research provides descriptions of symptoms that may vary from those more commonly seen in the nondisabled population—for example, people with intellectual disabilities experiencing depression frequently talk to themselves out loud rather than ruminate silently. This literature suggests that there may be variation in the typical symptom picture of a given disorder but that the experience of the nature of the disorder (e.g., depression, anxiety, even psychoses) is inherently the same.

A broad array of factors have been found to contribute to the higher-than-average rates of psychiatric disorders experienced by people with intellectual disabilities. It is important to note that these factors have been previously established to be contributory to depression and other psychiatric disorders for people in the general population. Sadly, these factors are even more prevalent among people with intellectual disabilities. These factors, as reported in Nezu et al. (1992), include

- low levels of social support;
- poorly developed social skills;
- a sense of learned helplessness (and correspondingly low sense of self-efficacy);
- low socioeconomic level;
- increased presence of physical disabilities (especially epilepsy);
- heightened family stress;
- heightened maternal stress;
- increased likelihood of central nervous system damage;
- increased presence of reading and language dysfunctions;
- decreased opportunities to learn adaptive coping styles;

- increased likelihood of chromosomal abnormalities, metabolic diseases, and infections; and
- decreased inhibition in responding to stressful events.

Finally, to this already lengthy list we may add higher-than-average rates of exposure to sexual abuse, known to be involved in the development of a wide range of psychiatric disorders in the general population.

It is against this backdrop of evolving awareness that our treatment of psychopathology and trauma in people with intellectual disabilities is set. As we began working with larger numbers of dually diagnosed individuals, that is, people with intellectual disabilities and psychiatric disorders, we found many of them had been victims of sexual abuse. This was particularly true for the female patients. We also began to receive a large number of referrals for males who had committed some type of sexually offensive behavior.

RELATIONSHIP BETWEEN SEXUAL ABUSE AND PSYCHIATRIC ILLNESS

Research suggests that the high rate of sexual abuse issues we found in the people with psychiatric and intellectual disabilities at our facility is not unusual. In general, people with psychological disorders are much more likely than nondisordered people to have experienced some form of sexual abuse (van der Kolk, 1996). In fact, the experience of trauma of any kind (i.e., sexual abuse, battering, the witnessing of domestic violence, and the like) has been implicated in the development of a broad range of psychological disorders (Herman, 1992b; van der Kolk, 1996; Walker, 1994). Van der Kolk (1996) and Herman (1992b), both renowned for their expertise in the area of psychological trauma, have noted that it has been consistently found that the majority of psychiatric inpatients have histories of severe trauma, frequently from within their own families.

Histories of sexual abuse have been implicated in the development of posttraumatic stress disorder (PTSD), depressive disorders, anxiety disorders, eating disorders, drug and alcohol addictions, and personality disorders, in addition to the development of long-term medical complications such as gastrointestinal disorders, reproductive problems, and even psychogenic seizure disorders (Root, 1991; van der Kolk, 1996; Walker, 1994). A recent study (Matich-Maroney, 2003) assessed the effects of sexual abuse on adults with intellectual disabilities by evaluating known victims for symptoms typically reported in the general sexual abuse literature. Eighteen adults with mental retardation were evaluated, along with 25 matched control groups with mental retardation and no known history of sexual abuse.

Compared with control groups, the adults with mental retardation who had experienced sexual abuse had higher rates of depression, anxiety, and sexual maladjustment (either sexually preoccupied, provocative, and inappropriate or, conversely, highly avoidant of all things sexual). They were more likely to carry dual diagnoses (psychiatric diagnoses in addition to the diagnosis of mental retardation) and to be prescribed psychotropic medications. The need for treatment for people who have experienced sexual abuse, including the many individuals with mental retardation who have undergone such damaging experiences, cannot be stated strongly enough.

With reference again to the extensive volume by Nezu et al. (1992), their review of the assessment and treatment of mental health problems in people with mental retardation reflects an absence of treatment initiatives for abuse survivors as of their 1992 printing. Monat-Haller (1992), in an important work covering a broad range of issues related to mental retardation and sexuality, noted that it is essential that people with mental retardation who experience sexual abuse be referred for treatment. She pointed out, however, that mental health professionals in the community are generally ill-prepared to treat individuals with mental retardation. Additionally, even the *Manual of Diagnosis and Professional Practice in Mental Retardation* (Jacobson & Mulick, 1996) published by the American Psychological Association (APA), considered to be the foremost compendium of research and practice for psychological practitioners in the field of intellectual disabilities, has only one reference to sexual abuse in its 540-page volume. This reference is contained in a chapter discussing the broad range of issues related to sexual development and the need for sexuality education. It stresses the importance of careful assessment of possible sexual abuse and asserts that intensive therapeutic approaches may be needed for survivors of sexual abuse as well as for offenders. Although it notes that pioneering efforts have been made regarding sexual skills training and techniques for dealing with inappropriate sexual behavior, it describes no published therapeutic approaches designed for treating sexual abuse survivors with intellectual disabilities.

In 1992 Richard Sobsey, known for his pioneering work with the Sexual Abuse and Disability Project at the University of Alberta in Canada, coauthored an important article on the need for sexual abuse treatment for survivors with intellectual disabilities (Mansell, Sobsey, & Calder, 1992). Because of the article's publication in a peer-reviewed APA journal, this effort began a call for attention to issues related to the sexual abuse of people with intellectual disabilities. The authors documented higher-than-average rates of sexual abuse among people with intellectual disabilities; the negative sequelae of sexual abuse, such as withdrawal, aggression, inappropriate sexual behavior, and psychological distress; the paucity of appropriate and available treatment; and the rationale for the modification of existing treatment models to aid recovery in survivors with intellectual disabilities.

A Canadian journal article (Perlman & Ericson, 1992) also documented the extent of sexual abuse in the intellectually disabled population, noting that a review of existing data suggests that one in three people with intellectual disabilities will be sexually abused before the age of 18. Perlman and Ericson noted that despite the longstanding belief that a diagnosis of mental retardation precluded psychotherapeutic intervention, recent evidence suggests that interdisciplinary therapeutic approaches have proved successful. These authors determined that the best predictor of recovery was a strong, validating support network, a factor we discuss in relation to group psychotherapy.

Ryan (1994), who has forged new ground in our understanding of PTSD disorder in people with intellectual disabilities, has detailed a six-point treatment protocol for survivors with PTSD (from sexual or other trauma). Briefly, Ryan recommends: (1) judicious use of medications; (2) identification and treatment of medical problems; (3) minimizing iatrogenic complications (e.g., insisting that an individual work alone for periods of time with a young male staff member, when it is clear that being alone with a young male triggers dissociative reactions); (4) provision of psychotherapy; (5) habilitative change to control dissociative triggers (as in the example with Martina, her living situation that isolated her in a basement was highly retraumatizing—each person's unique reactions and needs must be evaluated carefully to avoid further damage to the individual); and (6) program of education and support for staff. Of course, not all sexual abuse survivors have PTSD, and many, in fact, have varying diagnoses and needs, but Ryan's work and recommendations represent an important step in our evolving knowledge base in this area.

In addition, the NADD newsletter published an article discussing transference and countertransference issues that arise in the difficult work of treating abuse survivors with intellectual disabilities (Cox-Lindenbaum & Lindenbaum, 1996), suggesting that growth in this treatment area is continuing. And the ongoing efforts of Richard Sobsey, referenced earlier, and his colleague, Sheila Mansell, have resulted in a comprehensive volume with additional contributors (Mansell & Sobsey, 2001). These authors provide extensive documentation of the harmful effects of sexual abuse on people with intellectual disabilities, along with a discussion of their research findings on the patterns of abuse found in this population. The book goes on to provide a look at how individual therapy can be tailored to meet a patient's unique needs, as well as how family therapy and play therapy models can be used to enhance treatment success.

Even though modifications of conventional therapeutic models have been proposed, the literature reflects the absence of an established therapeutic model designed specifically to meet the needs of individuals with intellectual disabilities. This is an issue of particular concern in light of the growing documentation, as noted earlier, that people with intellectual disabilities, especially women with intellectual disabilities, experience higher rates of sexual abuse than women in the general population (Mansell & Sobsey, 2001; Mansell et al., 1992; Mansell, Sobsey, & Moskal, 1998). In fact, research by Furey (1994), like that of Sobsey and colleagues, indicates that women with mild mental retardation in particular experience the highest levels of sexual abuse. In Furey's study of 461 reported cases of sexual abuse of people with mental retardation, 72% of the victims were female, with the majority being women with mild mental retardation and having no additional hearing, visual, or mobility problems. The study also revealed that male victims were more likely to have severe retardation. Research by the Wisconsin Council on Developmental Disabilities (1991) suggested similarly high rates, estimating that up to 83% of women and 32% of men with intellectual disabilities experience sexual abuse at some point in their lives.

SEXUAL ABUSE PREVENTION TRAINING

One of the first published protocols for teaching adults with intellectual disabilities to protect themselves from sexual abuse was developed by Sgroi, Carey, and Wheaton (1989). Their model describes clearly defined learning objectives and uses teaching aids such as a song underscoring key concepts to be remembered, as well as anatomically correct dolls in avoidance-learning vignettes. Unlike the interactive group model we will be outlining in this book, however, their format follows a fairly traditional, didactic approach, with all information emanating from the trainer, and each participant needing to raise her hand to question or comment.

Avoiding sexual abuse is one of the many content areas outlined in the Circles curriculum (Walker-Hirsch, 1983, 1986, 1988, 1993), widely used in the human service field for its efficacy in teaching interpersonal skills and awareness to people with intellectual disabilities. Although the curriculum has a much broader scope with respect to interpersonal relations, it does describe how an individual should respond to unwanted touch or attempts at sexual intercourse. David Hingsburger (1995), a seminal disabilities advocate, has published a book describing key components of prevention training with adults with intellectual disabilities.

An article by Ragg, Mark, and Rowe (1991) documented the value of group therapy techniques to supplement traditional sex education for people with intellectual disabilities, noting increased sexual knowledge, attitudes, and skills as a result. Miltenberger and colleagues have used behavioral skills training to help adults with intellectual disabilities learn sexual abuse avoidance skills (Haseltine & Miltenberger, 1990; Lumley & Miltenberger, 1997, 1998; Miltenberger et al., 1999). In the 1999 study, Miltenberger et al. attempted to address the difficulties people with intellectual disabilities have in generalizing their training. After providing a group of women with 10 sessions of skills training in abuse avoidance, the researchers conducted an in situ assessment: A confederate, unknown to the participants and posing as a new staff member, would approach a participant and verbally present a simulated sexual abuse lure. (Note that these solicitations were pre-scripted and approved by the involved agency, human rights committee, and the University Institutional Review Board.) For participants who did not respond with an avoidance behavior, that is, failed to demonstrate generalization of the training to the new situation, the researchers then provided in situ training, again using confederates in a natural setting as opposed to the training site. The researchers found that in situ training resulted in generalized responding during naturalistic assessments.

MENTAL HEALTH AND SEXUAL OFFENSE BEHAVIOR

Concerning the relationship between sexual offense behaviors and people with intellectual disabilities, data are beginning to accumulate that suggest that men with mental retardation are somewhat more likely than nonintellectually impaired men to commit sexual offenses (Baroff, 1996; Day, 1997; Gardner, Graeber, & Machkovitz, 1998). These authors noted that among men imprisoned for crimes of a sexual nature, those with mental retardation are overrepresented. They stressed, however, that people with mental retardation are not guilty of greater amounts of criminal activity overall. In fact, the proportion of individuals with mental retardation in prison appears to be roughly equivalent to the proportion of individuals with mental retardation in the community. The distinction lies in the types of crimes committed. Baroff's research suggests that people with mental retardation are more likely than nonimpaired individuals to commit crimes against people. Conversely, they are less likely to commit crimes against public order (e.g., drug-dealing, fraud). Furthermore, the majority of offenses committed by individuals with mental retardation consist of misdemeanors, public disturbances, and less serious felonies (Gardner et al., 1998).

The higher-than-average rate of emotional disturbance in people with intellectual disabilities noted earlier appears to be even more pronounced in *offenders* with intellectual disabilities. In reviewing the relevant literature, Gardner et al. (1998) concluded that the rate of psychological disorders in offenders with intellectual disabilities is "exceptionally higher" (p. 350), with studies reporting prevalence rates ranging from 56% to 87%.

Early formulations concerning the psychological development of sexual offenders pioneered by Groth and Oliveri (1989) offered related observations. In the same volume, Sgroi (1989) offered one of the first published contributions devoted to the evaluation and treatment of the offender with intellectual disabilities. Groth and Oliveri identified two major categories of risk factors still considered viable today: biological defects and unresolved sexual trauma. The authors reported that the Sexual Disorders Clinic at Johns Hopkins Hospital in Baltimore has found a higher incidence of biological defects, such as genetic anomalies, chromosomal abnormalities, brain insult/dysfunction, and hormonal imbalances in clients treated for sexual offense problems than in clients treated for other types of psychological problems. This, of course, does not mean that people with mental retardation are inherently perverse or criminal; rather, the condition of mental retardation seems to cause a vulnerability that interferes with the understanding of, and expression of, one's sexuality. This vulnerability, and the interplay between cognitive impairment and emotional distress, are discussed at length in a chapter by London-based practitioner Valerie Sinason (1997).

Fago (1999), noting the frequent presence of long-standing learning problems in sexual offender populations, studied a group of offenders with respect to the prevalence of attention-deficit hyperactivity disorder (ADHD). He found that 77% of his sample of offenders had ADHD, a highly significant finding in that the rate of ADHD in the general population is approximately 18%. In general, there seems to be considerable support for the idea that neurodevelopmental deficits, while not inherently causal with respect to sex-offender behavior, do, in fact, increase the affected individual's vulnerability toward the development of such behaviors.

The second risk factor, unresolved sexual trauma, is also a factor in the development of sexual offense behaviors, though it certainly does not account for all cases. Ongoing research in this area has led to the awareness that offenders' childhood histories are replete with high levels of trauma of all types. Extremely high rates of sexual abuse and emotional abuse have been found in the histories of juvenile sexual offenders, with those who begin offending prior to age 12 and continue offending into adolescence having experienced the most severe and repeated emotional and sexual abuse (Burton, 2000). Thus, there is a significant prevalence of trauma in the histories of offenders, as well as in the general psychiatric population as noted earlier. The best thinking to date is that the experience of trauma seems to be a causal factor across the range of psychological disorders, and that even sexual trauma does not necessarily lead to the development of sex-offender behavior in all, or even most victims (van der Kolk, 1996). While noting that traumatized people may develop any of a range of psychological disorders, such as eating disorders, PTSD, anxiety, depression, addictions, and even sexual offense disorders, van der Kolk reported a tendency for trauma survivors, across the range of disorders, to re-enact the trauma in one of three ways. The survivor may (a) have a tendency to harm others, as seen with sexual offenders, perpetrators of domestic violence, and various types of violent criminals and juvenile delinquents; (b) have a tendency to be self-destructive, as seen in cases of suicide attempts, self-mutilation, and self-starving; or (c) have a tendency to be revictimized later in life. Specifically, prior rape victims are more likely to experience a future rape than are women who have never been raped. Also, women who were sexually or physically abused as children are more likely to be abused as adults (Carey, 1997; van der Kolk, 1996).

Finally, promising research has begun on the role of attachment, that is, the quality of the individual's relationship with his parents beginning from birth, and suggests that these key relationships play a critical role in the genesis of offense behavior, as well as other forms of pathology (Lewis, Amini, & Lannon, 2000; Marshall & Mazzucco, 1995; Smallbone & Dadds, 2000; Ward, Hudson, & Marshall, 1996; Ward, Hudson, Marshall, & Siegert, 1995). Van der Kolk (1996), following a review of the existing literature, wrote, "In children who have been exposed to severe stressors, the quality of the parental bond is probably the single most important determinant of long-term damage" (p. 185). We can look to this area of research for a growing understanding of the development of psychopathology versus healthy adjustment; moreover, its findings underscore the magnitude of establishing safe therapeutic relationships for patients with histories of trauma (Herman, 1992b; Turner, McFarlane, & van der Kolk, 1996).

TREATMENT INITIATIVES WITH SEX OFFENDERS WHO HAVE INTELLECTUAL DISABILITIES

A burgeoning area of literature can be found with respect to the treatment of, and understanding of, offenders with intellectual disabilities. Pioneering work by Haaven, Little, and Petre-Miller (1990) describes a residential treatment program for offenders with intellectual disabilities who would otherwise be incarcerated with little chance of rehabilitation. Their model consists of a comprehensive program of psychoeducational and psychotherapeutic interventions. Each client receives a thorough individual evaluation and is then incorporated into the program milieu. This is prioritized because every aspect of the client's life is relevant to his rehabilitation; so, for example, completing chores represents an opportunity to gain self-esteem from carrying out adult responsibilities. Treatment approaches include "re-parenting," or ongoing exposure to values and behaviors that model and reinforce empathy, openness, and honesty; changing the client's thinking and behavior through a modified cognitive restructuring approach designed to help him recognize and alter his own patterns; maximizing the client's ability to learn by connecting lessons with experiences that evoke emotions; and using other modes of the client's "multiple intelligences," such as art, music, role-playing, and other creative modalities. Finally, Haaven et al. made use of group process for modeling and reinforcing behavior change and fostering interpersonal skills. They also offered recommendations regarding assessment and transition to community placements.

G. D. Blasingame has created a two-volume set on the treatment of sexual offense problems in people with intellectual disabilities (reviewed in Prescott, 2002). Blasingame provided an overview of the literature with respect to both forensic and clinical issues. The second volume contains a manual for clinicians along with an overview of cognitive–behavioral and relapse prevention models. The manual even includes forms and worksheets for use in structuring the treatment.

The journal *Mental Health Aspects of Developmental Disabilities* published an issue (Luiselli, 2000) entirely devoted to sexually offending behavior in people with intellectual disabilities. The articles cover a range of topics, including pharmacological treatment, assessment of sexual deviance, paraphilias, and related personality disorders. In this journal, Seghorn and Ball (2000) delineated five different types of offenders with intellectual disabilities and echoed early efforts to categorize offenders with intellectual disabilities first documented by Groth and Oliveri (1989). These authors found that offenders with intellectual disabilities can generally be described by one of the following categories: (a) abuse-reactive offenders, who are individuals victimizing others following their own experience of victimization; (b) immature offenders, who do not meet the criteria for deviant sexuality but are displaying inappropriate sexual behavior because of ignorance regarding socially acceptable expressions of normal sexual urges; (c) impulsive offenders, whose neurodevelopmental disorders impair their ability to develop control over all of their impulses, sexual and otherwise; (d) sexually compulsive offenders, who use sexual release as a means of reducing highly distressing psychological states such as anxiety, depression, and a profound sense of personal inadequacy; and (e) sexually fixated/pedophilic offenders, who feel most comfortable in their relationships with children as opposed to adults and sexualize their relationships with children, feeling justified in sexually abusing them.

Nezu and Nezu (1994), whose review of the literature on mental health issues in people with intellectual disabilities was referenced earlier, have begun, along with a number of colleagues, to study the efficacy of group psychotherapy for offenders with intellectual disabilities (Friedman, Festinger, Nezu, McGuffin, & Nezu, 1999). Group psychotherapy for offenders with intellectual disabilities is also being used successfully by Cox-

Lindenbaum (2001) and is the subject of efficacy research in British systems as well (Rose, Jenkins, O'Connor, Jones, & Felce, 2002).

It is important to note that the thinking of the various authors on this topic is consistent with respect to the need for comprehensive services for the offender with intellectual disabilities, including the coordination of all the services supporting the client, for example, family members or residential staff who may be responsible for supervising a client, prescribing psychiatrist, mental health personnel, and program or employment-related personnel. In reviewing the literature and taking into account the higher-than-average rates of both sexual abuse and sexual offense behavior in people with intellectual disabilities, there is a decided need for therapeutic intervention with this population. To address this need, we review the specific workings of the interactive–behavioral model of group psychotherapy (Tomasulo, 1998a) and its relative utility in dealing with sexual abuse and related mental health problems in people with intellectual disabilities.

THE INTERACTIVE–BEHAVIORAL THERAPY MODEL: RATIONALE AND INITIAL RESEARCH

The interactive–behavioral therapy (IBT) model is a model of group psychotherapy that has evolved over the past 15 years through our work with individuals who are diagnosed with both intellectual disabilities and psychological disorders. The model's theoretical underpinnings, as well as many of its techniques, are drawn directly from psychodrama as originated by J. L. Moreno (Blatner & Blatner, 1988; Marineau, 1989). Certain adaptations to the model have been made to enhance its efficacy with the intellectually disabled population. The model is described at length in chapter 3 for those interested in learning how to conduct IBT groups. Further detail is provided as well in each of the chapters that address the use of IBT groups with specific patient populations.

The theoretical formulations of psychodrama have much to offer the treatment of people with intellectual disabilities. Moreno, like Freud, believed that one's early experiences were responsible for one's psychological development. He differed from Freud, however, in his ideas regarding the most effective ways to help people get better. Moreno believed that therapy ought to engage the person as completely as possible, and therefore the interactions between therapist and patient should not be limited to simply thinking and talking. Thinking and talking are cognitive activities; the individual is only engaged cognitively. However, if action is added, if the individual is invited to get up and demonstrate the problem, he or she is being engaged behaviorally, and ultimately, emotionally as well. The manner in which this enhanced engagement takes place will be the discussion of much of the rest of this book. For the purposes of this chapter, however, we would like to establish the unique utility of a psychodramatic therapy model with patients who have intellectual disabilities.

People with intellectual disabilities have a cognitive impairment, and cognition, of course, is the chief means of expression in traditional "talk" therapies. Thus, traditional therapies ask the individual to do therapeutic work in the area in which the patient with intellectual disabilities is most limited. By engaging the individual through behavioral and emotional means as well, we are increasing the individual's opportunity to do meaningful therapeutic work.

The IBT model has been investigated in recent studies with some promising results. Blaine (1993) tested the efficacy of an IBT group treating both intellectually disabled and nondisabled participants over 17 sessions. Using a number of measures, she concluded that both types of patients showed significant positive change from the therapy, and interestingly, those patients with intellectual disabilities demonstrated *higher* frequencies of most therapeutic factors. (Therapeutic factors are specific experiences that can occur in many types of therapy and that lead to psychological change. They are described in detail in chapter 3.) In addition, each patient set goals for himself, and then evaluated himself with regard to how successful he felt he had been. The final evaluations suggested that patients' achievements of their interpersonal goals in therapy exceeded their expectations.

Keller (1993) studied the emergence of therapeutic factors in a 12-week IBT group with participants diagnosed with both intellectual and psychiatric disorders. The emergence of therapeutic factors is frequently studied because it is considered a robust measure of the therapeutic value of a group. Keller had professional therapists review videotapes of group sessions and asked them to rate the tapes for the presence of various therapeutic factors. The therapists were blind to the nature of the study and to whether they were watching early or late-stage groups. The emergence of seven out of eight targeted therapeutic factors was reliably documented by the observers, suggesting that the therapeutic process does indeed evolve with participants who have intellectual disabilities.

The IBT model has also been found to be effective with another chronic population: people with chronic mental illness. Daniels (1998) tested the IBT model with a group of chronically mentally ill adults who carried diagnoses of schizophrenia or schizoaffective disorder. Multiple clinical rating scales were administered to measure changes in social functioning and negative symptomatology. Three hypotheses were tested, and each was supported by the ensuing data. Specifically, it was found that (a) IBT increases the overall social competence of people with chronic schizophrenia or schizoaffective disorders; (b) IBT improves the negative symptoms that are often associated with poor treatment outcome for people diagnosed with schizophrenia or schizoaffective disorders; and (c) IBT facilitates the emergence of those therapeutic factors found to enhance social competence in people with chronic schizophrenia and schizoaffective disorders. Note that both Blaine (1993) and Daniels (1998) did not limit their research to people with intellectual disabilities. Daniels's study suggests that the IBT model may provide a viable forum for people with chronic mental illness, whose treatment programs often include group psychotherapy.

The IBT model was studied by Carlin (1998), who explored its value in helping individuals with intellectual disabilities cope with bereavement. She found that all group members showed evidence of being able to engage in the bereavement process through three therapeutic factors specific to the grieving process: acknowledging the reality of death, recalling special characteristics about the deceased, and verbalizing feelings related to the loss. Additionally, a study by Oliver-Brannon (2000) compared IBT with behavior modification techniques in treating participants with dual diagnoses of mental retardation and psychiatric disorders. The study is limited by small sample size and nonrandom assignment, but data collection revealed that participants in the IBT group, compared with the behavior modification controls, evidenced greater reduction in target behaviors, increased problem-solving skills, and earlier return to the community.

The IBT model has been written about extensively in *Habilitative Mental Healthcare Newsletter* (now known as *Mental Health Aspects of Developmental Disabilities*; Razza & Tomasulo, 1996a, 1996b, 1996c; Tomasulo, 1994, 1997, 1998b; Tomasulo, Keller, & Pfadt, 1995), as well as in edited volumes on intellectual disabilities (Fletcher, 2000; Jacobson & Mulick, 1996; Tomasulo, 2000; Wiener, 1999). It is the subject of *Action Methods in Group Psychotherapy* (Tomasulo, 1998a) and has been taught to thousands of human service and mental health personnel through direct trainings and videotaped instruction (Tomasulo, 1992). It has been recommended as a valuable means of treating adults with intellectual disabilities who are at risk for suicide (Kirchner & Mueth, 2000).

GROUP THERAPY'S VALUE IN OFFENDER AND SURVIVOR TREATMENT

Even though IBT groups in particular appear to be valuable in treating people with intellectual disabilities, we should note that the literature on treatment of offenders and survivors in the general population points to group therapy as a significantly useful tool as well. Experts in offender treatment contend that group therapy is the treatment of choice for offenders (Sawyer, 2000), pointing out both the theoretical rationale and extensive reliance established offender programs have on group therapy. Sawyer noted that 86% of adult treatment programs and 89% of adolescent treatment programs use group as the primary treatment modality. In addition, a recent meta-analysis of 26 empirical studies using group psychotherapy with incarcerated offenders demonstrated the efficacy of group treatment along numerous outcome measures (Morgan & Flora, 2002). The analyzed studies looked at incarcerated offenders from the general population who had committed a range of offenses, including violent, nonviolent, sexual, and nonsexual crimes. The researchers found that group psychotherapy led to improvement on each of the variables measured: anger, anxiety, depression, interpersonal relations, locus of control, and self-esteem. More important, inmates mandated into treatment fared as well as those who were self-referred—a particularly hopeful finding in that many people with intellectual disabilities are not self-referred. Morgan and Flora (2002) concluded that "group psychotherapy is an effective treatment modality for potentially resistant offenders" (p. 214).

Similarly, trauma experts make the case for group therapy as especially helpful in treating people in the aftermath of trauma of all types, including that experienced by disaster workers, victims of disaster, motor vehicle accident survivors, combat survivors, homicide witnesses, and sexual abuse survivors (Young & Blake, 1999). Van der Kolk, McFarlane, and van der Hart (1996) and Herman (1992b) described the therapeutic needs of survivors in detail and made a formidable case for the unique treatment benefits group therapy offers. Van der Kolk (1996), stressing the tremendous difficulties trauma survivors often have in putting their experiences into verbal narrative, stated the following:

> Prone to action, and deficient in words, these patients can often express their internal states more articulately in physical movements or in pictures than in words. Utilizing drawings and *psychodrama* may help them develop a language that is essential for effective communication and for the symbolic transformation that can occur in psychotherapy. *Group psychotherapy* may also be effective in providing them both with (inter)action and with borrowed words to express emotional states. (p. 195, italics added)

In keeping with van der Kolk's thinking, efforts to assess the efficacy of using experiential approaches, such as psychodrama, in the treatment of trauma survivors suggest considerable merit (Hudgins & Drucker, 1998; Hudgins & Kipper, 1998). Although a detailed analysis of these works is beyond the scope of this chapter, the overall value of group treatment with survivors and offenders is an essential point to establish as we begin our journey into the use of group with the special population of people with intellectual disabilities. The establishment of group as a viable, and even preferred, treatment modality within the general population lends further support for the rationale behind providing group treatment with the intellectually disabled population. The unique features of group—for all populations—are detailed in chapter 3. Moreover, additional factors, which make group even more valuable for members with intellectual disabilities, are presented as well.

II

THE
INTERACTIVE–BEHAVIORAL
THERAPY MODEL AND
ITS APPLICATIONS

3

THE INTERACTIVE–BEHAVIORAL
THERAPY MODEL OF
GROUP PSYCHOTHERAPY

Just as despair can come to one only from other human beings,
hope, too, can be given to one only by other human beings.

—Elie Wiesel

As we have discussed in the first two chapters, the need for psychotherapy for people with both intellectual and psychiatric disorders can no longer be disregarded. Although early researchers (Browning, 1974) attempted to show the efficacy of individual and group psychotherapy for this population, it remained widely assumed that people with cognitive deficits would not profit from insight-oriented therapy. It is interesting to note that Browning's early edited volume contained a chapter on counseling people who have intellectual disabilities (Halpern & Berard, 1974). These authors noted that verbal counseling techniques could be successfully used with some individuals who have intellectual disabilities but that a very long time commitment would be necessary. They also presented the merits of behavioral techniques and play therapy. The authors reviewed more than 50 articles available at the time that looked at the efficacy of group therapy with this population. They noted:

> Since impairment in adaptive behavior is the primary deficit of the mentally retarded, group techniques are particularly useful with retarded clients in that one of the most appropriate goals of group counseling is to enhance the clients' social adaptation. The group should be structured directively by the counselor, and the procedures should be oriented more towards activity than discussion. (Halpern & Berard, 1974, p. 282)

Moreover, Halpern and Berard (1974) cited early research suggesting that, within the context of group therapy, "role playing" and "sociodrama" can be "readily employed" (p. 282). The authors went on to cite three major strengths of role-playing: (a) allowing the clinician to observe and diagnose interpersonal strengths and weaknesses, (b) enabling clients to become aware of the effects of their own social behaviors, and (c) providing clients with the opportunity to practice new interpersonal responses to problem situations. They concluded that "Role playing is an especially promising technique with retarded clients, in either group or individual settings. It can be used in many contexts, both diagnostically and therapeutically. Whenever possible, this approach should be utilized" (p. 283).

Unfortunately, as we have already noted, psychotherapy for people with intellectual disabilities did not evolve along a steady path of progress. The norm at mental health clinics for many years was to try to avoid providing mental health treatment for individuals with intellectual disabilities (Prout & Strohmer, 1994). People with mental retardation were generally viewed as being unsuitable candidates for psychotherapy, their limited verbal abilities often cited as the chief culprit, along with their presumed inability to achieve "insight." Further compounding the problem was a tendency on the part of practitioners to use artificial dichotomies between *mental illness* and *behavior disorders*, with those symptoms seen as behavior disorders being referred only for behavioral intervention (Hurley et al., 1996). Diagnostic overshadowing (Reiss, Levitan, & Szyszko, 1982), in which the condition of mental retardation is seen as responsible for many or all of an individual's symptoms, has also been a formidable obstacle in the accurate diagnosis and treatment of psychiatric disorders in members of this population.

Despite academic interest such as the early research just mentioned, virtually no integration of the literature on mental retardation made its way into clinical training programs. Clinicians by and large graduated from their professional training without ever having been introduced to the needs of people with intellectual disabilities and did not feel prepared to treat them. At the same time, outcome studies on psychotherapy efficacy routinely screened out potential people with mental retardation (Prout & Strohmer, 1994), thinking that the condition would interfere with their participation in or ability to benefit from the treatment or would negate the generalizability of the findings. Thus the dearth of treatment knowledge was perpetuated.

The result of the field's limited approach to treating people with intellectual disabilities was twofold. For individual treatment, behavior modification became the norm. In group treatment, social skills training became the treatment of choice. These treatment options left the therapist in the teacher or trainer role rather than the facilitator role. This was especially true for the social skills group leader. She would act more like an educator than an agent of therapeutic change. The primary focus of social skills training was on the curriculum, and only teacher-to-member, *not* member-to-member, interactions were regarded as a priority for learning.

The interactive–behavioral therapy (IBT) model, however, is a radical shift away from curriculum-based social skills training. Its theoretical foundations are drawn from traditional models of group psychotherapy. As such, the emphasis is on member-to-member interaction. Similarly, group process is prioritized over curriculum. Group psychotherapy pioneers, such as Irvin Yalom and J. L. Moreno, evolved their respective group therapy approaches informed by psychodynamic theory as developed by Freud and retooled by numerous followers such as Jung and Sullivan, to name a few (Blatner & Blatner, 1988; Yalom, 1995). The underlying philosophy common to these theories is that an individual's personality, and thus the individual's particular brand of psychopathology, develops through personal experiences with other people. Initially, this is primarily through experiences in the person's family of origin, but it continues to be affected by the multitude of interpersonal relationships one has in life. Because one's personality and particular style of interpersonal relating are developed in connection with other people, group therapy pioneers posited that changes in these styles can best be brought about in connection with others as well. The group therapy format allows for a controlled connection with others in which each individual's style of interrelating can be examined and altered. In the words of another early group therapy proponent, Cody Marsh, "By the crowd have they been broken, by the crowd shall they be healed" (see Blatner & Blatner, 1988, p. 193).

The core of the IBT model draws most heavily on the traditional models of group psychotherapy and psychodrama developed by Moreno. We then made modifications in design, technique, and implementation to enhance the possibility for change in people with intellectual disabilities.

MEMBER-TO-MEMBER INTERACTION

As we mentioned, the teacher/trainer model uses, in essence, a one-on-one teacher–student relationship in a group setting. This is an educational model that relies heavily on the curriculum and, for all practical purposes, ignores the rich group interactions between and among members. Indeed, the teachers in social skills training groups often focus on reducing member-to-member interaction, as it is seen as a form of distraction. The IBT model differs in two fundamental ways. First, it is not curriculum driven. It is a process-oriented method that allows for a wide variety of curricula to be used. This accounts for its use in such varied programs as AIDS training, anger management, advocacy support, relationship groups, vocational readiness, residential management, bereavement, sexual abuse survivors, employment groups, sex offenders, and other programs. By process-driven, we mean that the facilitator's primary responsibility is to establish those elements that will strengthen the group's dynamics first, with a secondary focus on dissemination of information relevant to any curriculum.

The second distinction is that the primary job of the facilitator is to extract herself from member-to-facilitator interactions, while enhancing the capacity for members to interact with each other. This shift in paradigm stresses the communication between peers rather than fostering the dialogue between teacher and student. In fact, studies on the IBT model (Keller, 1993) show that in IBT groups, interactions between facilitator and member *decrease* over time, whereas member-to-member interactions increase. This process strengthens members' abilities to listen to, and understand, peers rather than solely learning to follow a trainer's directions. The enhancement of member-to-member communication and listening lays the groundwork for important psychotherapeutic change that would not otherwise be possible.

THERAPEUTIC FACTORS AND PROCESS MODIFICATIONS

The first step in establishing the viability of the IBT model was to search for the emergence of therapeutic factors in groups with dually diagnosed individuals. The therapeutic factors are those features of the group process that have been shown to promote therapeutic change. Researchers in group psychotherapy such as Yalom (1995) and Bloch and Crouch (1985) have identified and studied these factors in psychotherapy groups with people who have psychiatric disorders but not mental retardation. Our goal was to see if these therapeutic factors would evolve in groups with members with intellectual disabilities as well.

In social skills training, the emphasis is on the material to be learned. In the IBT model, as in established group psychotherapy models, we are looking for factors emerging in the *interactions between members* that indicate the group's viability as a forum for self-expression and learning. In pilot studies to investigate this phenomenon we proposed three key ideas:

1. Emergence of therapeutic factors was not likely to happen in the brief time allotments used in previous studies. Rather than 6 or 8 sessions, our pilot studies lasted 12, 24, 36, and 48 sessions. It was reasoned that people with intellectual disabilities might require longer time periods for the emergence of these factors.
2. The use of action methods borrowed from the field of psycho-drama and sociodrama would be likely to enhance these factors

in group, and use of these methods would be central to the development of the model.

3. Modification of the standard group psychotherapy format would be required to accommodate the needs of this unique population.

Several groups were run in which action methods, particularly the use of the double (described later in this chapter) were used to provide support and cohesion for group members. Each group was videotaped and run by people proficient in the use of group dynamics, action methods, and intellectual disabilities. We continued the groups for a full year, by which time we had made some important observations. We found that all 14 of the established therapeutic factors had occurred and had been captured on videotape. There were several examples of each factor. Manifestation of these factors was often very concrete (e.g., one member passed a box of tissues to another who was crying, representing the therapeutic factor of altruism) but were, nonetheless, proof that factors demonstrating group viability evolved with this population. We also found that the traditional session format did not work as well for this population.

In traditional psychodrama, a session is composed of three stages: the warm-up, the enactment, and the sharing. The warm-up stage allows members to get ready to participate in an enactment; the enactment stage uses specific action techniques, including role-playing, doubling, and role-reversal, and heightens the emotional involvement of the group; and, finally, the sharing stage provides a way for the material to be discussed and assimilated into each member's own life. People with cognitive deficits often have limited capacity for assimilating meaning from the dramatic role-plays or the group process into their own lives. In some individuals, the capacity for reflection is thwarted by cognitive deficits resulting in limited ability for the abstract thinking such assimilation requires. To compensate for this limitation, we moved the enactment phase to a later point in the session. We found that a longer, more intense preparation for the enactment was necessary. We labeled this preparatory stage the orientation, as it gave members a chance to familiarize themselves with each other. In addition, it provided much-needed training for the members in sincerely paying attention to each other, not just to the facilitators, as years of school and "socialization" programs had conditioned them to do. Finally, we altered the traditional sharing stage because of its reliance on abstract thinking as noted earlier. We replaced it with a stage we called affirmation, and used it as an opportunity to reinforce each member for productive work done in the session. The result was a four-stage group process that allowed for two stages leading up to the enactment, and one stage following. The four stages in order of their sequence are the *orientation*,

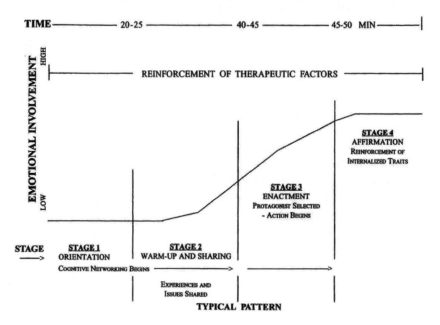

Figure 3.1. A typical pattern of the interactive–behavioral therapy group process. From "Group Therapy for People With Mental Retardation: The Interactive–Behavioral Therapy Model," by D. Tomasulo. In D. Wiener (Ed.), *Beyond Talk Therapy: Using Movement and Expressive Techniques in Clinical Practice,* 1999, p. 147. Copyright 1999 by the American Psychological Association. Reprinted with permission.

the *warm-up and sharing,* the *enactment,* and the *affirmation.* These four stages compose each session of IBT, with the total session time running between 50 and 60 minutes. The chart in Figure 3.1 shows the four stages, along with the degree of emotional involvement typically experienced with each stage. We discuss each of the stages next.

Orientation Stage

As these groups are *process-* rather than *content-*driven, the focus during the orientation stage is on strengthening communication skills. We have found that most beginning members are, unfortunately, accustomed to not being listened to. Moreover, they are not in the habit of listening to others, particularly to their peers. The group begins when the facilitator either notices one person is speaking already or asks who would like to begin. Once a member begins speaking, the facilitator needs to interrupt that person's discourse early on (usually within 15 to 20 seconds of their talking) and ask the group, "Who heard what (speaker's name) said?" The members in the group will then feed back to the person speaking what they heard. This feedback loop provides an opportunity for members to strengthen their listening skills while allowing the sender of the information an opportunity to clarify her remarks. Once satisfied that one or two members in the group have adequately heard her, the sender is then asked by the facilitator to choose the next person to send information. This allows the interaction between members to begin as soon as possible while keeping the facilitator out of the choosing process. As a new "sender" is chosen, others are asked to feed back what was heard. The process continues until each member in the group has had an opportunity to share, while along the way, the facilitator asks the members to orient toward one another by demonstrating eye contact and appropriate body positioning.

Depending on their levels of cognitive functioning, group members will vary in how much help they need learning to attend to each other. The goal of the orientation stage, however, is always to ready the members to participate in the IBT process. A list of the tasks that take place during the orientation stage (and following stages) appears in Appendix 3.1. The emergence of therapeutic factors begins in the orientation stage and will continue throughout the group. It is the primary task of the facilitator to identify behaviors that represent therapeutic factors and reinforce members at the time of their emergence; for example, "Ellen, I noticed you looked at Carmen the whole time she was talking today. You are really getting to be a good listener." In addition, the facilitator should repeat this specific accomplishment, and others that may have occurred, during the affirmation stage.

When beginning a new group, certain *executive functions* are best carried out during the orientation stage. By executive functions, we mean the facilitator's presentation of the fundamental rules and parameters of the group. For example, in each group, we, as facilitators, tell the members that there are two basic rules: safety and confidentiality. We explain that in order for group to be a safe place for each member there can be no physical violence or threats. We give concrete examples of these concepts and ask members to feed back what they have heard until it is clear that they understand what is meant. Violence or threats of violence toward group members, in or out of session, are grounds for termination from the group. Next we explain the concept of confidentiality, including the facilitator's professional responsibility in this regard and the members' responsibilities. We take great pains to clarify that members cannot talk about what other members say outside of group. To concretize this idea for lower functioning members, we stress that they should not repeat the names of other members outside of group. It is important to stress to the members that they *can*, if they wish, talk about *their own* group experience with others. This is an important distinction to clarify. Discussing our own business with others is always our right if we so choose. When this is not carefully clarified, members sometimes feel as if they must "keep secrets," as is so often the case in incestuous or alcoholic families. Members need to know they always have the right to discuss their own activities and feelings if they want to do so, and the confidentiality rule is to protect each member's right to be in charge of what is or is not said about them.

In new groups, we present this information during the orientation stage over the first few sessions. We repeat the information whenever a new member joins. Over the years we have found that veteran members will take on the responsibility of explaining these rules to newcomers—an effort we strongly affirm.

Additional parameters of the group can be given during the orientation stage, such as the time and length of the meetings and specific purpose or goals. The first meeting of a group for offenders, for example, or for abuse avoidance training will present specific details at this point. (In the chapters devoted to each of these types of groups, we discuss relevant information that we share.)

Typically members begin the orientation stage by sharing information that does not have powerful emotional meaning for them, and may even be rather superficial. This is termed *horizontal self-disclosure*; it is typical of the way people take the first steps of bridging the chasm between themselves and others, much like small talk at a cocktail party. Deeper, more emotionally meaningful material, termed *vertical self-disclosure*, comes later, once a sense of acceptance and safety is established. In groups with veteran members, of course, vertical disclosures often begin sooner in a session because the safety and security have been well established.

These initial disclosures during the orientation stage are used to build an agenda for the day's session, with each member having an opportunity to present what he would like to work on. We generally ask each member who has presented an issue to then choose another member and ask that person if he or she would like to present next. It is important to pay attention to the sociometry of these choices, that is, of who feels connected to or interested in whom, or if certain members are always chosen last, and so on. Once the group has started, we usually begin by asking if anyone would like to speak first, or if anyone has anything left from the last session that they feel needs more time. If two or more members respond that they would like to start, we begin fostering interaction and awareness of peers right at that point. We ask them to talk to each other about who should start off and to let us know the decision. Often one member will offer to let another start, and we make a point of affirming that member's support of the other.

Warm-Up and Sharing Stage

The warm-up and sharing stage is characterized by a shift from horizontal to vertical self-disclosure. The goal for this stage is for each member to clarify his or her agenda item or issue to be worked on for the day. For example, Gerry, who began the session talking about his fishing trip, now says that his mother hit him this past week, and he, after many months of successful self-control, hit her back. The facilitator's job during the warm-up and sharing is to acknowledge Gerry's honesty in bringing this up and to support this issue as a viable agenda item, checking to see who heard it. Following each member's presentation during this stage, a protagonist, or series of protagonists, may be chosen. The cognitive networking that began in the orientation stage continues in the warm-up and sharing stage, and in fact, will continue throughout the session.

Enactment Stage

In the enactment stage one or more of the issues presented during the warm-up and sharing is moved into action. The member whose issue will be addressed in the enactment is referred to as the *protagonist*. Other members who help by playing supporting roles are called *auxiliaries*.

The person chosen to be the protagonist should have an issue that appears to resonate with a good number of the members. The facilitator can choose the protagonist by observing which of the members are expressing feelings of distress or an interpersonal conflict. Sometimes members will directly request an opportunity to work on a problem through an enactment. A general guideline for the facilitator to use in choosing a protagonist is to look for someone who has a pressing need to work on that day, and who also appears to have the interest and attention of a good number of the other members.

In the enactment stage, we use a variety of action techniques that stimulate multiple senses, and as such, enhance both attention and memory. One of the primary action methods to be used during this period is that of the *double* (see Appendix 3.2). We describe an example of the enactment stage in which the action consists of doubling, as this is probably the easiest action technique for beginning therapists and members alike. In addition, it is extremely powerful and supportive and runs a very low risk of being threatening.

The double is used to create support for the protagonist by having another member, or the facilitator, stand behind the protagonist's chair and say the thoughts and feelings the protagonist may be having. Perhaps the most salient feature of the double technique is its ability to provide support.

It provides the facilitator freedom to add features to the group process that would not be possible without action techniques. The protagonist can be sitting or standing, and the double can assume the same physical stance as the protagonist, sitting or standing behind him. Assuming the same physical stance allows the double to "warm-up" to the internal state of the protagonist. This type of warm-up allows the person playing the double to mimic the protagonist in a way that gives clues to the internal state. All this, however, is but a readiness to understand the protagonist in a way that will provide an isomorphic condition, that is, one that matches the internal state of the protagonist. This condition allows the emotional expression, the emotional support, or the reorganization of perceptions to emerge more fully. If the double can create an atmosphere in which the protagonist feels supported and understood, the opportunity for change is greatly enhanced. The position of standing behind the protagonist is a powerful symbol of support and is the position most often used in doubling. The protagonist literally experiences someone "backing him up." Furthermore, the person doing the doubling has the opportunity to quite literally see things from the protagonist's perspective, to feel what it is like "from where he stands," and then to verbalize those feelings in the first person for the protagonist. It is a uniquely nonconfrontational and supportive stance.

The primary contraindication for this type of positioning is with cases in which it increases anxiety, as it may with people who are paranoid. In these instances, the doubling can be done from another position, such as from a seat next to the protagonist.

Appendix 3.2 outlines the ways in which the double may be chosen. Note that although the double is often a single individual, more than one member can double at one time. For example, two individuals may be asked to double for a protagonist to verbalize two conflicting feelings the protagonist may have. It is also possible to have two doubles voice the same emotion to represent the overwhelming force of the emotion—that is, to represent it "in stereo." Furthermore, any number of group members may be asked to double in an effort to help the protagonist experience such therapeutic factors as acceptance and universality with the other members. The facilitator asks individuals or pairs to take turns standing behind the protagonist in succession, verbalizing their understanding of the protagonist's feelings.

Perhaps one of the most common errors a group facilitator makes when first using action techniques is to have the protagonist engage in an interactive type of role-play too soon. This would include, for example, the types of role-plays in which the protagonist has to practice speaking up to a threatening figure such as a boss or a parent. Other examples might include having to reverse roles with a difficult figure in the protagonist's life, perhaps a domineering brother or a hostile coworker. Although it can be very helpful for a group facilitator to use role-playing to rehearse a new behavior or to act out an encounter, it is generally not the best place to start. Such a role-play may, on the surface, seem reasonable, but it may be too threatening for the protagonist to carry out in a new group. To successfully cope with highly stressful interpersonal issues, group members need to feel extremely comfortable and supported in the group. By far the safest action technique to use in new groups or with new members is the double. Doubling for the protagonist creates an atmosphere of support, which is arguably the single most important therapeutic feature of a group. If you are going to make an error, it is best to make it on the side of giving more, rather than less, support. Remember trust and safety are the cornerstone of your group. The double can help create this ambiance for the protagonist.

One example of the use of the double comes from our group for women with intellectual and psychiatric disabilities, many of whom have experienced sexual abuse. Erin, a relatively new member, was being asked about the problem she had described, with great hesitancy, some weeks before. Erin had told us she has a habit of talking to herself, and that this was a source of a great deal of shame and sadness for her. Her parents would yell at her and punish her by taking possessions away from her; her self-talk was a source of tremendous family strife and she felt helpless to change it.

Erin hid her face when asked to discuss the problem. She felt the same shame in group that she apparently was feeling at home. One of the other women, a long-time member, shared her very sincere empathy for Erin, having had the same problem for many years and experienced the wrath of her brother numerous times as a result. Others then joined in with examples from their own lives and expressed their understanding and acceptance. Nevertheless, Erin continued to hide her face in shame. We then asked the most vocal member, who had much the same experiences, to double for Erin. This member, Louise, stood behind Erin and said, "I feel so bad. Everybody thinks I'm weird because I talk to myself." We checked out the accuracy of this doubling with Erin, who agreed it was right. Erin removed her hand from her face. Louise continued in this manner with a few more first-person statements describing Erin's feelings.

After Louise sat back down, Erin looked at her and thanked her, her posture noticeably less constricted. She said she felt Louise understood, which clearly was not apparent to her before. She was not too sure about the others, however, despite their words, and so a number of other members took turns doubling for Erin. (This is an example of what is meant by multiple doubles.) Eventually, one of the doubles even made Erin laugh. Erin finally said she would like to talk about her problem, and she did so briefly. Most important, however, she experienced being truly supported on an issue that years of experience had taught her could bring only ridicule and pain. Her ability to talk about, understand, and work on the problem would evolve as a natural outgrowth of the support supplied to her regularly in this and successive sessions.

As you may sense, the enactment stage accelerates the emotional involvement of the members. (As noted earlier, the level of emotional involvement is diagrammed in Figure 3.1.) The level of emotional involvement builds as the session progresses, achieving its peak intensity during the enactment stage. Emotional involvement, as well as behavioral engagement, greatly enhances the power of the group, commanding members' attention, facilitating memory of the experience, and allowing for an opportunity to experience an altered and enhanced sense of self.

At the tail end of the enactment stage, great care is taken to affirm the protagonist for her effort in the group. Others are encouraged to say, "What was good . . ." about what the protagonist just did. Also, it is important to affirm each of the auxiliaries who did the doubling, as well as each of the members who gave their time and attention to the enactment. This process serves to complete the enactment stage and ushers in the affirmation stage in which members will be affirmed for their participation and be taught how to affirm one another. Other techniques that may be used in the enactment stage include the empty chair, role reversal, representational dramas, and the use of split doubles to represent internal conflicts. Also, auxiliaries can assist protagonists by playing the roles of other key people from the protagonist's life. We present some examples of these techniques in groups with offenders, survivors, and abuse avoidance and detail them in their respective chapters.

Affirmation Stage

The affirmation stage allows for feedback to be given to each member pertaining to his or her participation in the group. The facilitator provides each member with strong verbal acknowledgment for behaviors she displayed that reflect any of the therapeutic factors or show evidence of psychological growth. Group members are also asked to give feedback to each other about what they *liked* about a particular member's participation. During this period, the facilitator is highly directive, allowing no negative feedback to be given to any member. It is important to close the session with each member feeling good about himself. Moreover, each member should be able to take away at least one positive piece of an enhanced self-concept, for example, "Maybe I really am getting to be a good listener" or "Maybe I really am getting better at controlling my temper."

In addition to affirming an enhanced self-concept and helping members clarify specific strengths, the affirmation stage also serves to contain the affect generated during the enactment stage. We bring a sense of closure to the day's emotional material. It is not a time to bring up new material or to allow for controversy or criticism, because these would generate new emotional reactions. The feeling at the end of the session should be positive and growth affirming, with a sense of being done "for now," in the way a weekly television show is over. Members and facilitators are left looking forward to a continuing episode next week.

THERAPEUTIC FACTORS

Yalom (1995) has advanced perhaps the most comprehensive study of group psychotherapy research, including the formulation of a solid theoretical rationale for the use of group psychotherapy, extensive outcome research, and the delineation of therapeutic factors, that is, those components that actually account for patient improvement. Although many researchers have contributed to the field, the impact of Yalom's work has been felt throughout clinical and academic circles.

Therapeutic factors are components of group therapy that emerge during the group process. They are the specific components that benefit a member's condition. A therapeutic factor is the result of actions by the group facilitator, the members, or the individual. Yalom outlined and studied 11 of these factors; students of his have since defined additional factors as well. In this chapter we review a comprehensive list of 14 therapeutic factors, covering a wide range of interactive behaviors and conditions. Generally speaking, the more these factors are present in a group, the more therapeutic power the group has. The facilitator's job is to activate the emergence of these factors. Of all the therapeutic duties the facilitator must perform, activating the emergence of therapeutic factors is perhaps the most critical. How a facilitator may stimulate these factors is very broad in scope. In some instances, it may simply mean acknowledging that a factor has occurred, as in the following instance in which the therapist reinforces a demonstration of altruism. The facilitator may say, for example, "Carlos, I noticed you got right up and moved that empty chair away so that Ronnie could wheel his wheelchair into the circle. That was very nice of you." Other times the facilitator must be more directive and concrete in helping members to label what they have learned, as in the following case concerning the therapeutic factor of self-understanding. For example, in working with Helen—who feels highly dependent on others and tends to see herself as having been broken down by her life's many hardships—you note in today's group that she talked about removing a picture from her room to reduce some of her distress. During the affirmation stage, you feed this back to her in a way that highlights *her* role, *her* effort, and *her* ability to take action that improves her life. This is an important opportunity to make a dent in her damaged self-concept, and begin to instill in her some sense of self-efficacy. As facilitator, you might say, "Helen, I could hear how sad you were about what happened, but it's great that you were able to do something to make yourself feel better. You came up with the idea of removing the picture, you went ahead and took it down, and you helped yourself feel better. You are really getting better at coping." Patients such as Helen are often so locked into their self-perceptions that they fail to see the significance of behaviors that do not fit with that perception. Highlighting her own report of her experience in this way can have a powerful impact on the expansion of her self-understanding to include a sense of herself as a person with some competency.

We describe each of the 14 therapeutic factors in detail so that you can begin to become familiar with them. We also present some actual examples of these factors that we have observed in groups of people with intellectual disabilities.

1. Acceptance/Cohesion

In a cohesive group, members feel a sense of belonging and being valued by each other. This sense of being connected is usually fostered by interactions that are positive in nature. The feeling of trusting others and being safe is central to members' feelings of acceptance.

One of our groups for men who had committed sexual offenses had a relatively new member named Harold. Although in one of his first weeks in group Harold was able to admit his offense—grabbing his penis through his clothes while staring at young girls in a pool—he resisted discussing the problem again. He would begin with "fun," nonthreatening topics and stop there. When asked if he could do any work on his "problem," he dropped his head and covered his face with his hand. Tom, a long-term member of the group, started to tease Harold. Harold grew red in the face and would not look up. The facilitator asked him to try to look at Tom, and when he did he saw Tom smiling good-naturedly at him. Tom assured him that he and the others already knew what he did and verbalized the offense for him. Then he added that it was "OK," that they all like him anyway, and that they are here because they "have problems" too. Everyone reassured Harold that they liked him and that they knew he was in group to get better, as they were. The cohesiveness of this group gave Harold an experience of being accepted that far surpassed anything he was used to, and it allowed him to discuss his problem more easily in the following sessions.

2. Universality

The common acknowledgment of an experience by group members is referred to as universality. In a group session, Shari spoke of the humiliation of having been called "retarded" as a child by other kids waiting for the school bus. The moment Shari mentioned this she began to cry. The other members began to shake their heads and immediately offered her their experiences. People who have not had the experience of being called "retarded" cannot duplicate the support and understanding the other members gave her during this exchange. A therapist or support person could sympathize, but only others who actually lived through the same experience could validate Shari in the way she needed.

3. Altruism

As in the example where Carlos made room for Ronnie's wheelchair, members spontaneously help each other in group. This helping is usually unsolicited and is the result of an unselfish desire to be of assistance. Helping others without the need to have that help reciprocated is the cornerstone of altruism. It has therapeutic value for the recipient of the help, as well as for the member giving the help, who benefits from the awareness that he genuinely has something valuable to offer. This is a highly therapeutic experience for people with intellectual disabilities who frequently feel they have little to give others.

We have witnessed poignant examples of altruism in both our women's groups and our men's groups. Martina, whom we introduced in the first chapter, and many of the more veteran members, spontaneously offer emotional support and words of encouragement to newer members. They also frequently choose to share aspects of their own healing processes in an effort to help other members on their way. These altruistic acts powerfully assist the givers to enhance their own feelings of value and self-efficacy. Moreover, they offer real hope to the recipients who witness these people, with disabilities like themselves, in roles characterized by mastery and understanding. Similarly, the men are able to share from their own experiences of recovery from offense behaviors and, through their altruism toward other members, are able to give something that their nondisabled, female group facilitators can never give.

Altruism has a further advantage in that it multiplies; one act of altruism by one person leads to the generation of altruistic acts in others. The facilitator needs to keep a keen eye to instances of altruistic behavior and affirm each individual for his efforts.

4. Installation of Hope

Over time people will have positive changes occur in their lives as a result of having worked through an issue in the group. In addition, they will have had the opportunity to report on positive events or situations with which they have learned to cope in their lives. Each instance provides an opportunity for other members to witness this growth, and to glimpse a sense of hope for their own condition. For example, when Melanie, a newer member, lost her job and was feeling quite bad about herself, three of the longer term members discussed having been fired in past jobs. They also talked about having eventually found jobs that they could handle and hang on to. Melanie had simply assumed the others had never been fired. Their stories, and currently successful employment, allowed her to feel a measure of hope for her own future.

5. Guidance

Receiving guidance from other members is necessary, yet difficult to facilitate adequately. In rare instances, direct advice can be tolerated and actually useful. However, in the majority of cases, advice-giving is not helpful and often infuriating to the person at the receiving end. A far more effective form of feedback takes place when other members simply share their own related experiences.

One member of a men's group was describing difficulties he was having on his job. Some members were quick to advise him to quit; others started to say he should call his job coach. Clearly this member's issue was a common experience to many of the members and elicited a spontaneous outpouring of advice—advice that appeared to be annoying the member with the problem. The facilitator then asked one very vocal participant how he came to know so much about the problem. What he revealed was his own story. He himself had had similar problems on a job and ended up telling his job coach and setting up a meeting. When this member revealed his own story, he was sharing his real-life experience rather than simply telling the other member what to do. This sharing may end up providing the same guidance regarding the situation, but it does so in a much more palatable way. The recipient does not feel put down; he can see the other person has been in the same boat. Others can share their experiences in a similar way, thus allowing the member a broad range of options from people who have already been through the ordeal.

6. Catharsis

The purging of emotions has long been a central feature in the therapeutic arsenal of psychotherapy. An individual or group catharsis may occur, as well as positively or negatively charged purging. Many theories exist as to what allows for a catharsis to occur. However, it is important to understand that the benefit is not limited to the person having the catharsis. Witnessing a catharsis can mediate a positive change in the observers as well.

Habitually anxious and timid, Erin, whom we described earlier, talked about her parents in fearful tones. She was always trying to hide from them her habit of talking to herself in her room. Of course, they would "catch" her and yell at her fairly regularly. Anxiety was always present when she spoke; sometimes she would also express sadness over the situation. After a fairly long time in treatment and much supportive work, Erin was ready to speak to her "father," represented by an empty chair. She had never told him how she felt about his reproaches and longed to express herself although she was terrified to do so. She was even more anxious than usual as she began. With a supportive double helping her as she verbalized her feelings, she began to say more and more. Her fear then gave way to anger, an anger that grew to the point of rage. She let out a torrent of fury she had not consciously realized she was feeling. When she finished, she was supported for her efforts, and her awareness of her full range of feelings was reinforced. She felt a great deal of relief and a good deal less anxious immediately after, as is the case following a catharsis. Many others described similar feelings of anger toward authority figures that they could not express, and felt a sense of release as well, along with a new awareness of the need to work on their own problems. (Note that helping Erin figure out what to do with these newfound feelings was established as the subject of future sessions. She was affirmed for having faced her fear of speaking up and for becoming aware of her feelings of anger. She was told this did not mean she should immediately go home and act on them, but rather "put them on the agenda" for the weeks to come.)

7. Modeling

Other than the effort of one's own action, nothing has more impact than watching others struggle with pertinent issues in their lives. When members witness others developing, whether through a role-play or by relating an experience, they learn something themselves. And, the more the observers identify with the speaker, the more benefit they derive. This is another important reason for doing good cognitive networking: People will really get to know their fellow members and understand what they have in common. Their attention to others' discussions and enactments, such as Erin's described previously, will be heightened as a result.

8. Self-Understanding

Members learn important things about themselves in various ways during the group process, but chiefly through feedback from others in the group and experiences they have during enactments. Carol is used to thinking of herself as a "screw-up." The middle child between two sisters without disabilities, she has carried a sense of incompetence with her throughout her life, a self-concept that is continually perpetuated by her parents now that her sisters have moved out of the house. Yet in group she is able to be a highly "competent" member, attentive to others, admired for her helpful feedback, and able to say some challenging things to other members in respectful ways. She has worked hard to master competence with respect to the interpersonal skills demonstrated in group. Moreover, she has gained competence in her functioning outside of group, having gotten herself a job on her own and kept it for over three years, a dramatic improvement over her previous work history. She has gotten herself off social security entirely. And although her role in her family has not changed, her understanding of herself has grown as she has consistently been given feedback by members and facilitators regarding her "competent" behavior in session and in the workplace.

Another important example of self-understanding can be seen in the progress of a young man named Kevin. Kevin had been referred for making inappropriate displays of friendship and affection with young children. He had spontaneously hugged and tickled young children in the supermarket where he worked, in full view of their parents and other bystanders, apparently unaware of the usual social taboos. Despite warnings, he reverted to this behavior at work from time to time. He eventually lost his job. Similar problems occurred when Kevin was out in his neighborhood, with a neighbor once calling the police when Kevin hugged her young son. Although Kevin never attempted sexual behavior with a child, his overly affectionate manner with children continued to get him in trouble. In the initial phase of Kevin's treatment, he often described feeling perplexed that he had gotten into so much trouble because of his behavior with children. He felt he had never done any harm; he had never hurt a child or ever intended to hurt one. What had he done that was so bad?

Through the group process, Kevin was exposed to the stories of two other similarly naive members who had gotten into very similar predicaments. He (and the others) had the opportunity to explore their feelings, without fear of being reprimanded. Kevin was able, after a time, to say that he felt an "urge" to be with children. He felt free and happy with children, the way he did as a child. Timid, passive, and highly conditioned to having his life run by authoritative adults, Kevin also identified being very limited in his ability to express himself with adults. He had inhibitions with authority figures and peers alike, which played out in his group behavior as well. Kevin was able to work on developing his assertiveness and social interaction with adults, and he took some of his learning from group into his day-to-day behavior so that he was able to find work and social activities he could enjoy. He also learned that even if children in his neighborhood initiated contact with him, he needed to make an excuse and quickly leave the scene, because he would be tempted to hug or tickle them if he had close contact with them. The acceptance of the other men, who had similar difficulties, and were working along the same lines, gave Kevin a space that existed nowhere else in his life to explore his own feelings and to test out new behaviors. Kevin's self-understanding and sense of personal responsibility are now such that even with new job coaches assigned to him, Kevin takes responsibility for informing them that he has learned that he is a very good worker, but that he cannot ever work at a job where children are present. A further positive footnote is that Kevin for the last year or so has had a girlfriend his own age. His contact with her is quite limited because of their living situations; however, their mutual satisfaction points to considerable growth.

9. Learning From Interpersonal Action

Learning takes place as a by-product of trying to adapt to and relate constructively to the group. The format of the group allows for a relatively high degree of structure within which the group norms are set and members can learn through interaction how best to accommodate to the norms. As in Carol's example, her interpersonal efforts have been consistently affirmed when they demonstrated assertive, respectful feedback or the sharing of personal experiences. The member's actual behavior in the group allows for this growth process. Simply telling people to relate in this way would not actually help them learn how to do it. Carol has experienced the positive feedback and genuine admiration of her group for her improving efforts to interrelate, a true learning-by-doing. Moreover, the success of the interpersonal skills she has developed in group provides her with a greater repertoire of skills to use in work, family, and other nongroup situations.

10. Self-Disclosure

As we noted earlier, two types of self-disclosure occur in group: horizontal and vertical. Horizontal self-disclosure refers to the less emotionally charged interpersonal exchanges typical of casual social interaction, whereas vertical self-disclosure refers to personal information of greater emotional depth. Often vertical self-disclosure from one member can activate the same in others. This is another way in which the group process benefits the therapeutic process. A member's self-disclosure helps him by providing emotional release and allowing for the opportunity to experience being accepted even when one has bared "shameful" secrets. For the other members, however, it can be a helpful warm-up to beginning disclosures of their own. Therapists can enhance this process by affirming each member's efforts at self-disclosure and by pointing out how one member's disclosure led to another's. The former member stands to gain an enhanced sense of self through the awareness that she has played a beneficial role in another member's therapy.

One caveat to bear in mind regarding self-disclosure is that too much self-disclosure too fast by one member may cause that person to feel vulnerable. Sometimes, a member may jump right into an in-depth presentation of painful material and, soon after, begin to feel anxiety. Old fears from having been ridiculed or punished for self-expression may arise. Even in individual therapy, some patients fail to show up for the next session, leaving the therapist surprised and dismayed. "What happened?" the therapist wonders. "Things were going so well!"

It is wise to try to avoid, or at least offset, such anxieties through some proactive intervention. The therapist can ask the disclosing member to take a pause to check in with the others regarding their understanding of his discussion thus far. If, as the therapist, you have the sense that this has been an unusual amount of depth for this individual, or if the individual is new to group and disclosing for the first time, explain to him that people often have different feelings after doing so much work. They might feel very good and have feelings of relief. They might also feel somewhat uncomfortable or worried about what others think of them. It should be stressed to the individual that some amount of discomfort is normal. Having forewarned him in this way, the next step is to affirm that you are proud of him for the effort he made and to ask how he is feeling about it. Affirm his stated feelings. Then ask him if he is wondering how any of the others might be feeling about what he said. Guide the disclosing member to check with each of the others regarding their feelings at this point. Be sure to affirm the disclosing member and each of the others for relating their feelings. End with a reminder to the disclosing member that you and the group are proud of what he was able to say, and that if he has any uncomfortable feelings during the week, he should not worry. He should know he is respected for his efforts and should come in the next week and report back any difficult feelings he had.

11. Corrective Recapitulation of the Primary Family

This therapeutic factor refers to a member's ability to "work through" feelings established in the family of origin and come to a corrective understanding of those feelings within the group. The feelings will always be repeated in their original, problematic way first. For example, Robert, who is used to feeling that no one cares about him, expresses some of these same feelings in the group. That is, he begins to feel that people in the group do not care about him. Similarly, Dana, who has been betrayed by many members of her family, becomes exceedingly angry with another member over a slight mishap that she interprets as a purposeful betrayal. Once these dynamics are brought into the group, there is an opportunity to alter them.

Carol, whom we mentioned earlier, has always felt her two sisters got a great deal more from her parents than she did—more attention, more help, more recognition. She felt they were both favored over her, particularly her younger sister. As time went on in group, Carol was able to verbalize that she felt the other members "got more" than she did, in terms of time and attention, and even as far as services outside the group. Carol's verbalization of this feeling, which took her a long time to work up to, was affirmed. Only by her verbalizing this could it be addressed, uncomfortable as it was for us and the other members to feel accused of "playing favorites." From this followed a long process, revisited over many sessions, in which Carol's feelings were heard and fed back, supported by use of the doubling technique, and then likened to her feelings in her family. Even going through this process of honoring her perceptions and working with them begins to separate it from the family pattern, in which, of course, her perceptions would be denied. ("What do you mean, things aren't fair? Look at all we do for you!") The group's effort continually goes toward giving her a different experience and challenging her tendency to bring her old, established perceptions into the group. As Carol begins to truly feel the difference of her group experience, she can experience some sense of healing in this area, rather than being doomed to repeat her old pattern indefinitely.

Of course, not all individuals with intellectual disabilities will be able to fully understand the process we have just described. With more cognitively impaired individuals, however, we often find that even a very concrete change for the better can be made. For example, it is common for people with intellectual disabilities to feel they are the least successful, or least valuable, members of their families. Their felt sense of being successful in the group, and being truly valued there, even without a sophisticated understanding of all the dynamics, goes a long way toward healing their damaged sense of self.

12. Existential Factors

Group members share the common bonds of death, loneliness, and suffering. These are inevitable facts of life. The group experience allows for a secure environment as members grieve and share their experiences of loss with each other.

Brian was referred for treatment primarily because he could not tolerate any job stress. Although he had many work skills and good interpersonal skills for a young man with mild mental retardation, Brian would not last long in jobs. His last position ended when he simply walked off from his post as a supermarket cart collector and refused to go back. Later, when confronted by his job coach, he claimed he had been pressured to work overtime. He did not want the job coach's intervention, asserting that he just did not feel ready to work; he felt it had become nearly impossible for him to focus on a job because his father had died fairly recently. Although Brian attributed much of his distress to his father's death, the job coach suspected his claims were overblown because he had not lived with his father in many years. Moreover, his prior work history had also been poor.

Brian responded positively to the prospect of joining a therapy group. He described uncomfortable feelings of pressure when on jobs, feeling that his job coaches as well as his supervisors demanded too much of him. In addition, he expressed a great deal of sadness over his father's death and repeatedly detailed the events surrounding his learning about the death. He indeed proved to be quite preoccupied with the loss of his father. He disclosed that not long after the funeral, feeling very despondent, he bought a six-pack of beer and took it down to the beach. He sat on the sand, in the dark, drinking the beer alone. He was found by the police, who picked him up and then released him with only a verbal admonishment.

We worked at exploring the significance of Brian's father's death with him. Almost immediately, other members began to share their experiences with loss to support Brian. Artie had lost his father, and two other members had each lost both parents. In fact, the loss of the second parent had led to the distress that caused each of the latter two members to enter group. These members, having been dependent on their parents well into adult-hood, understood Brian's loss in a way that more independent adults could only imagine. These men experienced not only the loss of their most sig-nificant emotional attachments but major life transitions as well, as is often the case for adults with intellectual disabilities when they lose their parents. Unlike the job coach, these fellows did not question Brian's reaction; they demonstrated acceptance and understanding and shared their own grieving—and healing—processes.

As the weeks went on, we learned that Brian had been traumatized at a very young age by his mother's abandonment of him and his family. He became very attached to his father, but his father was apparently emotion-ally and financially unstable. He married and then divorced two or three more times. Throughout his childhood, Brian would alternate between various foster homes and his father's home. Ultimately, the foster mother he had as a teenager became his sponsor when Brian reached adulthood. Thus we came to learn of Brian's early traumatic experiences regarding attachment and loss, which seemed to be related to his own job instability as well as to his traumatic reaction to his father's death—the father he never really had. The group gave Brian a place to talk about his fears with others he could identify with. He was truly supported by the other members and was never judged. He grew to look forward to the group and would openly discuss how connected and supported he felt. Brian never tried using alcohol again and has taken on a very supportive role with new members who enter the group. He has independently found volunteer work for himself, which he is able to feel good about.

13. Imparting of Information

This is the didactic element in the group. If you are facilitating anger management, AIDS training, sex education, advocacy, or literally any other topic, you may introduce the group to the topic or specific information and then allow for the warm-up and sharing and the enactment to follow from this orientation. Many "teachable moments" occur as a result of therapeutic work because of the emotional state evoked. For example, a purely didactic approach might allow for role training as a means of teaching a person with intellectual disabilities what to do if offered a bribe for sexual favors. However, actually allowing that same person to play a role in which she is confronted with a perpetrator offering a bribe and beginning to pressure her will induce a feeling of anxiety or apprehension. Then, with the group's help, when the individual experiences successfully getting away, she will feel a sense of relief. No didactic discussion alone can match the learning power associated with such a dramatic level of feeling change. Important pieces of learning can be mastered with the help of increased emotional readiness. In the chapter on sexual abuse avoidance training (chap. 6, this volume), we detail this therapeutic factor in action as we incorporate the practice of specific self-protective behaviors into the group format.

14. Development of Social Skills

This factor refers to the feedback available to members concerning social interaction. As we have discussed, there is a great deal of attention given to social skill development during group, primarily through affirmation for behavioral improvements, such as maintaining eye contact while speaking and listening, listening without interrupting, and so on. The group experience offers an opportunity for the development of these skills that cannot be found in didactic or trainer-centered models. In fact, we have found that as time has gone on, members will often begin to help other members improve their social skills during session. For example, Lisa, modeling the prompts given by the group facilitators, will often remind Fred that he should look at her while he is talking to her. She is on the alert to catch him when his eyes drift back to the floor and will cheerfully say, "Hey, Fred, I'm over here. Look up!"

THERAPEUTIC FACTORS AND THE
THERAPY PROCESS

In the chapters that follow, we delineate, step by step, the stages of an IBT group, through the description of actual group sessions we have conducted. In doing so, we also illustrate specific techniques from psychodrama that have been found to promote therapeutic change in people with intellectual disabilities. Note that we have organized this book into separate chapters on the basis of group members' issues, that is, offender, survivor, and prevention groups. IBT prevention groups differ from treatment groups in key ways that are discussed at length in chapter 6 on sexual abuse avoidance training. However, IBT treatment groups, whether for offenders or survivors (and keep in mind, many people are both), or for any patients across a broad array of psychological disorders, are essentially the same with respect to theoretical underpinnings, session format and stages, and techniques. We tend to form groups based on the common experiences of the members chiefly to enhance the experience of universality and member comfort. Our groups for offenders typically contain some men who have committed sexual offenses, some with aggressive behavior problems that are not sexual in nature, and others whose disorders include such things as self-injurious behavior, anxiety, agitation, verbal outbursts, and decreased tolerance for ordinary work and social stress. This same group of men will contain some who meet the diagnostic criteria for impulse control disorders, some who are better classified by anxiety disorders, and others who primarily have a mood disorder. A similar array of disorders characterizes our groups for survivors and includes some members who are diagnosed with posttraumatic stress disorder as well.

We say more about making intake decisions in this and following chapters. Our point at this juncture is to encourage readers who are learning to facilitate treatment groups to read the chapters on survivors as well as on offenders. Each chapter helps to round out a clinical understanding of the group process and essential techniques and strengthens the foundation for skills that will be useful for treating a majority of individuals with dual diagnoses.

GROUP THERAPY OR INDIVIDUAL:
CONSIDERATIONS FOR TREATMENT PLANNING

Before we go on to detail the applications of the IBT model, we would like to address the issue of treatment modality. Who should be referred to group?

Yalom (1995) asserted that, despite considerable research, determining which patients will benefit most from group therapy remains a murky process. In fact, after an exhaustive study of the literature, Yalom concluded that "on the issue of selection of patients, empirical research has failed to deliver" (p. 218). Yalom's thinking is that each group, and each individual in each group, is so "exquisitely complex" (p. 218) that the accurate measurement of key variables—variables that would mark an individual as a potentially successful group candidate—remains elusive.

One factor, however, that provides something of a guideline, as per Yalom's research and our own experience, is deviance from the group. That is, an individual who is significantly deviant from the other group members is least likely to benefit from the group and most likely to drop out prematurely. By "deviant," we mean only that the individual is different, in critical ways, from the other members. We are using the word deviant in the statistical sense. An individual who is moderately depressed but has no addictions would be the deviant in a group for mentally ill chemical abusers.

Furthermore, reviewing our own experience with patients who have psychological disorders and intellectual disabilities, we have had the worst outcomes with patients who were highly paranoid; specifically, paranoid to the point of having psychotic delusions. We have often had people with nonparanoid psychotic disorders, on medication, who functioned successfully in group. Sadly, however, we had dismal experiences with two cases in which the individuals, both with only mild mental retardation, had poor histories of medication compliance and tendencies toward paranoid delusions.

In both cases, one male and one female, we managed to maintain them in their respective groups a number of years, with uneven but gradual improvement in their abilities to take in support, to disclose painful experiences, and to relate to others. Because of their willingness to come to group over such long periods, and to struggle through some uncomfortable work, we developed a sense that the struggle was truly worthwhile. Yet in both cases, intense paranoid reactions to interpersonal dynamics with other members ultimately erupted. Both members hastily withdrew, and much difficult work, with each of these members and the remaining group members, needed to be done in the aftermath. In time, each individual was ultimately able to accept individual treatment and continue to make progress. The woman was able to do so within a few weeks, but the man returned to his former isolative state for a long period before being able to reengage.

We share this information in the hope of providing at least some limited guidance on the issue of determining whether an individual ought to be considered for group therapy. Certainly, many patients who may be able to benefit from group therapy may present themselves for treatment to an agency that has no appropriate group for them. The absence of an appropriate treatment group is a common reason for providing individual therapy. If your agency or clinic has some groups running, but the new patient you are evaluating seems to be deviant in some key way from other members in each of the groups, individual therapy should be offered.

As we have already made clear, our experience in working with hundreds of people with intellectual disabilities and psychological disorders has generated in us a decided preference for group work over individual treatment in most cases. Many of the therapeutic factors discussed in this chapter are unique to group psychotherapy. We advocate for the development of a range of treatment groups so that as many individuals as possible may have the opportunity to receive the benefit of group therapy. With few exceptions, such as severely paranoid individuals bordering on the psychotic level of personality organization—who should not be treated in group even with other paranoid individuals—we have found decided advantages with group treatment.

Another key diagnostic category for which group is likely to be contraindicated is sociopathy. Sociopathic members can be damaging to a group of nonsociopaths, although treatment in a group composed entirely of sociopaths may be preferable to individual treatment (Yalom, 1995). In our experience, sociopathy is relatively rare in the intellectually disabled population. We have never encountered enough referrals to form a group and have only treated these patients individually. If there is any suspicion that a new referral may be sociopathic, it is best to treat him individually until such concern is safely ruled out.

As we note elsewhere in this book, we have found that some variation in intellectual functioning can be tolerated, and even beneficial, within a group. Again, it is important not to have only one individual with an IQ that is extremely different from the others. What seems to work is if members represent a modest range, with a few people at various points along the range. For example, group has been successful with a few people who are at the mid-range of moderate mental retardation, a few at the high end of the moderate range, and a few at various points in the mild range. Similarly, we have run "lower functioning" groups with individuals ranging across various levels of moderate and severe mental retardation.

Additionally, as Yalom (1995) stressed, some range with respect to personality dynamics is also beneficial. If every member of a group has, say, a depressive character style, or an anxious style, or an avoidant style, or a manic style, the range of what members can offer to each other is grossly restricted. However, if variation in character styles exists among the membership, individuals will be able to offer each other different viewpoints on a given issue, as well as different modes of coping with stress and of problem solving.

Perhaps we can conceptualize the ideal group organization as one in which there is (a) moderate heterogeneity with respect to intellectual functioning; (b) moderate heterogeneity with respect to level of personality organization (or ego functioning)—those with more serious pathologies, that is, severely characterological and psychotically organized patients grouped separately from those with milder pathologies, that is, neurotic to moderately characterological individuals; and (c) a high degree of heterogeneity regarding character styles.

A final important point to consider in determining the best course of therapy is to bear in mind the general efficacy of group psychotherapy. We reported in chapter 2 that experts in sexual offense treatment (Sawyer, 2000) and in the treatment of trauma survivors (Harney & Harvey, 1999; van der Kolk, 1996) regard group psychotherapy as the treatment of choice in a majority of cases. Moreover, research into group therapy generally for patients with all types of psychological disorders points to a high degree of efficacy. Yalom (1995) presented the results of research that reviewed 32 well-controlled studies comparing individual and group psychotherapy. The results indicated that group therapy and individual therapy were equally effective in 75% of the studies; in the remaining 25% group therapy was *more* effective. Similarly, McDermut, Miller, and Brown (2001) conducted a meta-analysis of 48 studies and found that group therapy for depression was as efficacious as individual therapy, and the effect sizes suggested that the average treated participant was better off than 85% of the untreated participants. The authors concluded that the group therapy was particularly advantageous because of the savings in time and money.

Of course, all of the previously described research on group therapy's efficacy with trauma survivors, offenders, and general psychiatric patients has been conducted with nondisabled participants. We have detailed earlier the unique benefits group psychotherapy has to offer to people with intellectual disabilities, and, although efficacy research on the relative merits of group versus individual therapy for this population has yet to be done, the existing literature as well as our experience lead us to believe that group therapy has a distinct advantage.

We recommend every effort be made to create therapy groups that can accommodate a majority of people with intellectual disabilities. We recommend individual therapy for those patients who are not a good fit with existing groups and for severely paranoid or sociopathic individuals. In addition, we recommend individual treatment as a first course of action toward the following ends: (a) further assessing the patient to determine treatment needs (i.e., individual or group therapy, behavioral intervention, or need for family/caregiver involvement); (b) orienting the individual toward the therapy process; and (c) helping the individual to identify treatment goals. Some individuals may need very little time with this, whereas others may need extended sessions.

Finally, we should add that it is not uncommon for individuals who are good candidates for group to be anxious and resistant to your efforts to include them. It is often best to encourage these individuals to try group; more often than not, it is exactly what is needed. With such patients we use a limited number of individual sessions to explore the specifics of the fear and to dispel misconceptions. Then we present the individual with a plan to test out group that includes a safety valve. We tell him that we would like him to go to four sessions and have him make a decision after that time. If he still does not feel good about group, then we will make another plan for his treatment.

If we feel group is in the patient's best interest, and if we have an appropriate group running, we move rather quickly toward having the individual try out the group as part of his decision-making process rather than attempt to dispel all of his fears in advance. Talking about group is no match for actually experiencing it, and for most people the experience puts an end to this anticipatory anxiety. In addition, the freedom to opt out after four weeks helps the patient feel an important sense of control. At the end of four sessions, the individual can make a truly informed decision to accept or reject group treatment. A great majority choose to accept it.

We revisit the subject of group candidacy in chapters 4, 5, and 6, reviewing and elaborating on concepts presented here. Determining which treatment will best serve the needs of a given individual is inarguably a matter of great importance, deserving careful thought as well as research.

SUMMARY

A good deal of territory was covered in this chapter. Before presenting applications of the IBT model, we would like to encapsulate what we have put forth so far. In this chapter we considered the historical background concerning therapeutic treatment for people with intellectual disabilities and psychological disorders. We described the therapeutic rationale for a particular model of psychotherapy, IBT, and explored the model's therapeutic value with respect to 14 previously determined factors indicative of treatment efficacy.

To begin to familiarize clinicians with the model's workings, we described the four stages of a session, using case examples from actual sessions to give a feel for the process. Finally, we discussed the matter of determining treatment modality, examining the relative merits of group and individual psychotherapy.

We turn next to an in-depth discussion of the IBT group process.

APPENDIX 3.1:
SESSION STAGES AND ASSOCIATED TASKS

Stage 1: Orientation

Leaders clarify:
Rules (safety and confidentiality)
Meeting schedule
Nature of the group (e.g., offender treatment or avoidance training, etc.)
Leaders facilitate cognitive networking:
Affirm members for attending to each other
Encourage members to choose speakers
Leaders make mental note regarding:
Sociometry of choices

Stage 2: Warm-Up and Sharing

Leaders: Acknowledge and affirm deepening disclosure
Note member interest in potential protagonist
Suggest moving protagonist's issue into action

Stage 3: Enactment

Leaders invite action by:
Helping protagonist demonstrate issue psychodramatically
Inviting auxiliaries to participate
Leaders build support for protagonist by:
Doubling or having members double
Verbally affirming protagonist

Stage 4: Affirmation

Leaders affirm each member for:
Efforts at participation
Demonstration of therapeutic factors
Leaders encourage members to affirm each other

APPENDIX 3.2:
THE DOUBLE

Functions of the Doubling Technique

Provides emotional support for protagonist
Gives voice to feelings
Clarifies or reorganizes perceptions

Processes and Techniques Used in Doubling

Restating (to demonstrate understanding of protagonist)
Speaking the unspoken (to express what protagonist feels but cannot say)
Exaggerating (to assert loudly what protagonist presents timidly)
Amplifying (to highlight key parts of protagonist's statements)
Verbalizing the resistance (to clarify impediments to therapeutic change)
Clarifying conflict (to voice competing emotions or ambivalence)
Introducing alternatives (to voice ways to reframe protagonist's perceptions of self or situation)
(*Note: The member doubling checks accuracy of each doubled statement with protagonist; protagonist may repeat key statements.*)

Selection of the Double

The facilitator may choose the double
The protagonist may choose the double
A member may volunteer to double
The facilitator may double
The protagonist may double for himself

Types of Double

Single Double (one person stands behind protagonist, making statements as per techniques (see above)
Paired Double (two people stand behind protagonist, to amplify or exaggerate one feeling/perception, or to voice conflicting feelings/perceptions)
Multiple Double (usually a series of single doubles in succession to heighten universality; may also be a "chorus" of members doubling at once)

4

GROUP TREATMENT FOR TRAUMA AND SEXUAL ABUSE SURVIVORS WITH INTELLECTUAL DISABILITIES

Give sorrow words. The grief that does not speak
Whispers the o'er fraught heart and bids it break.
—William Shakespeare

Before a presentation of our group treatment model for trauma survivors, a brief review of some of the relevant findings from trauma research, and from intellectual disabilities research, is in order. As we discussed previously, many people with intellectual disabilities experience sexual abuse; in fact, as we saw in chapter 2, growing research suggests that people with intellectual disabilities are subjected to higher rates of sexual abuse than are nondisabled individuals (Furey, 1994; Mansell & Sobsey, 2001). Of course, sexual abuse is not the only form of trauma to which people—disabled and nondisabled—are exposed, although in present-day, American society data point to sexual abuse as the most common form of trauma experienced by women, whereas males are more likely to experience combat-related trauma and noncombat violence such as witnessing homicide or severe injury (McFarlane & DeGirolamo, 1996). Traumatic experiences resulting from accidents, surviving terrorist attacks, and experiencing natural disasters account for additional cases among both men and women.

Many people who experience traumatic events develop posttraumatic stress disorder (PTSD); however, as we noted in chapter 2, PTSD is only one of many disorders that can result from traumatic experiences. Traumatic exposure has been shown to lead to such conditions as borderline personality disorder, dissociative disorders, somatization disorder, self-mutilation, eating disorders, substance abuse disorders, panic and anxiety disorders, phobias, and protracted states of depression (Herman, 1992a; Mayou, 2001; van der Kolk, 1996). Research suggests that even those trauma survivors whose symptomatology fails to meet all the diagnostic criteria for PTSD may still warrant psychological treatment in that many exhibit severe emotional distress and suicidal ideation (Marshall et al., 2001).

We discuss two points related to these findings. First, we need to recognize that individuals with varying psychological symptoms may be victims of traumatic exposure. Second, we need to consider that a variety of experiences may constitute a traumatic event.

With regard to the first point, it is important to remember that, as we screen individuals for services, those who do not meet the criteria for PTSD may still have experienced traumatic exposure. If emotional distress or significant symptoms are present, treatment should be made available. In addition, these individuals may or may not meet the criteria for another psychiatric diagnosis. In any case, if an individual has experienced a trauma, disclosure of the traumatic experience will often take place during the course of psychotherapy, once the patient feels safe.

Regarding the second point, we need to consider that what constitutes a traumatic event cannot be neatly or narrowly defined in terms of a limited number of experiences. Even the fourth edition of the *Diagnostic and Statistical Manual of Mental Disorders* (*DSM–IV*; American Psychiatric Association, 1994), the standard diagnostic reference in the mental health field, defines traumatic exposure in rather broad strokes. The manual categorizes trauma as the experience of "actual or threatened death or serious injury, or a threat to the physical integrity of self or others" (p. 427). It goes on to state that the individual's response to the event must have "involved intense fear, helplessness, or horror," adding that "in children, this may be expressed instead by disorganized or agitated behavior" (p. 428).

THE NATURE OF TRAUMA AND ITS INTERFACE WITH INTELLECTUAL DISABILITIES

What do we know of the types of trauma most often experienced by people with intellectual disabilities? We know that sexual abuse, the most common form of trauma for women in the general population, is much more common for women with intellectual disabilities. We also know that men with intellectual disabilities seem to be at somewhat higher risk for sexual abuse than men in the general population. At the same time, men with intellectual disabilities are less likely than nondisabled men to experience service-related trauma (through combat, police work, and the like). Finally, people with intellectual disabilities, like many people from the general population, are often subjected to traumatic experiences in the form of abuse (both sexual and nonsexual) and neglect during childhood. As noted in chapter 2, van der Kolk (1996) and Herman (1992a) pointed out that a significant majority of psychiatric patients have histories of trauma, frequently as a result of abuse and neglect in their own families of origin. Trauma researchers (Raphael, Wilson, Meldrum, & McFarlane, 1996) have also noted that personal traumas, such as the abuse of a child, motor vehicle accidents, or rapes and assaults experienced by adults, typically draw little or no public attention, with the exception of a few sensationalized cases. Raphael et al. pointed out that such experiences can be very isolating; they do not garner attention or support for victims, despite the fact that the total number of people exposed to these events is greater than the number exposed to large-scale disasters.

As we noted in chapter 2, people with intellectual disabilities are more likely to have experienced many of the life stressors and health complications known to increase vulnerability to psychiatric disorders. Research into factors that may predispose to the development of PTSD also raises the possibility that people with intellectual disabilities are at increased risk for this disorder in additional ways. For example, in the general population exposure to certain key life events during childhood have been found to predict both an increased likelihood of experiencing later trauma and an increased likelihood of developing PTSD after exposure to trauma. These key life events consist of negative parenting behavior, early separation from parents, parental poverty, and lower educational levels (Shalev, 1996). As discussed in chapter 2, the heightened levels of family and maternal stress in homes with an intellectually disabled child would increase the child's exposure to negative parenting behavior. Increased levels of separation from parents are more common in the lives of children with intellectual disabilities because of higher rates of both institutionalization and hospitalizations. Finally, parental poverty and lower educational levels are both related to lower socioeconomic level, a factor that increases vulnerability to life stress and to the development of psychiatric disorders, and that is more prevalent among people with intellectual disabilities than the general population (Nezu, Nezu, & Gill-Weiss, 1992).

As if these strikes against individuals with intellectual disabilities were not enough, trauma research with military personnel also suggests that people with lower IQ scores are more likely to develop PTSD following combat exposure than are people with IQ scores at the higher ranges of intelligence (Macklin et al., 1998). It is likely that lower levels of intelligence would increase vulnerability to psychopathology following other forms of trauma as well. In a related vein, a preliminary survey by Carlson (1998), and observations reported by Murphy and Razza (1998), suggest that domestic violence victims with intellectual disabilities appear to be even more vulnerable to psychological, physical, and sexual abuse than nondisabled women, and that they are similarly, but more severely, affected.

The lives of people with intellectual disabilities are further complicated by the sometimes traumatizing effects of developmental milestones. Research suggests that psychological crises commonly occur in people with intellectual disabilities in relation to developmental milestones such as puberty and adolescence, being surpassed by younger siblings, out-of-home placement, and death of parents (Levitas & Gilson, 2001). These milestones often constitute extreme stressors in the lives of people with intellectual disabilities, taxing them beyond their ability to cope. Levitas and Gilson noted that such developmental crises often precipitate mental health consultations and hospitalizations, yet their role in the genesis of the patient's symptoms is frequently overlooked. Moreover, these authors underscore the anguish that family members of people with intellectual disabilities often experience at various points in time. They point out how traumatizing family members find such milestones as the initial shock of learning that their child is mentally retarded; coping with the realities of school, such as classification and special needs; dealing with the transition from school to unknown possibilities; and the loss of dreams regarding whom the child might have been. Thus, the intellectually disabled individual, already compromised in regard to his or her ability to cope with stress and trauma, is likely to be growing up in a family that is compromised by its own suffering as well.

We are left to consider that a broad range of experiences may be traumatizing and that, for people with intellectual disabilities, the risk that a given experience will be traumatizing may well be heightened. In our experience with people who have intellectual disabilities, we often see symptoms suggestive of traumatic exposure, without clear-cut documentation that traumatic experiences took place. In light of the research mentioned here, it may well be that many people with intellectual disabilities display reactions suggestive of trauma in response to events that may not ordinarily be thought of as traumatizing. Moreover, people with intellectual disabilities are sometimes poor historians; salient events may not be spontaneously presented. Furthermore, the construction of a meaningful life narrative, in which key events are clarified and their effects understood and acknowledged, may take the work of a lengthy therapy. (Of course, this is often the case for nondisabled patients as well.)

In our work with people who have intellectual disabilities, sexual abuse, in many and varied forms, is by far the most common form of trauma we see. Other experiences, which seem to have been traumatizing based on the symptomatic presentation of the patients involved, have included such things as physical battering, chronic exposure to denigrating verbal abuse, and death of parents along with subsequent relocation.

It is not uncommon for adults with intellectual disabilities to present with the agitation and disorganized behavior noted in the *DSM–IV* criteria for children who have been exposed to trauma. Research has found that, for people with intellectual disabilities, agitation and disorganized behavior are more common symptoms of depressive episodes, manic episodes, anxiety disorders, and PTSD (Nugent, 1997) than they are for patients without intellectual disabilities. The common referral problem of self-injurious behavior is now understood to be, in some cases, a symptom of depression, mania, anxiety, or PTSD, and preliminary research suggests that some proportion of cases of self-injurious behavior may be due to sexual victimization (Burke & Bedard, 1995).

BEGINNING TREATMENT:
SAFETY AND CONFIDENTIALITY

Previously, we have discussed the importance of establishing the safety and confidentiality of the group. This is perhaps the best place to start a discussion of therapy groups for survivors of interpersonal trauma because it is so crucial to the process. Safety and confidentiality are the absolute foundations of a therapy group for people who have been sexually abused or who have experienced other forms of trauma at the hands of another person, such as battering. In the absence of safety and confidentiality, no real therapeutic work will be done.

People who have been sexually abused have experienced the most intimate physical and psychological form of interpersonal harm. They know, from actual, lived experience, that people cannot always be trusted, and now they are being asked to trust a group of people they have just met. They know that people are capable of doing great harm, and now they are being asked to rely on a group of people for help. Of course, an individual's fears regarding the prospect of some form of betrayal is not likely to be limited to the other members alone. Research has shown that many of those who sexually abuse people with intellectual disabilities are staff members and other professionals involved with the individual. Mansell and Sobsey (2001), whose pioneering work was noted in chapter 2, reported the results of a survey of 215 victims of sexual abuse or assault, conducted through the Abuse and Disability Project at the University of Alberta, Alberta, Canada. The sample included people from Canada, the United States, and New Zealand. Mansell and Sobsey reported that disability service providers, such as personal care attendants, psychiatrists, and residential staff, constituted 26.3% of the abusers; specialized foster parents (or sponsors) 6%; and specialized transportation providers 5.1%. Note that research on the abuse of people with intellectual disabilities, such as that by Mansell and Sobsey (2001), and by Furey (1994), who investigated 461 reports of sexual abuse over a five-year period, shows that most offenders are known to the victim. (This is regularly found in studies of child abuse as well.) Abusers have been found to come from all categories of relationship to the victim, including paid professionals and support staff, volunteers, family members and extended family, acquaintances, and neighbors. In Furey's research, only 8% of the abusers were strangers, and in Mansell and Sobsey's report, strangers accounted for a mere 6.8%. Our clients, therefore, may already have had experiences with service providers that would cause them to be wary of their new group facilitators. Vigilant respect for boundaries is required of those of us leading groups for abused individuals. Even seemingly minor infringements, such as responding to a staff member's question about the individual during a casual interaction in the hall, could contribute to the individual's distrust of the group leader.

Although the parameters of safety and confidentiality must be discussed in session, discussion alone is not sufficient to make members feel that they are safe. Each member's sense of safety in the group develops through repeated experiences in the group in which they are treated with respect for their person, their feelings, and their boundaries.

We begin our groups with an explanation of the confidentiality rule, making sure each member understands the responsibility not to talk about the other members outside of session. The experience, over time, of facilitators and members proving trustworthy in this regard ensures that the group experience is respectful for each member. Such respect is often unique in a participant's experience. Moreover, it is only in a climate of such dependable respect that members can share their most painful and shameful life events, and venture to do the work of rebuilding themselves.

As we have stated, when explaining the confidentiality rule to more impaired individuals, it is helpful to tell them not to repeat any member's name outside of group. Members need to be told that they are free to discuss their *own* group experiences with other people in their lives, however, if they desire. They should not be made to feel they must "keep secrets." This is an important distinction to clarify because victims of sexual abuse are so often forced by perpetrators to keep the abuse secret or face greater harm.

Each time a new member joins the group, we take the opportunity to revisit the confidentiality discussion. In groups with veteran members, we have found that the members themselves will frequently initiate the discussion during a new member's first session.

We have found it necessary to speak to caregivers who work with our group members regarding patient confidentiality. It is generally helpful at the outset of treatment to tell staff and family who bring the group member in for treatment that we keep the details of the sessions confidential, and, just as we tell the group members, we only break confidentiality for one of two reasons. First, in situations in which the member and facilitators agree it is in the member's best interest to discuss a certain issue with others, and the member gives her consent; and second, in cases in which imminent harm will come to the patient or someone else if the information is kept confidential. Imminent harm generally means urgent suicidal or homicidal risk, or the risk of abuse of a minor. Of course, mental health practitioners are required to abide by the reporting statutes relevant to their particular license and state and should plan their confidentially discussions accordingly.

This should not be taken to mean that there is no place for communication between group facilitators and the staff and others who help support the individual. Many members, after becoming involved in group, request that we attend meetings, such as those held for their individual habilitation plans, along with them. They feel so strongly supported by the group, and by those of us leading the group, that they feel the facilitator's presence would be an asset at their meetings. In these cases we discuss with the individual exactly what we will and will not say in advance of the meeting. During the meeting we limit our role to two functions: (a) supporting the individual as she expresses her feelings and point of view and (b) asserting that the individual is making good use of her therapy and is a valued member.

Returning to the initial discussion of safety, the final issue pertains to each member's right to be free from physical aggression, threats of aggression, or verbal abuse in session. This also means, however, that members carry the same responsibility toward each other outside of group. Group cannot be a safe place if even one member harms, threatens, or is verbally hostile to one other member.

In our experience with groups of women, we have rarely encountered problems with verbal or physical aggression. We have, however, had reports of confidentiality violations. For example, one group member, Wanda, had become friendly with another, named Anne. Wanda and Anne began to talk with each other fairly regularly on the phone. On one occasion, Wanda even spoke to Anne's boyfriend on the phone while he was at Anne's apartment. Wanda made the mistake, however, of bringing up a topic with the young man that she only knew about because of her group membership. The boyfriend became angry with Anne for what she had said in the group. Anne brought the problem up at the next session. Everyone felt that the mistake had been an innocent, albeit thoughtless one, and decided to let Wanda continue her group membership. Wanda acknowledged her mistake and apologized. As facilitators, we encourage the group members to discuss their feelings and arrive at a consensus regarding the offending member. We have come to feel that the cognitive impairments of some people with intellectual disabilities make learning the confidentiality issues more difficult, and thus an opportunity to learn through a trial such as this seems warranted. This opportunity for another chance cannot be given at the other members' expense, however, and can only be done when all members concur. In the case of Wanda, she ultimately re-offended, breaking the confidentiality of another member. She was then asked to leave the group.

A small number of other members, from both survivor and offender groups, have had to leave group because of continued problems with confidentiality. More often than not, however, members have learned the rule after one or two mistakes. For the member who must leave the group, an individual follow-up session or several sessions should be scheduled to fully explore the individual's understanding of what happened, as well as her feelings about it. An assessment of the need for continued therapy can be done again at that time, and individual sessions offered if deemed necessary. In one case, a male member had garnered a growing animosity because of his repeated confidentiality transgressions. He truly regretted his behavior and demonstrated a strong sense of connection to the men in the group. Unfortunately, his keen interest in the others, coupled with his poor impulse control, led to more transgressions than the membership could forgive. Because of his expressed desire to continue in group, we transferred him to another group, reviewing with him what he needed to do to maintain his membership. He was successfully able to redress his problem as a result and was grateful for the opportunity to start over.

The example of Wanda and Anne brings up a related issue. It is important to tell members that their contacts with each other outside of group should be brought up and shared with the rest of the group in the next session. As facilitators, we tend to be encouraging of members' efforts to engage in supportive relationships with each other outside of group, with the knowledge that such relationships may complicate the therapy process. In fact, group therapy experts working with the general population often advise members not to get closely involved with one another as this may compromise what they feel comfortable saying in group. In any case, because facilitators cannot control members' behavior outside of group, it is wise to recommend from the beginning that their extra-group activities be disclosed in group. Over the years we have found that more good than harm comes from the relationships that members have developed. Very few of the members who begin treatment have healthy, dependable relationships with peers. Learning how to develop mutually satisfying relationships is always an important goal for therapy and seems to be helped considerably by both members experiencing the same type of interpersonal learning in group.

Related to this issue is the fact that people with intellectual disabilities tend to be involved in many different types of groups with one another. Recreation, day program, and residential programs serving people with intellectual disabilities all draw from the same population within a county or limited geographic region. Because their numbers are few, people with intellectual disabilities often cannot avoid having contact with each other outside of their therapy group. Although individuals from the general population typically have a broad range of options for negotiating their free time and their choice of work environment, and can expect to have no other contact with members of their therapy group, people with intellectual disabilities generally live their lives within much smaller circles. As such, it is even more important to prepare members for maintaining the confidentiality rule in various settings and to help them learn how to manage friendships successfully.

GROUP COMPOSITION

As we indicated in chapter 3, how to determine who is a good candidate for group psychotherapy has been a topic of considerable research, with rather murky results. Yalom (1995), whom we referred to earlier, and who has established himself as the foremost researcher in the field of group psychotherapy, has conducted an enormous amount of research in this area and has also evaluated the research of scores of other clinicians. His conclusion was that few hard-and-fast criteria can be counted on to distinguish good group therapy candidates from poor ones, and he felt that, in general, the therapist's best course of action is to determine which patients "cannot possibly work in a therapy group and should be excluded. And then they should proceed to accept all other patients" (p. 219). Admittedly, this is a crude assessment strategy. What makes for a candidate who cannot possibly work in a therapy group? Essentially, Yalom found that the "deviant," that is, the individual *most unlike* the other members, is the most likely to terminate prematurely and to have an unsuccessful group therapy experience. This does not mean the individual is deviant on some absolute measure; it only refers to the individual's status compared with the rest of the group. For example, imagine a group for combat survivors with PTSD containing seven members who are extremely chronic, unable to work, and subsisting on disability checks. If a patient were referred for the eighth slot who manages his PTSD with only occasional periods of panic and insomnia, and works full time, *that* patient would be the group deviant.

As we have noted, in all of our groups, whether for survivors, offenders, or other forms of psychopathology, we find that the group can well tolerate a moderate range both with respect to severity of symptoms and to level of intellectual functioning. For example, a group in which roughly half of the members can be classified in the range of mild mental retardation and the other half in moderate mental retardation tends to be workable. No one person is extremely deviant from the rest, and the range of intellectual functioning allows for sufficient communication. We do not screen out candidates on the basis of prior intelligence testing, however. An individual whose records indicate an IQ score in the range of severe mental retardation would still be evaluated for group because experience has taught us that IQ score reports are not good screening tools for psychotherapy. Some individuals with surprisingly low scores are able to comprehend and communicate sufficiently to engage in the group process.

Each person referred for therapy is given an individual assessment by the primary group facilitator prior to beginning group. An individual whose cognitive functioning is such that she is completely unable to describe any of her experience in words is then generally referred for a behavioral intervention. An individual whose verbal ability is extremely limited (such as a tendency toward accurate but one-word responding) and needs consistent direction for fundamental interpersonal skills (e.g., habitually looks at the floor while speaking) may still be accepted for group therapy. We tend to keep a number of groups running so that we can accommodate a range of needs. An individual whose interpersonal skills are severely limited and requires a great deal of work on skill development to function in group is generally accepted into a group in which other members have similar needs. In both "lower functioning" and "higher functioning" groups, however, we include individuals across something of a range. We have found that the members at the upper levels of skill development (in relation to their group) offer potent models for less developed members and positively influence the evolution of the group's functioning. These more skilled members benefit from the expanded sense of self they develop as a result of making their contributions.

In screening women referred for therapy, there will inevitably be cases of known sexual abuse, as well as cases with no known sexual abuse. Much has been written on the subject of group therapy for abuse survivors in the general population, however, as we mentioned in chapter 2, there is limited literature on group therapy for trauma or sexual abuse survivors with intellectual disabilities. As a result, the intake process we have evolved, while drawing heavily from the work of trauma experts such as Judith Herman (1992a) and Bessel van der Kolk (1996), has also been shaped by our experiences with survivors who have intellectual disabilities.

We have found that many women referred for therapy with no known sexual abuse ultimately disclose prior abuse experiences. Sometimes these disclosures are made during the initial interview. In other cases, they come after rather long periods of group membership. In these cases it seems that a prolonged period of integration into the group is needed before these individuals feel safe enough to begin discussion of their trauma.

There have been women, as well, whom we have taken into our survivor's group (we call it simply the *women's group*) who never report sexual trauma, even after long-term group membership and significant symptom reduction. Initially, we take these women in because they present a serious symptom picture, often including posttraumatic symptoms, severe depression or anxiety, self-abusive behavior, and often hostile or unpredictable interpersonal behavior. Despite competent work skills, these women frequently have difficulty maintaining job placements because of their interpersonal hostility or reactivity. Essentially, then, we include women in the group whose symptom picture and cognitive functioning fit, within rather wide margins, the general patterns of the other group members. The cause of the individual's distress and dysfunction, that is, sexual abuse or some other form of trauma, does not have to be determined in advance for the individual to have a successful group experience. Similarly, group members need not have experienced the very same types of trauma to work effectively together. A person with distressing symptoms needs to begin treatment as soon as possible and is likely to derive great benefit from being in a group with others who have experienced similar distress and made improvement.

GROUP PROCESS: A SESSION CLOSE UP

Sessions follow the four-stage format described in chapter 3. During the orientation stage, members tend to bring up topics of immediate concern. Some of these topics seem directly related to abusive experiences or traumatic exposure; however, many do not. Beginning therapists sometimes think that the presentation of topics other than abuse represents resistance and call for the member to be redirected back to the issue of abuse. Actual experience with successful group participants has demonstrated otherwise, however. The experience of sexual abuse and other traumas such as battering and verbal abuse, especially when experienced chronically throughout one's developmental years, cause symptoms that affect day-to-day functioning and personal relationships. How members manage everyday life events bears directly on their recovery. Direct discussion of memories of abuse is just one facet of the recovery process.

A closer look at an actual session illustrates this point and provides a sense of the flow of the group process. The particular session we are about to examine occurred in a long-term, ongoing group. Carol, whom we introduced in chapter 3, is the second of three sisters. She habitually feels devalued by her family because of her disability and feels she is not loved like her two sisters, particularly her younger sister whom Carol describes as the favorite.

Carol's symptoms generally include frequent experiences of anxiety, periodic depressed mood, initial insomnia, and compulsive eating, especially when highly stressed. She is able to identify these problems as issues she needs to work on. Additionally, Carol is quite limited in her ability to deal with stressful interpersonal encounters. Despite adequate verbal skills, Carol has great difficulty verbalizing her personal feelings to others and frequently suffers because she fails to express herself. She has become increasingly aware, through the group, that this is an area she needs to address. In addition, Carol lies quite regularly. This appears to be a long-standing habit she developed because of the tremendous anxiety she has about being direct with her feelings.

Carol has a boyfriend of many years and is working on increasing her assertiveness with him. A low point for Carol occurred several years ago when Carol played strip poker with her boyfriend and one of his male friends. They had played this game many times, often chiding Carol that she would have to have sex with the friend if she lost. This one particular time, Carol felt she had lost so badly she could not get out of the consequence. Verbally, but not physically pressured by both her boyfriend and the friend, she cooperated in having sex with the friend while her boyfriend waited downstairs. She soon found herself feeling enraged at her boyfriend for not having stopped the friend and for, instead, having encouraged them both to go through with the act. Sadly, she had no way of anticipating how bad this experience would make her feel about herself for a long time to come.

During the particular session we are about to detail, Carol's focus was on her feelings about work. Instead of her usual complaints about the job, in which she also feels devalued and disrespected, she announced that she was simply going to quit. This was distressing to us as group leaders. Carol had made tremendous progress in the past three years. She had found a job as a supermarket cashier on her own and had maintained it successfully, with the help of a limited amount of job coaching added later. She was taken off Social Security as a result of the increasing hours she was able to work over the years, and at this point was in a union and had full benefits, including her own insurance. At age 33, this accomplishment stood in marked contrast to her prior work history. Over the years since her high school graduation, Carol had gotten and lost numerous part-time positions. Her skill level was rarely the problem. Interpersonal relationships led to her downfall. Carol was quick to feel slighted. She would react to this by doing anything but directly addressing the problem. She would withdraw, use passive-aggressive means of expressing her anger, and occasionally lash out by leaving hostile phone messages when she could no longer contain her resentment.

Of course, our feelings about Carol's announcement, however relevant, were not the place to start. We directed ourselves to the task of facilitating the warm-up and sharing stage by encouraging Carol to give the group more detail on her thinking. Carol cited examples in which she felt her manager did not treat her with respect. She also expressed feeling overwhelmed by the total amount of work she had to do each week. Carol's parents insisted she do many hours of free babysitting for her younger sister's two children.

Between the babysitting and her supermarket job, Carol had little time to herself. Carol consistently maintained that there was no negotiating with her parents, so if she wanted time for herself, she had to take it out of the job. Her manager, unfortunately, was not always accommodating, which led to Carol's sense of being taken advantage of at work as well. Finally, Carol had a job coach from whom she wanted more support. She was angry with her as well for not understanding her need for emotional support. Of course, she had not communicated this need to the job coach, who had essentially withdrawn after ensuring that Carol's work skills were adequate.

As Carol outlined her frustration and intention to quit, other members spontaneously responded to her. These unsolicited expressions of support can go unrecognized by novice group leaders for the valuable gifts they are. Well-intentioned, but clinically naïve, referring parties will often inform us that a new referral *needs* individual therapy, because of the seriousness of her problem. They assume that group therapy is a watered-down version of the "real thing." But there is a beautiful and healing presence in the group that those who have not taken part in one do not know. The other members, who have lived with some of the same anguish, can offer things that many of us trained professionals cannot.

Louise, a long-time group member, was moved by Carol's anguish and volunteered to provide some doubling for Carol's emotions. As the double, she stood behind Carol and verbalized Carol's own feelings. Remember that this is done in the first person, so that the protagonist hears statements that she can directly repeat, if she agrees with them. Louise said, "I'm really mad. I just can't stand it anymore." (If the protagonist disagrees with the statement, she is asked to correct it.) In this case, Louise was already well tuned in to Carol's emotional state, and Carol found the doubling to be quite supportive.

As noted in chapter 3, doubling has a number of desirable effects. The protagonist knows with certainty that she has been heard and is understood. Moreover, the double can verbalize emotional extremes that the protagonist might not be saying. For example, in facilitating this segment, I asked Louise what she, as Carol's double, might want to say if she did not have to worry about any consequences. Louise said, "Screw all of you! I'm going to do what I want to do, and you can all go to hell!" Carol laughed for the first time that day and said, "Yeah, that's it." Louise then spontaneously added, "At least you know we love you here. We know what you're going through."

Other members verbalized support for Carol as Louise sat back down. Most of the women easily identified with feeling used and understood Carol's desire to simply run away from the perceived oppression. However, one member, Martina, whom we discussed at length in chapter 1, was able to look at the problem from a different perspective. She brought out how far Carol had come, keeping this job for so long and getting off Social Security.

This was a difficult position to take in this particular group. Most of the members were simply caught up in Carol's emotional state of resentment, which she targeted against the job. She was far too frightened by her parents to directly present her resentments to them. But Martina, having made some progress in this area herself, was able to say that Carol might really need to tell her parents how drained and angry she was from all the hours of free babysitting she had to do; that her increased work hours were very demanding and needed to be prioritized. Of course, Martina's language was somewhat plainer, but she made a critical point.

At this juncture, because Carol had already been well supported by the membership, she was in a somewhat better emotional state to take in an alternative perspective. In addition, Martina deserved to be given some support for having been the sole voice for an unpopular, but important, position. Leone, the cofacilitator, took this opportunity to voice her concerns and echoed Martina's comments. Leone's words provided Martina with support for having had the courage to express her feelings. Additionally, Leone's repetition and affirmation of Martina's concern provided Carol with a second opportunity to consider this perspective.

The warm, supportive feeling that had been engendered began to change as the members sensed Carol's obvious tension in the face of these concerns. Yet there was reason to be hopeful. Despite the rashness of her decision to quit, there was already one big advantage over Carol's old behavior pattern: She had told us her plans before acting on them. In the past, Carol would quit in haste or get herself fired. Now she had a group of people she could confide in, so the opportunity to alter her usual process existed.

To facilitate this juncture, I turned to Carol, slowing down the action briefly, and commented on the process thus far. Addressing her, I said, "Carol, you have done a great thing for yourself today. You reached a crisis, and before acting on it, you brought it in here. That's a big change for you. We know that you are used to acting quickly on things, because you can't tell your parents. They always criticize your ideas. But you trusted us with this problem. You were able to get lots of support for your feelings, and you are even getting some new ideas. [Turning toward the other members, and gesturing toward each in turn] I want to thank all the group members for giving so much time and so much help. I think we can all see that you are trying to solve your problems better by thinking them through with the group first. That's a good change."

Carol was able to feel good about framing her process in this way. This comment also united the members under the broader umbrella of a well-rounded group who wants to provide both emotional support and new perspectives to help a member through a crisis. (Note, it is important, as Yalom, 1995, has stressed, that the facilitator seize opportunities to make unifying group-process comments such as these whenever possible. They greatly advance the functioning of the group and provide a healthy way to contain individual differences as well as to derive benefit from these differences.) I then asked Carol how she felt about the feedback from Martina and the cotherapist. Carol hesitated, but then stated something to the effect of, "I know they have a good point. And Leone is like a mom; I guess she's worried about me."

Because Carol had many prior supportive experiences with Leone, as well as with the group, she was able to be somewhat open to differing ideas. This also represented good progress in her therapy. I asked Leone to verbalize again what she and Martina were thinking. I then asked Carol if *she* could double for Leone. Of course, this is quite a switch. Carol is actually the protagonist in this session. However, she generally feels positive about Leone, which lends a readiness to being able to double for her. Also, Carol's response to having been asked how she felt about the feedback is telling. She did not describe her own emotional state. She instead jumped into what Leone might be feeling, that is, "I guess she's worried about me."

Having Carol double for Leone gave Carol the opportunity to voice a different perspective than her own, without being asked to give her own up. It was essential for Carol to feel her own opinion had value and was respected, even though it was not the *only* opinion.

To do the doubling, Carol was asked if she could leave her seat for a moment—and, along with it, her set of feelings. Her empty chair would continue to represent her and her position. To emphasize this, we pulled her chair slightly into the center of the group circle, setting it so that it faced Leone. Carol was asked to go over and stand behind Leone's chair, in the position of the double. As Carol stood behind Leone's chair, I stood next to her for support. I told her that I would like her to represent Leone's feelings from this position and to try putting them into words. To facilitate this, I helped Carol warm up to the role by stating that Leone has a long history of supporting her and seems to have some important concerns. Carol nodded, clearly feeling the same way. I then asked Carol to describe some of what Leone might be feeling.

Carol, as Leone's double, addressed the empty chair she had vacated, stating, "You have a good job now, and you make good money—better than minimum wage. Maybe you won't get another job this good." As the facilitator, I stood next to Carol and repeated her exact words for emphasis. Leone nodded in agreement. I then cued Carol to express some of Leone's *feelings*, because she had actually started with thoughts. I said, "And as you think about this and look at Carol (represented by her now empty chair) you feel . . ." We all waited for a few long seconds. Then Carol stated, "Worried."

"Yes, worried," I repeated, and Leone nodded again. Cuing her further, I said, "Worried that . . ." Carol sighed and paused for a moment, then said,

"Worried that she might quit this job and not find another one. Then she'll really crack up." I repeated this as well. Of course, this was quite a bit stronger than Leone's actual worries, but because Carol was the true protagonist, it is *her* deep-seated worries that count. By expressing them from the safety of Leone's role, she was able to share the fear she had been keeping underneath.

To bring the enactment to an ending that would help Carol contain both the rash impulse to quit and the fear of "cracking up," I asked Carol, still as Leone's double, how she feels about Carol as a person. "I like her," Carol was able to say. "I like her a lot, and I know she's trying really hard." Both Leone and I reinforced this by adding some additional positive statements regarding Leone's respect and concern for Carol. Carol was then asked to return to her seat.

The tone at this point was quite happy, but with the sense of happiness one has at the end of an exhausting race. "Whew!" Carol remarked as she sat down. The rest of the members audibly exhaled as well. Following this, we asked the group members what each of them liked about Carol's work. This is generally the next step after an enactment. The protagonist is in a vulnerable position when doing an enactment. It is essential to provide support and affirmation directly following the drama. To avoid exposing the protagonist to critical comments at this vulnerable time, questions to the group must be carefully worded. For example, if a facilitator were simply to ask, "What do you think of Carol's role-play? Can anyone give her some feedback?" a member might voice an idea that they think would have been better than what Carol did. Members might say, for example, "She should just go up to her boss and tell her off" or "She should move out and live on her own." The moments following an enactment, however, are not the time for alternative ideas, even if they are good ones. It is a time to affirm the protagonist for what she did that was good that day, that represented progress in her development.

Each member should be encouraged to share her positive feedback. This allows the protagonist to get maximum benefit from the group and also ensures that each member's opinion is heard and valued. The members should be thanked by the facilitator for having given the protagonist time to focus on her problem. They should also be thanked for their feedback after the drama.

Following Carol's enactment, some of the members said that Carol did a good job of talking about her problem, and others were impressed at how well she could double for Leone. We made sure Carol received affirmation for having been able to try on the differing viewpoint that Leone and Martina expressed. We gave her recognition for the difficult task of doing all this thinking while she was really yearning to just take off and quit.

With these affirmations for Carol's efforts and progress, Carol's turn as protagonist was brought to an end. The session continued with other members sharing some additional things about themselves, such as updates by some of the members who did not have pressing dilemmas that week. Generally, only one issue is developed into an enactment in any given session. The session closed with the usual affirmations for each individual's effort.

GROUP PROCESS: ADDITIONAL ASPECTS AND TECHNIQUES

In the previous example, we described some psychodramatic techniques, that is, use of the double and use of the empty chair. We also used a technique from the general group therapy literature as outlined by Yalom (1995): the group process comment.

We used the double in two ways. First, doubling was used to help Carol feel clearly understood and know that her feelings were being validated. This was accomplished by Louise's efforts when she stood behind Carol and voiced Carol's feelings. Second, we used doubling to help Carol try on an alternative perspective to her own. Carol stood in the position of the double behind Leone and verbalized Leone's feelings. The use of the empty chair provided a "seat" for Carol's original feelings and allowed for a continued representation of those feelings while Carol tried on an alternative view.

The group process comment facilitated two important aspects of the session. First, it allowed for a slowing down of the action, thus avoiding what might have become an emotionally charged conflict around the differing viewpoints. This slowing down helped Carol see the beneficial aspects and genuine caring behind the alternative perspective, rather than railing against it as she might have if her parents or a job coach had offered it. Second, the group process comment had the added advantage of unifying all the members around the common goal of helping Carol cope with her crisis. All members were able to feel good about what they had to offer and about the diversity of their contributions.

An earlier session of the same women's group, with many, but not all, of the same women, provides another example of how the group process may be used with this population. A member, Dana, entered in an unusually distressed state. She reported that the day before she had been accosted at the bus stop. Dana has cerebral palsy and uses a wheelchair for ambulation. She had been waiting at a public bus stop for the bus that would take her to her part-time job at the mall. A man came up behind her and reached down inside of her pants. She screamed and attempted to wheel herself away. She took appropriate action to report the man, whom she had seen before because he often rode the same bus and also worked at the mall.

Despite having taken good action to report the incident, Dana was still, understandably, upset by it. She was encouraged to describe the experience, as well as her feelings about it. After Dana presented this, Martina responded to her by sharing that she had been sexually abused by her cousin when she was a child. This was the first time Martina had disclosed the abuse in the group. She had previously discussed it only in individual sessions, in which she had made it her goal to find the courage to bring the issue up in group. In facilitating this, I began by stating first that a great deal of important work was being done in group that day; Dana had had the courage to tell us about her experience, as well as having taken good action for herself, and Martina had had the courage to tell us about her abuse as well. I stated that Martina must indeed have a great deal of feeling for Dana, because this was the first time she had ever discussed her abuse in group, despite having been a member for quite a while. I made the connection between Dana's pain and Martina's compassion for that pain as a way of highlighting the positive aspects of the group process that helped Martina break her long-held silence. This type of framing helps both members increase their conscious awareness of their connection to each other, and helps the remaining members see the connective threads between them. (In fact, Martina and Dana were the only two members in wheelchairs, probably further enhancing their sense of connection.) Without this focus on relationships, there can be a tendency to see members' presentations as nothing more than "taking turns," or, in the worst case, to become competitive cries for attention.

The next step is to honor both presentations as important topics to be worked on in that session as well as in sessions to come. The facilitator needs to verbalize this directly and affirm each participant for presenting important topics to be worked on in group.

In facilitating a group in which a member suddenly discloses a powerful experience such as incest, there is a pull toward delving into that issue with the member as one might in an individual session. Furthermore, just as the therapist has an emotional response to the disclosure, so indeed do the other participants. After affirming the member for the disclosure, and establishing it as an important agenda item, it is time to check in with the other members. In the example with Dana and Martina, after allowing them some time to express their own feelings, the next step was to ask the other members how they felt about what each of the women had said. Again, it is important to prevent comments that might feel hurtful to the disclosing members; they are in an emotionally vulnerable state because of the disclosures. In addition to protecting the members who made the disclosures, the facilitator's other chief responsibility at this point is to help the observing members identify and express any feelings of their own that might have come up as a result.

In such situations, the therapist might prompt reflection by saying, for example, "Dana and Martina, since you have each told us such important things, I'd like to take a moment to check in and see how everyone is feeling at this point." Some members may spontaneously begin to share their feelings following this, which the facilitator can then affirm. Others sometimes respond by asking questions about the disclosure or by giving advice. It is necessary for the facilitator to be fairly directive when this happens. Questions lead the group back to an exploration of the disclosing member's issue, which should not be done before each member has had a chance to share her feelings. Also, advice-giving runs the risk of being critical. It is best for the facilitator to respond to questions or advice-giving by saying, "That's an important point" (or, "That's a good question"), but for right now I wanted to check on how you are feeling about hearing all this. Think for a minute. How do you feel inside?"

This focus on the internal state usually helps the member verbalize a feeling, which can then be affirmed. In the session with Dana and Martina, each of the members eventually disclosed feelings, such as being scared, mad, and sad. Sometimes, an individual sits quietly through this part of the session. The facilitator then needs to address this member to be sure her feelings are expressed. Still other members may be reminded of their own abuse experiences and may say a bit about them. Once everyone has described their reactions, the facilitator can make another unifying comment regarding the various feelings. The point of this comment should be that we all have important emotional reactions to hearing about abuse, and it is good that we can share these reactions and support each other.

In addition to providing the members with a sense of support and containment for their feelings, the other advantage of checking in with each of the members is to help them become skilled at identifying their own emotional states. Many members go through their days with little conscious awareness of what they are feeling; that is, they are not in the habit of connecting their thinking to their feeling. They have the feeling and then simply react to it, sometimes with problematic behavior. An important goal of therapy is to help members learn to identify and label their own emotional states. Following this, they can be helped to identify better behavioral alternatives to these states.

SUMMARY

In keeping with the theme of thoughts about emotion, recall Figure 3.1 (see chap. 3, this volume) in which the emotional intensity of a session is diagrammed. The warm-up and sharing stage begins to generate an intensification of feeling, which reaches a high point during the enactment stage.

In moving through the session with Carol, the group members' emotional engagement was felt during the warm-up and sharing as they reacted to Carol's presentation—already highly emotionally charged for her. The emotional charge was channeled into an atmosphere of support for Carol—so much support, in fact, that she was able to consider a different *thought,* a reframing of her dilemma. As the feeling tone settled down during the affirmation stage, Carol was left actually feeling differently about the problem. She was noticeably calmer, no doubt from feeling truly heard, understood, and supported, in contrast to how she usually feels. The other members, because of their connection to Carol, felt good, too, and felt good about themselves for their contributions. Thus, the emotional experience, managed therapeutically, allows for new ways of thinking, and ultimately, new ways of behaving, in session and beyond.

In the next chapter, we explore a treatment group for offenders with intellectual disabilities. Even though the therapy process, session stages, and techniques are essentially the same, the nature of the offenders' problems necessitates additional treatment components that we outline in detail.

5

GROUP TREATMENT FOR OFFENDERS WITH INTELLECTUAL DISABILITIES

Knowing your own darkness is the best method for dealing with the darkness of other people.

—Carl Jung

When an individual is referred for services because he has committed a sexual offense, the intake process is somewhat more complicated than for an individual whose symptoms hurt only himself. For therapy to be successful, a team effort is usually needed. Successful therapy is predicated on reliable supervision and monitoring of the individual's behavior, especially in the early stages. Before discussing the therapy process, we examine the initial interview and service coordination that lay the groundwork for treatment success.

INITIAL INTAKE PROCESS

The initial interview with the individual, detailed in chapter 7, is the first level of the intake process. When the referral is made, it is a good idea to ask the referring party to have the individual or his guardian sign a release allowing any pertinent paperwork to be forwarded in advance of the interview. This not only prepares the clinician for the interview but also increases the likelihood that relevant reports—police reports, social work assessments, psychological evaluations—will in fact be sent. Once individuals have been accepted for treatment, it is often harder to try to obtain records. Before the client is accepted, there is generally a sense of urgency on the part of referring personnel who feel pressure to get the individual into treatment. This is the clinician's opportunity to compile records that might help in developing the best treatment strategy for the case.

As with any initial assessment, the need for medication should be considered and referral to a psychiatrist be made if necessary. Sex offenders, as a group, have high rates of comorbid psychiatric disorders. Most notably, recent research has found extremely high rates of attention-deficit hyperactivity disorder (ADHD; Fago, 1999). Sex offenders also tend to have higher than average rates of anxiety disorders, impulse control disorders, substance abuse disorders, mood disorders, and psychoses (Raymond, Coleman, Ohler King, Christenson, & Miner, 1999).

It is possible that some percentage of referred offenders may have sociopathic personality organizations. In this case, there is a complete absence of felt remorse or guilt, although these offenders may verbalize feelings of guilt because they perceive that to be what interviewers want to hear. Among people with intellectual disabilities, we have found very few cases of sociopathy, but in determining the treatment of choice for any given referral, sociopathy should be ruled out prior to making plans to include the newcomer into a treatment group. Yalom (1995) stressed that sociopathic personalities should not be included in treatment groups for nonsociopaths, although a group strictly limited to sociopaths can be preferential to individual treatment for many sociopaths (Yalom, 1995).

The next step in the intake process is to assemble a meeting of all parties involved with the individual. During the initial interview it is necessary to inform the client that, because he has a problem that hurts other people, his admission into the group rests on his agreeing to a team meeting to discuss his treatment. It is essential to have the client (or his legal guardian if he is not a self-guardian) sign releases at this time to allow for communication between the treating clinician and other team members. It is also important to be direct with the client about the need for monitoring of his behavior. We generally stress to the client that this is the first step in helping him protect himself from making another mistake.

When assembling the team meeting, each facet of the individual's life should be represented. This may mean family members or group home staff, job coach, case manager, and legal guardian if the person has one. Each team member's responsibility in supervising the individual should be clarified and agreed on. It is also helpful to use this meeting as an opportunity to make clear to the individual the exact relationship between his offense behaviors and their consequences. For example, many individuals have been referred to us just after losing a job because of sexually offensive behavior. With the entire team present, it should be made clear to the individual that he is no longer working at his job because of his behavior. The behavior and its consequences need to be described in concrete terms. For example,

"Alan, you got fired from Shop-Rite because you grabbed a woman's breast and tried to kiss her." It is then necessary to check back with Alan, asking him to repeat his understanding of why he was fired.

The team member closest to the problem is in the best position to deliver the information. In the previous example, Alan needs to hear from his job coach why he lost his job. In the best of all possible situations, he would have already heard this from his boss. We find, fairly often, however, that employers shy away from direct discussion with the individual about the aberrant behavior. This is understandable; it is no doubt uncomfortable for an employer to discuss sexual misconduct with an employee who has an intellectual disability. However, some employers have been amenable to talking with us or with a job coach about the individual and have agreed to then give the individual the necessary feedback themselves. In such cases, we have found that a powerful impact is made on the individual. Hearing the bottom line from the boss seems to be much more meaningful to many individuals. Often the individual is so habituated to hearing feedback from staff that it is easy for him to minimize it. Some even deny the reality of the actual firing or other consequence and blame the job coach or parent for removing them from the job or the activity without grounds.

In any case, it is a poor strategy for the clinician beginning treatment with the individual to be the first to confront him with the reality of his behavior and its consequences. If the individual experiences confrontation regarding his behavior *only* in the context of therapy, he comes to associate therapy with this discomfort. This leads him to want to avoid the very therapy he needs. Furthermore, there is no serious challenge to his psychological denial if the involved parties are not confronting him. However, if the individual has been confronted with his problem by his job coach, and preferably his employer as well, he experiences the discomfort in association with his own behavior and job loss. The therapist is then in a position to present the therapy as a means of helping the individual to correct this problem behavior. The therapy can, and should, be presented as a source of support to the individual who is in crisis because of a behavior problem.

In our experience it has sometimes been the case that staff members, teachers, and family members have mistakenly thought that the treating clinicians will completely take over the job of talking to the individual about his offense behavior. Even during the course of therapy, problem behaviors displayed by the individual at work or in the residence have sometimes been reported to us without having been discussed with the individual. Staff members may feel they are doing the right thing, of course, and assume that only the clinicians are sufficiently trained to address the issue with the client. Certainly, it is the clinician's responsibility to explore the problem at length and help the individual improve his functioning. It remains essential, however, that the individual be presented with his problem behavior by the observing party (i.e., staff or family member), so that he feels the dissonance his behavior causes right in his environment. A follow-up call to the treating clinician can be a helpful and even appropriate means of simply keeping the clinician abreast of the situation. We make a point of advising staff members that they are an integral part of the client's treatment and that their ability to address the client's behavior problem in his environment greatly supports the therapy.

THE INTAKE PROCESS WITH OFFENDERS WHO DENY

Some individuals, from the very first meeting, hang their heads and admit their wrongdoings with great embarrassment. Others admit to one charge, specifically the one in which they were caught, and deny or minimize having a history of similar offenses. Still others deny any wrongdoing at all, even when supplied with clear evidence by involved parties.

Historically, sex offender treatment protocols have stressed admission of guilt as the very foundation on which successful treatment rests and often require such admission prior to starting treatment. There is no doubt that the individual's ability to acknowledge his own offense is central to his recovery. However, experience has taught us that this acknowledgment— that is, actually becoming fully aware of his problem and being able to own up to and verbalize the problem—is a therapeutic accomplishment that often evolves as a *result* of psychotherapy. In other words, we have learned that acknowledgment and admission of the offense do not have to take place *before* psychotherapy for therapy to be successful. Such admission frequently occurs *during* a successful therapeutic experience.

Tough and Hingsburger (1999), whose advocacy concerning sexual issues and intellectual disabilities we discussed earlier, have similarly found that, in counseling offenders with intellectual disabilities, those who deny may sometimes be treated successfully. By successfully, Tough and Hings-burger mean that the individual ceases to perform offense behaviors. In some cases, they noted that the behavior change takes place while the client continues to deny or minimize the problem. Tough and Hingsburger posited that treatment ought not be contingent on admission of guilt because sexual offending presents such great risks to others with whom the client may be in contact.

We agree that risks to the community can, and should, be prioritized by providing treatment to offenders, regardless of their initial ability to admit guilt. This may, at first, sound contradictory to our earlier recommendation that the individual be presented with his behavior and consequences at a team meeting prior to treatment starting. We have found, however, that many individuals will agree to this forum and even express an under-standing of the relationship between their behavior and its consequences, yet still try to deny the problem during the early stages of treatment. Quite frequently, they deny that they have ever had similar problems in the past. We treat this denial through the group process, and we discuss some examples in detail. As long as the individual agrees to allow communication among clinicians and the other team members and participates in the initial team meeting in which his offense and supervision needs are discussed, we consider him a viable candidate for psychotherapy.

TREATMENT STRATEGIES WITH OFFENDERS WHO DENY

Nathan was referred for therapy by his workshop counselor. It was reported that Nathan had made verbal statements of a sexual nature to a 5-year-old girl at a McDonald's. The girl's mother complained about Nathan, and Nathan was escorted out of the building. Furthermore, Nathan was informed that if he ever attempted to enter that McDonald's again, the police would be called.

Nathan lived in an apartment with his mother and stepfather. He had two brothers who no longer lived at home. His mother quickly became very restrictive regarding his activities, and the workshop provided a reasonably well-supervised workday, including transportation.

When Nathan entered the group, he appeared downcast. He stated that a child at McDonald's "told lies" about him and got him "in trouble." We simply reminded Nathan that his workshop counselor had told us, in his presence, that he had been barred from his local McDonald's because he had gotten into trouble there. We then allowed the group process to unfold. Other, more senior, members would disclose problems they had during the week. Some members would discuss their progress, and we would review their earlier problems to point out how well they were now doing. For example, Sean would tell us that he saw children when he was out running but had made a point of not crossing the street to their side. He was even able to say he wanted to stop and talk to them but did not. Other members, as well as the two of us facilitating the group, would make a point of contrasting Sean's new behavior with his past behavior and affirming him for his good work.

By simply sitting in the group and bearing witness to the process, Nathan had the opportunity to experience some important vicarious learn-ing. He learned that no matter what a member disclosed, he was not con-demned. No member was diminished in the least, or scolded or threatened. This was clearly a new experience for Nathan, one he observed with obvious fascination. Nathan was able to see that any progress a member made was applauded, and just as important, these other members had made mistakes similar to his.

The day came when Nathan told us that he had gotten into trouble at the mall, even before the incident at McDonald's. He disclosed that he would frequently hang out in the mall's video arcade and watch kids play video games. One time (at least) he followed some kids as they left the arcade and continued to watch them as they traveled around the mall. Before long, he found himself being physically led out of the mall by two security guards. As with McDonald's, he was told that the police would be called should he return.

As soon as Nathan disclosed this, we commended him for his honesty. We made a point of stating that he had the courage to tell us this, even though it was clearly uncomfortable for him. We then turned to the other members and asked them for feedback, in the same manner as we do following an enactment. We asked one member, Mike, if he knew what was so good about what Nathan just did in group. Mike was able to say, "He told the truth." We acknowledged Mike's response and then asked if he could tell Nathan that directly. Looking right at Nathan, Mike said, "You told the truth." Both members were then thanked for these efforts. Feedback was similarly elicited from the other members.

The point here is that the disclosure of such important, and obviously shameful, material leaves an individual feeling vulnerable in much the same way that baring one's feelings through an enactment does. If the individual is criticized or embarrassed by the responses he receives to his disclosure, he is likely to shut down again. However, by giving the individual a supportive response, and one that affirms his honesty, his ability to self-disclose will be enhanced.

Of course, some members may spontaneously criticize the disclosing member and say something to the effect of, "That's not right. You can go to jail for that." At times, especially with members who are in denial about the seriousness of their problems, this feedback can be a helpful part of the process. The clinician needs to be observant regarding the disclosing individual's understanding of his actions, as well as his feelings about them. Suppose, for example, that Mike had said, "Nathan, you shouldn't do that; you could go to jail." The facilitator's job in this case is to extract the good from this comment and then quickly return to having Nathan's honesty affirmed. A helpful response from the facilitator might be, "That's true, Mike, he could go to jail if he does it again. That's why it's so good that Nathan's talking about it and getting help. What did he do *in this group today* that was good?"

The opportunity for vicarious learning is a powerful tool not available in individual psychotherapy. From the time a new member first enters the group, he is able to witness other members making disclosures and receiving affirmation for doing so. This is a particular advantage in ongoing, as opposed to time-limited, groups. In ongoing groups, there are always some veteran members who are accustomed to the process and are able to speak candidly about their offenses and problem behaviors. The new member sees right away that open discussions of problems and wrongdoings are met with respect and concern for the individual, thereby diminishing part of the reason for denying.

Within a few months Nathan told us what he had actually said during the incident at McDonald's. He had asked the little girl what color underwear she had on. We took this opportunity to affirm him for being able to tell the truth and for his awareness that what he did was wrong. Since that time, Nathan has disclosed numerous earlier incidents, as well as fantasies that he has had. He works sincerely in therapy, and his behavior, although still requiring considerable support and structure, is greatly improved.

Al serves as another example of an offender who initially could not disclose his transgressions. He, too, was referred by his workshop counselor. The counselor reported that Al often sexually accosted women at the workshop. Sometimes, he was aggressive and would grab a woman's breast or crotch. Other times he was extremely gentle, stroking someone's hair and speaking softly to the person. He would perform such behavior, however, despite protests by the woman involved and her requests that he stop.

During Al's early weeks in the group, he presented complete denial of any wrongdoing. While he paid attention to the group process and witnessed affirmation and respect toward other members' disclosures, he remained adamant that he had done nothing wrong. Even when members made overtures, such as, "It's okay, Al. We've all made mistakes. That's why we're here," Al would not budge. Needless to say, the other members started to become annoyed with him.

To cement his position, Al began wearing a policeman's hat and badge to group, telling us that he did not ever have to worry about getting into trouble because his uncle was a police officer. He would never end up in jail. (In fact, the uncle—actually the husband of a cousin—had apparently given him the police items years ago. Al had lost both his parents and no longer had any relatives who would come to a meeting for him or even visit him. He had to be given a state guardian and was living with a sponsor arranged for him by the state Division of Developmental Disabilities.)

During one week, a member who had been in group quite a while, was pressing Al to talk. Al, as usual, refused. We asked the other member, Carlos, if he could double for Al. Carlos was asked to stand behind Al's chair. He was then asked if he could say what Al might be feeling right at that moment. Carlos needed help to warm up to this task. We asked Carlos if he could remember how he felt when he first started group. Carlos thought for a minute. Then he said, "I didn't like it." We acknowledged this and then asked Carlos to say this again, as though he were Al. As the facilitator, I (Nancy Razza) repeated, "I don't like this." Carlos, still standing behind Al in the position of the double, then said, "I don't like this." I then asked Al if this was how he felt, if this was right or wrong. Al said, "It's right; I don't like this."

"Good," I affirmed. "So Carlos knows how you feel." Then, turning back to Carlos, I asked, "Is there anything else you think Al might be feeling right now? We keep trying to make him talk, and he doesn't like it. How do you think that makes him feel?" Carlos then said, "Mad." I asked Carlos to say this for Al. "I feel mad," he said. I then asked Al if this was right. "That's right," Al said. "I'm mad alright." At this point I thanked Carlos for his help and asked him to sit back down.

I then asked Al if he thought any of the other members might understand some of his feelings the way Carlos did. He could only reply that he did not know. Another member volunteered to double, and we invited him to do so. We continued in this manner until each of the members had gotten up and doubled for Al. Through the use of multiple doubles, Al experienced each of the members making an effort to understand and verbalize his feelings. This was an important step because Al had said he "didn't know" if any of the members really understood how he felt. He needed to have the experience of his feelings being understood exactly as he felt them in the moment to begin to feel that this group could be a safe place for him. Many weeks went by in this fashion, with the chief action for Al being the emotional support of the group rather than his own disclosure.

Al's level of protesting diminished somewhat. He also began to show interest in some of the other members, which was affirmed strongly. Eventually, we added another technique. We told Al, as we often did, that the cofacilitator had gotten another call from his workshop staff. Our general practice was to inform him of the call and ask him if he would be willing to talk with the group about the problem reported by his staff. Before we describe the next technique, however, this point requires some discussion. It is often the case that workshop counselors or other staff call to inform us of problems that occur with group members during the week. As we described earlier, we make sure that the staff member also discusses the matter with the individual, if they have not done so already. We then inform the individual during the group session that we received a call from their workshop staff or other concerned party, and we ask him if the issue is one he is willing to work on that day. We do not share the problem with the group ourselves, because it is the individual's right and his responsibility. This is a fine line to draw. We are letting the individual, as well as the rest of the group, know that his behavior was problematic enough for his workshop counselor to call, yet we stop short of disclosing the problem without his permission. In this way, we oppose his denial, yet we show respect for his boundaries. Our goal here is twofold: (a) to maintain an honest environment by consistently expressing our awareness of serious problems and (b) to demonstrate clear respect for each individual's personal boundaries by not disclosing details without his permission. Needless to say, boundary violations are the very essence of sexual offense problems. In Al's case, he was demonstrating his own boundary problems by approaching and touching nonconsenting women, and, like so many other offenders, had been the victim of sexual boundary violations himself. Although there is no perfect solution to this dilemma, attempting to maintain some respect for the individual's boundaries in the group setting has important therapeutic significance.

With respect to the latest phone call received from Al's workshop counselor, we informed Al during the session that the counselor had called again to report a problem. As usual, we asked Al if he would discuss the problem with the group, and, as usual, he declined. This week, however, we felt it was time to encourage him more strongly. Al's comfort level with the group had grown through the doubling and other positive experiences he had had with us. He evidenced this increased comfort by demonstrating real attentiveness and even compassion toward other members and reduced complaining about having to come to group when he walked through the door.

Given these observations, we told Al that we would like to help him find a way to discuss his problem in group and stated that this discussion would be a way to help him get better, just as he had seen other members get better by working on their problems. The cofacilitator, who had received the call, asked Al if she could help him relate the problem by standing behind him. Since Al was now quite familiar with the experience of doubling, she explained that, with his permission, she would stand behind him, in the position of the double, and describe the problem.

Al consented. This represented tremendous progress on his part. The cofacilitator got up and stood behind Al's chair. She began to speak as though she were Al and started with her sense of his feelings in that moment. She stated, "This is so hard. I wish I could just get out of here and never come back." She then asked Al if this was right; if this was how he felt. Al nodded. He was hanging his head and staring at the floor, apparently feeling some of the anguish of his situation instead of just denying it. The cofacilitator continued. "Everybody makes a big deal out of nothing. I touched some girl's hair; it's no big deal." The cofacilitator then paused to check with Al again, to see if this was how he felt. Al replied, "Yeah, it's no big deal."

Because Al was accepting the process and agreeing with the statements, the cofacilitator continued. "I really like that girl, and I wanted her to be my girlfriend. But, now she's mad at me, my workshop staff is mad at me, and everyone in this group is going to be mad at me, too. That's why I don't like to talk about these things." This was quite a lot of material for Al to work with, and so the cofacilitator said each statement slowly, bending down to see if Al was continuing to nod as she spoke. Al did in fact continue to nod, and he continued to hang his head, sadly staring at the floor. To give the doubling a sense of closure, the cofacilitator then stated, quite solemnly, "I guess I made a mistake." Al nodded again. She then asked Al if he would repeat that statement himself. "You try it," she coached him: "*I guess I made a mistake.*" Al drew in a heavy sigh. "I guess I made a mistake," he said softly.

The cofacilitator then sat down. As the facilitator, I immediately affirmed Al for the hard work he had done, and then made a point of thanking each of the other members who had given their time and attention in support of Al's work. We then began the process of asking each of the members to discuss what they felt Al had done that was good that day, and we encouraged each member to give that positive feedback directly to Al. As we have noted previously, the question to the group members is always phrased in the affirmative so that feedback to the protagonist is supportive of his growth. The vulnerability of the protagonist after his enactment is too great for any feedback that might directly threaten his sense of self. In addition to working against the development of a healthier sense of self, it encourages the individual to go back to his more regressed modes of defending himself. For example, in this case, if Al felt attacked following his first efforts to acknowledge his problem, he would likely conclude that he had been right all along to deny his problem because people cannot be trusted; they will kick him when he is down. He would not be likely to open up and try again.

To conclude the affirmation section, we thanked each of the group members for giving Al their time and attention as he worked on his problem. We made a point of impressing on Al how proud we were of him for being able to admit to a mistake. We addressed his fears regarding "everyone being mad" at him by clarifying that he had done the right thing in disclosing that he had touched someone's hair. We affirmed that he was still a valued member of the group and that he had taken a big step toward getting better.

GENERALIZATION PROBLEMS

During the course of our work with offenders who have intellectual disabilities, we have seen significant reductions in the referral problems, on average, for a majority of the treated individuals. The problem of generalization of the learning has presented itself, however, in many forms and deserves some discussion.

Because of their cognitive impairments, most individuals whose intellectual functioning falls within the range of mental retardation cannot carry out abstract reasoning. Many, but not all, nondisabled people develop the capacity for abstract thinking during adolescence and young adulthood. This ability allows one to think through the relationship between elements, even when those elements cannot be experienced in concrete reality. For example, a person capable of abstract reasoning can understand the concept that if A = B and B = C, then A = C. However, the learning ability of a person whose level of thinking has not evolved to this point is limited to that which he directly experiences. This type of thinking is categorized as *concrete*, from the original classification described by Piaget (see Berger, 2001). If we extend this understanding to our work with offenders with intellectual disabilities, we can see the potential problems. For example, a nondisabled offender is likely to be able to understand the concept that any sexual activity with a minor is against the law. He will have hard work before him with respect to various therapeutic tasks, such as learning how to avoid putting himself at risk for re-offending, identifying his emotional triggers, developing safe alternative behaviors and emotional supports, and so on. It is unlikely, however, that the nondisabled offender would have trouble grasping the implications of the initial concept, that is, that any sexual activity with a minor is illegal. He could, in all likelihood, acknowledge the implications that result from this law, across a range of conditions in which he might consider becoming involved with children. The offender with intellectual disabilities, however, must work at all of the same therapeutic tasks as the nondisabled offender, but with the additional obstacle of not necessarily understanding all the implications of the law. The offender with intellectual disabilities often has difficulty understanding that if something is wrong in one situation with one person, it may also be wrong in another situation with another person.

Let us examine the concept that any sexual activity with a minor is against the law. This invariably becomes the subject of discussion during some group sessions. Members will verbalize their understanding of this concept. Some of the men will say, "I know; you can't have sex with kids. You could go to jail for that." We, of course, affirm this understanding and check to see if the other members heard and understood. After providing considerable detail and citing examples of what this concept means, we then ask questions to explore the members' understanding. We might ask, for instance, "How about if the kid says it's OK to touch him; is it still against the law? What if your boss tells you to have sex with a child; is that OK? Or, what if it's a teenager; is it OK to have sex with a teenager?" These are hard questions for a person who cannot think abstractly. In fact, many of the questions we ask come from actual examples of situations our members have shared. Many of our group members have struggled with questions like these even after months of work in group and good behavior in the community. A person who can reason, who can carry out abstract thinking, can comprehend intellectually the idea that if *any* sexual activity with a minor is against the law, then each of these examples is against the law because each of them asks about sexual activity with a minor, with the possible exception of the question concerning teenagers. A person who can reason would know the particular concerns regarding the issue of involvement with teenagers; that is, that some teenagers are technically minors and some are not. A person with limited cognitive abilities, however, may well be unable to grasp the general concept and therefore would be unable to apply it across situations.

THE INTERSECTION OF COGNITIVE LIMITATIONS AND PSYCHOLOGICAL DEFENSES: TREATMENT TECHNIQUES

Our group members have taught us a great deal about the ways in which cognitive limitations interfere with generalization of learning. For example, Aaron was referred for services when he was a 20-year-old special education high school student. He had grabbed his speech therapist's breast while alone with her during a session and sent her screaming down the hall. He had also tried to touch a female neighbor, who quickly called the police. Aaron then was taught that before attempting any physical contact with a woman, he should ask her permission. Tragically, he made the mistake of asking his niece if he could touch her. She agreed. She was 8 years old.

Aaron suffered tremendously when his family learned what he had done. He had been quite confused by pieces of information that had been presented to him, such as the importance of asking a person first before touching and the prohibition against having sex with children. He did not "have sex"—he had asked to touch her genitalia. Furthermore, Aaron gave every indication that he still thought of himself as a kid, despite being 20 years old. It was a new and very problematic issue for Aaron to think of himself as an adult. He certainly did not seem to have any adult rights. What's more, he was still in high school. (Many students with intellectual disabilities are maintained in high school until the legal limit of age 21.) In addition to his difficulties in forming an adult identity, Aaron was also being confronted with the fact that even becoming involved with a willing female classmate could be a punishable offense if the girl was under age 18.

An examination of a group therapy session gives us a closer look at some of the problems related to limited conceptual understanding and poor generalization of learning. Aaron's functioning also demonstrates the defensive use of denial and avoidance commonly seen in this population. In describing the session, we present psychodramatic techniques used to engage this particular client whose cognitive limitations and psychological defenses are so typical of offenders with intellectual disabilities.

During the early stages of his therapy, Aaron's behavior during group was extremely withdrawn. He often sat with his hands over his face. He denied any problems and generally tried to tune out anything that was said to him. One week, Gene, a male psychologist who knew Aaron well, joined the coleader and myself in running the group. The psychologist felt a great deal of investment in Aaron and had in fact referred him to the group after doing some individual work with him.

As this particular session began, Gene was talking about the need to discuss feelings in group, and that sexual feelings in particular needed to be talked about. He was trying to make the point that *talking* in group about sexual feelings would be helpful and would not get Aaron into trouble the way *acting* on his sexual feelings had.

All these words, however, only had the effect of further shutting Aaron down. He was sitting slumped over in his chair, his face in his hands. He was not responding to Gene's requests that he speak about his feelings. In fact, he appeared to be trying not to hear what Gene was saying.

To facilitate some positive movement, I asked Gene if he could double for Aaron. After securing Aaron's permission, Gene assumed the position of the double by standing behind Aaron's chair. Aaron, of course, remained seated. I moved into the chair Gene had been using and began to play *his* role by restating the same words Gene had expressed to Aaron. I stated how it was OK to talk about sexual feelings in group, and then began to press Gene to talk, just as Gene had pressed Aaron. Remember that now Gene is doubling for Aaron; this means that he must speak as though he *is* Aaron and say out loud the feelings he believes Aaron is having. We made a point of reminding Aaron that he was now "off the hook," that he no longer had to respond. Gene had to be his double and do the responding for him.

Gene responded to my pleas to talk by saying what he thought Aaron was feeling at the moment. "I don't want to talk about it. I always get in trouble because of my sexy thoughts." (Note the use of the word *sexy* rather than *sexual*. When Aaron refers to sexual feelings, he uses the word *sexy*, and so Gene used this word as well.) After Gene made this statement, he checked with Aaron to see if it accurately represented how he felt. He asked Aaron if it was right or wrong. Aaron said, "Right." As the doubling had begun, Aaron had lifted his head up somewhat and removed his hands from his face.

We proceeded in this fashion, with my playing Gene's old role and trying to convince "Aaron" (actually Gene) to talk. Gene continued playing

Aaron's role. In playing the role, Gene verbalized the fear he believed Aaron felt, and continually checked with Aaron to see if his words accurately reflected his feelings. As the process went on, Aaron became increasingly involved; he held his head up, listened with interest, and responded when Gene asked if his descriptions of Aaron's feelings had been right or wrong. Eventually, I asked Aaron if he could repeat a few of Gene's words himself. This request invited a deeper level of participation and was a step toward deepening Aaron's emotional experience in the moment. Aaron was able to repeat a simple feeling statement expressed in the first person by Gene: "I feel really bad about what I did, and I don't like to talk about it."

We immediately affirmed Aaron for this verbalization. We then ended this phase of the enactment and asked Aaron if he would be willing to now play the role of the psychologist, that is, to sit in Gene's original chair and speak as though he were Gene. This meant that I would leave the role of playing Gene and vacate the chair. Aaron agreed to play the role of Gene, and I offered to help him. Gene continued to play the role of Aaron and moved from the position of standing behind Aaron's chair to actually sitting in it. Note that throughout the enactment we keep the chairs in their original positions, with each chair consistently representing only one individual. Thus, the chair originally used by Aaron always represents Aaron. It is kept in the same spot that it was in when Aaron first used it. Anyone who plays the role of Aaron sits in that very chair and keeps it in its original position. Anyone who doubles for Aaron stands behind that chair. Similarly, anyone playing the role of Gene sits in the original chair Gene used. In this way there is a concrete representation of the involved individuals.

Essentially, in asking Aaron to play Gene's role, we are asking him to reverse roles with Gene. This can be a threatening proposition in some cases and should not be used as a technique without considerable experience with the patient. Whereas doubling is generally a safe and supportive psychodramatic technique, role reversal can be anxiety provoking because it asks the patient to take on the salient characteristics of another person. This can be distressing when the other person's role toward the patient has been critical, abusive, or hurtful in any way. Role reversal should not be undertaken too early in the patient's therapy experience and should only be done after the patient has experienced sufficient support for his own position.

In this case, we felt Aaron had been well supported by Gene's doubling, as well as by his considerable months of experience with him. We chose to ask Aaron to play Gene's role primarily to get a sense of how he experienced Gene. In playing Gene's role, Aaron would have to make statements he felt Gene would make, thus giving us an idea of how he perceived Gene. It would also give Aaron the opportunity to experience being in the role of the authority, of the one who could ask the questions and demand answers. We felt Aaron might derive some psychological benefit from trying this role on, because he seemed so oppressed by his usual role in life of being the one who is always at the receiving end of the questions and demands. Finally, in asking Aaron to play Gene's role, we were inviting him into a still deeper level of involvement in his treatment and in his emotional experience of the moment.

So in this second phase of the enactment, Aaron played Gene, the psychologist, and sat in Gene's chair. I supported Aaron in this role and stood behind him. Gene played the role of Aaron, the patient, and sat in Aaron's chair. I asked Aaron to speak the way Gene spoke. Aaron was initially inhibited in this role. He looked at Gene but seemed not to know what to say. I offered some statements that echoed Gene's original words: "Aaron, I want you to talk to us about your sexual feelings. You are in group now; you're supposed to talk about your problems." Gene responded as though he were Aaron, putting into words Aaron's feelings of resistance: "I don't want to talk about it. I always get in trouble because of my sexy thoughts. I'm not going to say them in here."

I continued to verbalize Gene's role to make it easier for Aaron to play it, and Gene continued to play Aaron. After a few exchanges, I asked Aaron, in Gene's role, if he could try saying something to get "Aaron" to talk. Eventually, Aaron, from the role of Gene, began to verbalize numerous ideas. At first he said, "Come on, why don't you talk about it?" He later offered, "It's OK; we'll help you." Gene, in the role of Aaron, continued to express feelings of fear regarding talking and a desire to avoid the subject altogether. Note that Gene's role as Aaron was limited to saying only those things that represented exactly what Aaron originally demonstrated. In this case, then, Gene, in playing Aaron, could only verbalize resistance, fear, and avoidance. He could not deviate in his responses from those originally presented by Aaron.

In this way, Gene continued to play the role as Aaron originally did, with the only difference being that Gene said *with words* the emotions and defenses Aaron demonstrated. Aaron, however, in his role of Gene, began to feel increasingly comfortable and was able to say more and more. The other cofacilitator and I strongly affirmed anything Aaron said in his role as psychologist, stating, "Good question! You're really doing a good job of trying to get him to speak," and other positive remarks to encourage him.

Aaron, as he played Gene, said a few times that the group will help him. He said this in a gentle tone, suggesting that, perhaps, he did perceive the group as being a place where people really do want to help him. Later, Aaron came up with some questions of his own that he, playing the psychologist, addressed to Aaron, the patient, as he was played by Gene.

In the role of the psychologist, Aaron began a series of questions. He asked if it would be OK to touch his boss, or if it would be OK to touch a female customer if the other guys told him to. Gene, in the role of Aaron, continued to say that he did not know what to do and that he did not want to talk about it. However, through the questions Aaron came up with in his role as psychologist, we learned many of the questions that run through Aaron's mind. We got a sense of some of the fantasies he has, as well as his struggle to determine what is right and what is wrong. In playing the role of the psychologist, Aaron became freed up to say things he had not been able to say before. He did not realize he was sharing so much of his own internal process by making up these "good questions."

As this process continued, I asked Aaron, who was still in the psychologist role, how he thought Aaron (that is, the patient played by Gene) was feeling. "Sad," he said, without a moment's hesitation. Now we had an understanding of Aaron's affective state, one that he had not been able to verbalize from his own role. From the safety of a different role, Aaron was able to tell us how he actually felt.

"Sad," I repeated, reinforcing this understanding. "It makes sense that he would be sad about this problem." I made this statement to provide Aaron with affirmation for being able to identify and verbalize the emotion he had when he focused his attention on the problem. Clearly the sadness was with Aaron even at the beginning of the group when he was not able to speak at all. Usually when Aaron appeared sad he withdrew, looked down at the floor, sometimes covering his face, and was silent. His ability to put his feeling into words represented an important therapeutic accomplishment and deserved reinforcement.

In an effort to help Aaron clarify those things that contribute to his sadness, I asked Aaron, who was still in Gene's role, "Do you think he's sad because he's always getting in trouble?" Aaron, as Gene, nodded his head. I continued by asking, "What else do you think makes him sad?"

"Everybody's mad at him," he replied. I again reinforced this understanding by repeating it. "Everybody's mad at him," I said, "and he feels sad." The tone at this point was quite somber, with our words being spoken rather slowly. At this point, Gene, in his role as Aaron, began to elaborate on all the people who were mad at him: the speech teacher, the neighbor, his sister and brother-in-law, and so on. Having verbalized this, Gene deviated too far from the type of information Aaron himself had originally presented. Suddenly, Aaron became defensive. He began to speak as though he were himself, breaking from his role as Gene, the psychologist. He began to deny that he had ever touched the speech teacher. "No, I don't! I don't touch Cathy, the speech (teacher)!" Clearly, the elaboration of the many people who were mad at Aaron had threatened Aaron's sense of safety. His behavior was telling us he had done enough for one day. The task now was to close down the enactment, and the emotional intensity, in a way that would affirm the good efforts Aaron had made, as well as bring him to a more peaceful emotional state.

Speaking to Aaron, who was still technically in the role of Gene, and in his chair, I said to him, "It's time for us to bring this to an end. Please look at Aaron (still played by Gene) and say the last thing you want to say to him for now." Aaron looked at Gene and said, "Just keep your hands off. Don't touch *nobody*."

I thanked Aaron and asked him to return to his own seat. Gene, of course, returned to his original seat as well. Aaron let out a huge sigh; actually, I think we all did. We immediately provided praise and affirmation to Aaron for all his efforts. Note that this positive feedback enumerates and highlights specific behaviors Aaron portrayed. We made statements such as, "You did a great job playing Gene; you were able to ask good questions; you were able to say what Aaron was feeling." These help to reinforce the patient's understanding of his accomplishments, as well as to help him feel good about them. Furthermore, we make the point of affirming a positive sense of self, by praising a core characteristic of the person. We might say, for example, "Aaron, you really are a person who is willing to work hard to get better." This type of affirmation speaks to a deeper level of the person than do affirmations related to his overt behavior alone. It lets the person know that his therapists and fellow group members see goodness in him and challenges his sense of himself as "bad." Many of the offenders have a sense of self, an identity, in which they feel they are bad. It is hard to make major life changes when one feels innately bad. Through the therapeutic process, this "bad" sense of self can be repeatedly challenged, and the goodness in the person—that is, the efforts to help himself, to control his behavior, to admit to his wrongdoings, to support his fellow members, and so on—can be presented and affirmed, thus helping the individual evolve a healthier sense of self.

Finally, as always, it is very important to acknowledge the efforts of all the group members who witness an enactment. Members should be thanked for allowing the protagonist to have uninterrupted time and for having shown support through giving their time and attention. They should also be asked to give their positive feedback and should be acknowledged for these contributions as well.

LEARNING FROM OUR TECHNIQUES
AND OUR MISTAKES

In reviewing the session with Aaron, we described how Gene's spontaneous elaboration of the many people angry with Aaron caused him to "de-role." This enactment, we feel, is a valuable teaching tool because it demonstrates how much therapeutic work can be done with a withdrawn and resistant client using psychodramatic techniques, but it also shows how easy it is to slip up. After Aaron, from the safe role of the psychologist, states that everyone is mad at him—a threatening issue for him indeed— the actual psychologist, Gene, starts to list the names of the people he knows, from prior experience, to be mad at Aaron. This was too threatening for Aaron. A therapeutic strategy would have been to simply stay with repeating Aaron's exact words, without elaborating, and affirming him for saying them. In any case, we were still able to "save" the enactment by bringing it quickly to an end, and then moving to the affirmation. The same type of ending would have been used even if things had been ideal. That is, we invite the protagonist to "say the last thing you want to say for now" to whomever the other figure is, whether the other is a representation of the self, as it was in this example, or a representation of a different person. "Saying the last thing you want to say for now" allows the protagonist to be in command of the ending, without feeling pressured to come up with a perfect or final ending.

TREATING THE WHOLE PERSON

It is important to conceptualize psychotherapy for offenders as a broad-based endeavor in which the patient's psychological development and overall healthy functioning are the end goals. Sessions should not be limited to discussions of sexual offense issues only, nor should every nonoffense issue a member brings up be interpreted as "avoidance" of the offense problem. People with intellectual disabilities who commit sexual offenses typically have poor psychological functioning, a damaged sense of self, inadequate interpersonal skills, and a need for treatment that improves their overall functioning. Remember our earlier discussion regarding the high rates of psychological disorders among offenders in the general population. Certainly many offenders with intellectual disabilities can be expected to be suffering from some type of psychological distress that affects their functioning, in addition to the limitations in learning and problem solving associated with their cognitive impairment.

Many of the offenders with intellectual disabilities with whom we have worked come from homes in which a parent was alcoholic, abusive, or both, as is often the case for nondisabled offenders. These individuals have an identity that has been compromised not only by their failure to be "normal"— a shameful life experience for so many of our members—but also by the experience of growing up amid chaos, witnessing and surviving physical brutality. Even for those members whose households were not chaotic or abusive, it seems there was a glaring absence of a caretaker who could tune into the individual's particular needs, provide acceptance of them, and help the individual learn how to understand and cope with his own needs adaptively.

As the group member develops an increasingly healthy sense of self and learns skills for relating to others, his likelihood of relapsing into old maladaptive behaviors decreases. Of course, under stress, or when the individual's usual structure changes, there is always an increased risk that he will regress, at least temporarily. We generally explain to the patient, as well as to family and support staff, that it is best to continue the patient in therapy for some time, even once the referring problem seems to be under control. This is especially important when the behavioral improvement leads to a life change, such as a new job, which is so often the case. We like to have the member begin the job with the safety net of the group still in place. In this way the member can come in and discuss his experiences on the new job. We use this opportunity to affirm his successes, as well as to invite him to discuss difficulties he is experiencing. Our goal at this point is to intervene proactively in helping the member to cope with interpersonal difficulties and other dilemmas that arise in the new situation.

Generalization of learning, as we noted earlier, is difficult for many people with intellectual disabilities. Even though a problem on a new job may seem strikingly similar to a problem at the old job, for example, being teased by a coworker, the member may struggle to bring to bear what he has learned in the new environment. Continued group involvement can often make the difference between a successful transition and a failed one.

SUMMARY

Offenders with intellectual disabilities pose a number of challenges to treatment and require a system of intervention that encompasses support staff, such as residential, day treatment, and vocational staff, family members, and psychotherapy. In addition, many offenders may require medication for psychiatric conditions. Supervision and monitoring by involved staff and family members is as essential as psychotherapy, especially in the early stages of treatment. It is imperative that the need for supervision be communicated to involved parties on the treatment team.

Many offenders with intellectual disabilities need lengthy involvement in treatment because of difficulties in generalizing what they learn about offense behavior to new situations. At the same time, however, we have found that great gains can result from extended treatment. Veteran members, who have learned how to avoid re-offending and can talk about themselves with genuine understanding, are valuable agents of support and change for new group members. Not only do these experienced members aid the process for newer ones, but their continued group involvement helps to keep them from falling back into old patterns of behavior. In this regard, they are much like long-term members of Alcoholics Anonymous who maintain their sobriety with ongoing attendance and the sponsorship of new members. The presence of longer term members, who have experienced some success, lends an air of hopefulness to a group for offenders; they are the therapist's allies, bringing a sense of recovery to the room.

6

SEXUAL ABUSE
AVOIDANCE TRAINING

Only in relationship can you know yourself, not in abstraction, and
certainly not in isolation.

—J. Krishnamurti

In earlier chapters, we described J. L. Moreno's (see Blatner & Blatner,
1988; Marineau, 1989) original model of psychodrama along with the modifications we constructed for people with intellectual disabilities. The modified model constitutes the group therapy format we have come to call the
interactive–behavioral therapy (IBT) model and have described in detail.

Along with his development of psychodrama, Moreno created a related
form of group intervention that he called sociodrama (see Blatner & Blatner,
1988; Sternberg & Garcia, 2000). As we discussed earlier, Moreno's philosophy of psychological development posited that social interactions—the
experiences we have with other people throughout our development—make
up the very core of our being. The sum total of our interpersonal experiences
shapes our sense of self and our functioning. From this philosophical orientation, group therapy as a treatment approach for psychological problems
naturally followed suit. Moreno's thinking was that because a person's psychological development evolved through his experiences with other people,
changes in psychological functioning would evolve through new types of
experiences with other people.

Because of the centrality of social experience to psychological functioning (for which there is mounting research support and to which a great
many theorists subscribe), Moreno wanted to help people improve their
abilities to take on and carry out social roles. Whereas psychodrama was

created in an effort to provide psychotherapy for people in distress, socio-drama was created as a means through which people could try on various social roles in a safe environment. In this regard, sociodrama represents a proactive effort to safeguard against distress that might result from inexperi-ence with the demands of certain social roles. Moreno contended that the development of skill and confidence in the various social roles one plays in life would add to one's overall psychological health and functioning, even in otherwise well-functioning people.

Among its many applications, sociodrama has been used effectively in such endeavors as preparing police academy trainees to deescalate domestic conflicts and providing recently divorced women with practice in transitioning to the new roles that follow the ending of a long-term marriage (Sternberg & Garcia, 2000). Whereas psychodrama concerns itself with the individual's internal world, sociodrama is focused on the person's external world. In a psychodrama session, the issues discussed and the enactments portrayed arise from within an individual member, from the individual's store of memories, emotions, and experiences. In sociodrama, however, the issues and dramas arise from the group member's shared need to learn and practice new social roles. For this reason, sociodrama represents an ideal vehicle for providing individuals with intellectual disabilities the opportunity to develop skills that would help them protect themselves in potentially abusive situations.

THE INTERACTIVE–BEHAVIORAL THERAPY MODEL AND SEXUAL ABUSE AVOIDANCE TRAINING

Because of the successful experiences we had with the IBT model in working with people with intellectual disabilities, we decided to use essen-tially the same format for conducting sexual abuse avoidance training groups. We drew from Moreno's model of sociodrama described previously and incorporated it into the four-stage IBT format we detailed in chapter 3. The use of the orientation stage, already found to be an essential addition to the traditional model when working with cognitively impaired members, became all the more important as we began to draw groups of individuals with intellectual disabilities together to teach them self-protection skills. Unlike police academy trainees or divorced women seeking help in reenter-ing the dating world, our group members did not come in asking for help in dealing with potentially abusive interactions. Other people, largely residential and day program staff, who heard about the project and wanted to afford their clients the opportunity for training, referred individuals to the groups. We discuss this issue further in the orientation stage section later in the chapter.

Using the IBT model for sexual abuse avoidance training differs from many other sexual abuse avoidance training formats largely in that it is not curriculum bound. Issues and dramas arise from the members and group leaders during the course of their interactions. The overriding goal is to ensure that each of the members is emotionally connected to the experience in the moment. The more closely the dramas are connected to the individual's experience, the greater the emotional involvement will be. The emotional experience of dread a member has when confronted with a threat from an authority figure, followed by the rush of relief that is felt when she experiences getting away, provides an aid to memory no didactic format can match. We describe ways in which we enhance the emotional experience in the sections to follow.

Moreno developed his theories regarding the importance of behavioral and emotional engagement from his observations of people with whom he worked. It is interesting that research that has been conducted in recent years lends support to his early thinking. Specifically, studies on the efficacy of child sexual abuse prevention programs suggest that models with behavioral and emotional components have, in fact, the best outcomes. Among the many topics analyzed by Goleman (1995) in his comprehensive study of emotion is the subject of child sexual abuse prevention programs. Citing the limitations of purely cognitive or didactic prevention training models, Goleman (1995) stated, "Information is not enough" (p. 257) and reported that,

> By contrast, children given more comprehensive training—including related emotional and social competencies—were better able to protect themselves against the threat of being victimized: they were far more likely to demand to be left alone, to yell or fight back, to threaten to tell, and to actually tell if something bad did happen to them. . . . Those children who got the more comprehensive programs were three times more likely than those in minimal programs to report abuse. (p. 258)

Goleman explained that it is not enough for a child to simply be told about "good" versus "bad" touch; children need to learn that they must pay attention to when a situation *feels* wrong to them, which it often does even before physical touching begins. Children need to have the experience of acting on their own feelings of distress, even when the offending adult may be telling them that everything is "okay." Children who have the opportunity to focus on their own feelings in role-plays, and then have the experience of acting on them by removing themselves and reporting the problem, have the added benefit of experiencing their own feelings as powerful guides to what they should do and have the experience of adults supporting them for acting on their own emotional awareness. Their self-confidence soars along with their skill level. The very best of these programs were given over a series of sessions, rather than in one shot, and taught parents to give children the same messages on self-protection that the program gave. Later in this chapter, we return to the topic of child sexual abuse prevention training programs and explore additional ways in which they can inform our work with adults with intellectual disabilities.

As we have noted, the emphasis on emotional engagement leads us to draw the role-plays from ideas generated by the members in the session rather than from a checklist of possible scenes. We should add, of course, that group leaders bring their own store of experiences and thinking to the sessions, and as such can shepherd the group to cover areas that might have received only minimal attention. For example, if most of the enactments have involved male perpetrators, a group leader may introduce similar scenes using female perpetrators. If a number of scenes have taken place in residential settings, then facilitators can gear new scenes to enact problems on job sites. Some scenes may involve bribes and lures; others may involve threats. Still others may involve multiple perpetrators. Group leaders take off from and enhance members' contributions, paying vigilant attention to the types of problems members bring up and ensuring that a full range of alternative dilemmas is explored.

On a related note, it is important to acknowledge that interactive–behavioral sexual abuse avoidance training (IB/SAAT) groups are proposed as an adjunctive program to sexual education. We are strong supporters of sexual education as a core component of the educational curriculum for all students, and we feel that it ought to be taught in an in-depth and repeated fashion over a period of years, geared to the students' growing capacity for self-awareness and for social norms regarding sexual behavior, as well as for the feelings and bodily changes that go along with sexual maturation. Sexual abuse avoidance training groups cannot take the place of general sexuality education. They offer, however, a helpful vehicle for providing people with intellectual disabilities with an experiential format for learning self-protection.

WHO IS A CANDIDATE FOR SEXUAL ABUSE AVOIDANCE TRAINING?

Perhaps a better question would be, who is *not* a candidate for this training? Certainly, everyone is potentially at risk for sexual abuse, but as we saw earlier, not everyone is at *equal* risk. Individuals with intellectual disabilities, especially females with intellectual disabilities, appear to be at great risk. For this reason, we feel the goal should be to provide the training to as many people with intellectual disabilities as possible, with certain key exceptions.

In pilot testing this model, we worked with young adults, middle-age adults, and older adults with varying degrees of mental retardation. Similar to our criteria with the IBT groups, we did not include individuals with a complete absence of verbal ability. We did, however, include even those with minimal expressive and receptive skills, as well as those at the higher end of verbal abilities. The primary exclusionary criterion is serious psychiatric instability. There is no certain way to determine how an individual in severe emotional distress would react to the training, nor is there good reason to believe the individual would be in a good position to learn new skills while actively in distress. Individuals demonstrating serious psychological symptoms need to be referred for psychological or psychiatric evaluation and may possibly be good candidates for IBT *psychotherapy* groups. Similarly, individuals known to have experienced serious sexual abuse, and who display symptoms suggestive of trauma, are in need of an IBT psychotherapy group, or some type of therapy, rather than a sexual abuse avoidance training group.

We tested our model on young adults, the youngest of whom were approximately ages 18 to 21. We did not test our model on young adolescents or children. There are important considerations here regarding exposure of young people, especially those whose intellectual level is even younger than their chronological age, to potentially stressful interpersonal experiences. At the same time, we know that even young children with intellectual disabilities are all too often the victims of sexual abuse. Our thinking at this point, however, is based on our awareness of the child protective movement and its analysis of children's training programs. We delineate these recommendations in a later section. Our recommendation at this juncture is that IBT sexual abuse avoidance training groups be limited to adults, with the youngest end of the range being those in their last years of a special ed high school program (approximately ages 18 to 21). In addition, although there is something to be gained by the sharing of experiences across generations, we have found members to be most comfortable when the age range is only moderate in these sessions.

THE FOUR STAGES OF AN IBT SEXUAL ABUSE AVOIDANCE TRAINING GROUP

In conducting IB/SAAT groups, we made a distinction in the usual IBT format. We began each group with one set of approximately eight new members and kept that set of members exclusively until completion, approximately 12 sessions later. Unlike our practice with IBT psychotherapy groups, we did not retain members based on individual need, nor did we keep "veteran" members in group to support their progress and aid newcomers. Because we were interested in testing the efficacy of this model for sexual abuse avoidance training, we ran each series for approximately 12 sessions, and then, following a three-month hiatus, brought the group members back to see how much of the skill was retained, as well as to provide "booster" sessions. It is quite likely, however, that using the same open-ended format as we do with the IBT therapy groups would be as useful or even more useful than running time-limited, closed-session series. The optimal number of sessions and the value of closed versus open-ended series are questions we hope to address in future research.

We used the same four-stage format as in IBT groups and describe these stages in detail because they are sociodramatic, rather than psychodramatic, as in the IBT therapy groups. This distinction changes the role of the facilitators in a few ways that will be clarified in the discussion that follows.

Stage One: Orientation

As previously described, the orientation stage begins each session. In chapter 3, we stressed the importance of the orientation stage in helping members learn to pay attention to each other rather than solely to the group facilitators. The same techniques and processes pertain to the facilitation of sexual abuse avoidance training groups and are no less essential. Learning to listen to each other helps members gain valuable interpersonal skills. Moreover, the act of truly attending to others helps members—as it does all of us—to develop emotional connections. These connections increase members' vicarious learning opportunities. For example, once Helen begins to feel connected to Joni, she benefits from observing Joni's learning experiences, as well as from engaging in her own. Because she cares about Joni, she feels concerned when Joni is confronted with a role-play scene in which a man offers her candy for sex. She is likely to feel worried when Joni hesitates following the offer, then cheerful and even proud when Joni suddenly runs to safety. In this way, the range of learning experiences is manifold.

In addition to the techniques and processes of the orientation stage described in chapter 3, sexual abuse avoidance training groups have a further element that must be incorporated into the orientation stage. It is, perhaps, the most difficult aspect of this stage, especially in the first meeting: the task of clarifying to the new members the nature of the group. The group facilitators bear the burden of explaining to the members the goals as well as the processes of the group, and ensuring that the members understand and agree. As we noted earlier, few, if any, of the members joining these groups are ever self-referred. Therefore, it is incumbent on the group facilitators to make certain that the members understand what their participation in the group will entail and that their involvement is voluntary. Signed informed-consent forms, by the involved individuals and their legal guardians, are recommended.

Once again, in explaining the nature of the group to new members, it is important to ask them to repeat back what they are hearing. It is also important to let them know what they can do if they do not want to participate or change their minds at any point in the future. Be certain that members can state in their own words what their options are. As soon as some members begin to demonstrate understanding of the nature of the group, it is good practice to have those members explain it to others who may not yet be clear. This facilitates the group process by initiating member-to-member interaction.

Stage Two: Warm-Up and Sharing

The warm-up and sharing stage of a session in IB/SAAT groups is somewhat more structured than it is in IBT psychotherapy groups. IBT psychotherapy groups generally begin with an open-ended sort of question, designed to encourage members to share their unique, internal concerns. In an IB/SAAT group, however, facilitators begin each session, during the orientation stage, with a review of the purpose of the group. As the weeks progress, facilitators can start the session by asking what members remember about the work that was done the week before. Facilitators can also ask members if they have ever been in threatening situations like those worked on in previous sessions.

Member-Generated Issues

It is critical to remember that, inevitably, some percentage of the group members will have had sexually abusive experiences at some point in their histories. It is likely that some of the members may share these experiences during the sessions. The facilitators must be alert to the level of distress these individuals display. As noted earlier, training is no substitute for psychotherapy. Even though most individuals in severe psychological distress will probably be screened out and referred for treatment prior to the group's onset, facilitators should stay alert to the possibility that some members' need for treatment may not become apparent until later in the series of sessions. A referral for psychotherapy, or at least an evaluation, may be needed at that point. In our experience, we have found that many members had sexually abusive experiences, along a broad continuum of intensity, that they were able to identify once examples of abuse were discussed and enacted. Similarly, some members were able to describe potentially harmful experiences from which they had been able to get away.

In cases in which members are able to describe abusive or potentially abusive situations they have encountered, without signs or symptoms of serious psychological distress, facilitators can use these examples as the basis of enactments. Real-life encounters make for powerful learning tools. A number of such episodes were ultimately disclosed as our IB/SAAT groups went on. For example, after a few IB/SAAT sessions, one young woman related that a man had once fondled her breast while she was seated next to him on a bus. She had not previously reported this to anyone, and she was not able to be clear about how long ago the event occurred. Although the memory of the episode still appeared to be uncomfortable for her, she was able, as a result of the sessions, to appropriately identify it as a form of sexual abuse and was able to relate it without severe distress. Also, her records, screening interview, and behavior in the group thus far revealed no signs of serious psychological disturbance. Accordingly, this woman's abuse experience lent itself to being reworked into a learning experience for the group. We thanked her for sharing it and asked her if we could work on it through role-plays so that other members could learn ways to protect themselves and cope with such experiences. In so doing, we progressed from the warm-up and sharing stage to the enactment stage and engaged the group members in an emotionally meaningful learning experience.

In using scenes based on a member's experience, it is very important not to present any feedback that might in any way be perceived as critical by the member who shared the experience. In the example with the young woman accosted on the bus, it is important that she not feel criticized for not having told anyone sooner or for not having switched her seat to get away from the offender. The member sharing the experience should be thanked for bringing the experience to the group so that all the members can benefit from learning how to handle it. It is a good idea to affirm the member directly following her initial presentation of the experience, and then again later, after the experience has been reworked through the group process, stressing its utility in helping everyone become better prepared for future problems.

Facilitator-Generated Issues and Sociodramatic Techniques

In some sessions, it may be desirable to use alternate modes of engaging members in the warm-up and sharing stage. In early sessions, members may not be able to identify examples they can share. Furthermore, as sessions progress, it may become clear to the facilitators that much of the work has been limited to only certain types of cases. Specifically, after a few weeks, the facilitators may note that each of the enactments done in earlier sessions focused on a community setting such as the workshop or the dance, with none of the dramas having involved abuse in the home. In this regard, it would be important to generate enactments that portray potentially abusive scenes in the home, including the full range of "homes" the group members live in, such as supervised apartment, group home, family home, sponsor home, or other.

Whenever a topic is facilitator-introduced, the interactive process among group members will need a little boost. Facilitators can encourage a member-to-member focus through the use of sociodramatic techniques. For example, one of the facilitators can ask the group to consider a question that directs them to think about the other members in the group. The question should always be framed positively. Examples of this type of question include, "Who in this group has been doing a good job in the role-plays?" or, "Who in this group would you like to have with you if you needed help in a scary situation?" or simply, "Who would you like to see do a role-play today?" A facilitator can use this type of question to introduce a situation in need of work. To do so, the facilitator might say something such as, "Look around the room, and think about which person here could do a good job of keeping safe if someone tried to grab them at the bus stop. Who do you think could keep themselves safe?" Then, as the members are considering their answers, the facilitator should ask them all to stand. The facilitator continues by instructing the members to walk up to the person they want to choose. That is, each member should go and stand next to the person they feel would keep safe at the bus stop. Members should be encouraged to move around the circle to the person of their choice. Until group members become familiar with this type of exercise, it is usually a good idea to ask one member at a time to make his choice. If the facilitator asks Mike to pick a person he feels can do a good job of keeping safe, and Mike chooses Carl, then Mike is directed to stand next to Carl. Carl can then be asked whom he chooses, and he should be reminded that he can choose anyone in the group, including Mike. Let's say Carl chooses Eleanor. Carl is then directed to walk over and stand next to Eleanor; Mike is directed to follow Carl to continue demonstrating that Mike's choice is Carl. When the process is complete, the members will be standing in the form of a "sculpture" representing their choices.

At this point, with the members still standing next to their chosen individuals, the facilitator can focus members' attention on the experience of being chosen. For example, the facilitator can say, "Carl, Mike chose you as someone who would be able to keep himself safe at the bus stop. How does that make you feel?" Each member should be spoken to in this manner, clarifying to them the reason he or she was chosen and eliciting his or her feelings regarding being chosen.

The importance of this sociodramatic experience for the members lies in its capacity for focusing members' awareness on one another, actively engaging them with one another, and providing the positive emotional experience that comes with choosing and being chosen. However, there is important information for the facilitator concerning the sociometry, or pattern of relationships, in the group. Who was chosen? Were some individuals chosen by multiple members, while others were not chosen at all? Were some choices reciprocal? Perhaps some individuals were chosen despite having demonstrated *poor* abuse avoidance skills in previous role-plays. Especially in early groups, members often make choices based on how well they like another person rather than on the question that was posed. Remember that the facilitator should not comment on any individual's choice. The facilitator's responsibility is to make a mental note of the relationships and the relative connectivity of the group. In particular, facilitators need to be aware of members who are rarely chosen and remain peripheral. It will prove equally important and interesting to note how the patterns of choice vary over time.

With respect to moving from sociodramatic choices into enactment, a few simple caveats should be kept in mind. Facilitators are advised to resist the temptation to pull outliers (members not chosen by anyone) into the group by casting them in starring roles in the next enactment. Protagonists ought to be those members with the most sociodramatic "pull," that is, those people chosen by the most members. If three members choose Brian, and each of the other members are chosen by only one person or are not chosen at all, Brian should be asked to take the lead in the next role-play. Also, in cases in which each member is chosen by only one person, but a "chain" has formed, the best bet for protagonist is the person at the end of the chain. In other words, if Mark chooses Lea, Lea chooses Mary, and Mary chooses Jim, then Jim is the person who should be asked to be the next protagonist.

The logic to this approach is that the person who is at the center of most people's interest will draw the most attention when carrying out an enactment. The more members are interested in and feel connected to the protagonist, the more they will pay attention to the enactment. Furthermore, they will be more emotionally engaged in the enactment they are observing, which maximizes the likelihood of their learning from it.

It is not wise for a facilitator to choose an outlier or a peripheral member to play the protagonist's role, even though the facilitator may feel that person "needs" the experience. In the absence of sound integration in the membership, the experience is likely to be lacking in support for that protagonist, as well as lacking in emotional engagement for the others, as we have described. To help peripheral members deepen their relationship to the others, a better strategy is to assist them in doubling for others as a first step. As we have described in earlier sections, doubles can be chosen by the protagonist and also by the facilitator. In situations in which you, as facilitator, determine that the protagonist's feelings stand a good chance of being understood by the peripheral member, invite the peripheral member to stand with you behind the protagonist, in the position of the double.

Then ask that member if he can verbalize how the protagonist might feel, coaching him if necessary. As with any situation involving doubling, have the double (the peripheral member) check out with the protagonist if he "got it right," and have the protagonist repeat the verbalized feelings that he agrees with. Make a point of affirming the double for the effort, for his ability to understand the feelings, and so on. As members begin to see this once peripheral member as someone who understands them, their interest in him will begin to grow.

Stage Three: Enactment

As we have stressed, it is essential that the enacted experience is one to which each of the other members feels some connection, and as always, group facilitators must keep an eye on the responsiveness of the observing members to the issue presented. In our IB/SAAT groups, we included both men and women in roughly equal numbers in each group, which allowed for a broader range of experiences to be shared, as well as for broader types of problem-solving alternatives to be generated. Moreover, it avoids reinforcing the stereotype that sexual victimization is a risk exclusive to women.

Moving Into Action

Ultimately, members related a variety of sexually victimizing, or potentially victimizing, experiences, many of which we had anticipated, but a number of which we did not. One that came as a surprise to us had to do with what some of the members referred to as the "kissing closet" at one of the weekly dances. In the kissing closet, a participant at the dance, usually a male, would hide out and stalk female prey. A nearby female would periodically be pulled into the closet where she would be kissed and fondled. From what we heard, it sounded as though a few females found this to be an enjoyable encounter and participated willingly. Many others found this to be repulsive and even frightening. The sharing of feelings around it, and the enactments we carried out, helped members not only in learning how to cope more effectively if they were pulled into the closet against their wishes, but also helped expand members' awareness that not everyone felt the same way about the experience. This was an especially important piece of learning for some of the men for whom the kissing closet had always seemed to be pure fun. As members develop emotional connections to each other, their sensitivity to each other's feelings deepens significantly. Telling Mike, a young man who finds the kissing closet to be the height of excitement, that some women do not like it may amount to no more than empty words. But for Mike to get to know and like Lydia, and then see her become visibly shaken when confronted with a role-play of the kissing closet, is a learning experience that powerfully alters his previous, one-sided view of the issue.

The kissing closet proved to be an emotionally engaging issue for most of the members and provided ideal material with which to build an array of enactments. We examine one such enactment in detail to clarify the workings of this stage.

Example of an Enactment Stage, Step by Step

Margaret, a 30-year-old woman with moderate mental retardation, began to describe an apparently uncomfortable experience with the kissing closet during the warm-up and sharing stage of a session one week. The cofacilitator and I (Nancy Razza) were unclear about what she, with considerable difficulty, was trying to explain. Another group member, Charlie, caught on to what Margaret was reporting, and said, "Oh, yeah. You mean the kissing closet." A few other comments were then made by some of the members, and questions and information exchanged between facilitators and members, ultimately clarifying the nature of the kissing closet just described. Following this clarification, we turned back to Margaret, asking her to state how she felt about her experience.

Margaret dropped her head and looked at the floor. "He was bothering me. I don't like it."

"It's good you can tell us, Margaret," said the cofacilitator. "You are doing the right thing talking about it." Next, to add support for Margaret and deepen member-to-member connection, the cofacilitator asked, "Margaret, who in this room do you think understands how you feel about the kissing closet? Look around the room and pick somebody you think understands how you feel."

Margaret lifted her head and looked directly at another female member seated across from her. She then began to restate her feelings to that individual rather than to respond as requested. The cofacilitator helped to redirect her by saying, "OK, Margaret, you have told us how you feel, and right now you are looking at Kelly to see if she understands you. Let's check it out with her. Kelly, do you know how Margaret feels about what happened in the kissing closet?"

Kelly replied, "She feels bad."

"Good, Kelly," the cofacilitator responded. "Now, ask Margaret if you got that right."

Kelly looked at Margaret. "You feel bad?"

"Yeah," Margaret said flatly.

"OK," the cofacilitator said at that point. "That was good. Margaret, you were able to tell us how you feel, and Kelly, you were able to understand it." The cofacilitator then asked Margaret to check out other members' understanding in a similar fashion. Margaret did so. The cofacilitator then said, "Margaret, it sounds like a lot of people understand that you feel bad about the kissing closet. Would it be all right if we did a role-play to try to find some new ways to deal with it? Maybe we can find a way that you can get away from the guy in the closet. Some of the other women would like to be able to get away, too."

Margaret was agreeable. Conditions were conducive to beginning an enactment in that most of the group members had an interest in the topic, and many could understand Margaret's feeling about it. As we began to set the wheels in motion, however, there was an important choice point here for the facilitators, as is often the case. Should Margaret be the protagonist? In a sense, she already was, because it was her issue, and she presented it. At some point, it would probably be therapeutic for her to relive a version of it through an enactment and then be given the chance to reenact the scene with new, more adaptive strategies. It can be daunting, however, to have to go right into a scene such as this, already loaded with negative emotional experience. Because this group is a forum for training, the involvement of another member in the protagonist role heightens the learning experience for yet another individual. So we suggested to Margaret that we could begin either with her as the protagonist or with someone else of her choosing playing the role. Giving Margaret the opportunity to make this decision is a good first step toward moving her out of the victim role, which she apparently felt in the "closet." Margaret responded by saying that she would like Kelly to take the role, and so we asked Kelly if she would be willing to try it. Note that each participant must be asked, not directed, to take part in an enactment. If an individual refuses, her refusal needs to be accepted. Another member can then be requested to play the part.

After establishing that Kelly would play the protagonist's role, we asked Margaret to help set the "stage" for the role-play so that it would be similar to the way things were at the dance. She pointed to a corner of the room, just beyond the group circle, as the area where the "closet" would be located. We moved a large chair over to the corner to represent the closet; standing behind the chair represented standing in the closet. We then checked with the rest of the members to be sure that everyone understood the scene we had set up.

At this point, the "stage" was set, and the protagonist was established. We now needed someone to play the part of the perpetrator. This brings us to another critical point. It is generally not a good idea for group members to play negatively charged roles such as that of a perpetrator. Even when the person playing the role fully understands that he is "only acting" and realizes that he is doing so for a good purpose, the experience of acting out such an aversive role can leave an uncomfortable residue. Members often volunteer to play these roles, but our experience leads us to recommend against it. In fact, the negative after-effects are not limited to group members. Without exception, each of us on staff who shared in playing the perpetrator roles felt drained after the experience. The emotional involvement of these enactments, so valuable as a learning vehicle, takes a toll when the role is a negative one. In fact, debriefing after the enactment is essential, which we discuss in the next section.

The use of two facilitators, helpful in any type of IBT group, is vital to the success of the SAAT group. With cofacilitation, one facilitator can remain in the facilitator role and help to direct the enactment, while the other takes on the role of the perpetrator. In Margaret's scene with the "kissing closet," I played the role of the perpetrator, while my cofacilitator, Leone, continued to direct the group.

We found it helpful to keep a few costuming supplies on hand for use in augmenting the character of the perpetrator. In this case, I wore a man's jacket and baseball cap. I stood behind the chair that had been positioned to represent the closet. The cofacilitator asked Margaret to set up the dance scene. She asked Margaret to position Kelly on the "dance floor," near the kissing closet, and then asked her to invite a few other members onto the dance floor to give the feeling of really being at the dance. The cofacilitator then directed all of the members to dance, talk, and behave as they normally do at the dance. After a few minutes of their involvement in dancing and socializing, I, as the perpetrator, began to verbally coax Kelly toward the "closet." I whispered to her, and when I had gotten her attention, signaled to her that she should be quiet and not tell anybody about my presence. I then reached out and lightly touched her arm (the only physical contact we ever present in these enactments is a light touch on the arm, hand, or shoulder). Kelly did not know what to do. She simply stood and stared at me. Aware of Kelly's apparent anxiety and inability to respond adaptively, the cofacilitator directed the group by saying, "OK, let's freeze the action." (The word *freeze* was one we had already taught to the group and used consistently to mean that everybody should stop the action, but stay exactly in place.) She continued. "Let's look at what is happening. Margaret, what is happening to Kelly?"

"The man is bothering her," Margaret replied.

"That's right," the cofacilitator continued. She then asked Margaret if she would stand behind Kelly and say how she is feeling.

"She doesn't like it," Margaret said.

"OK," said the cofacilitator. "Margaret, ask Kelly if that's right." Margaret checked this out with Kelly, who confirmed and then repeated the statement.

The cofacilitator affirmed Margaret and Kelly for their efforts. She then asked Kelly if she thought anyone else could understand how she was feeling in the situation. Kelly chose Liz, another member on the dance floor. Liz was asked if she could stand behind Kelly as Margaret had and say how she thought Kelly was feeling. Liz was able to say, "Scared," which was then confirmed and repeated by Kelly. Note that all this time the scene did not change. Kelly was still standing with the perpetrator's hand on her arm, and all of the members playing ancillary roles kept their positions. The reason for freezing the scene at this point is that we want members to become aware of the fear that is experienced at the very beginning of the potential entrapment. The first response to the fear is often to stop in one's tracks, like a deer in the headlights, as Kelly did. Our goal is to help members learn that this fear can also be a signal to do more adaptive things, such as to run away and seek help.

After identifying Kelly's emotion and offering supportive doubling for the emotion, we asked Kelly what she wanted to do when the scene started back up again. She said she wanted to get away. The director then announced that the "freeze" was over and everyone should get back to dancing as they had been. Continuing in the perpetrator role, I whispered to Kelly that I wanted her to come into the closet, that it would be fun, that I would give her candy, and so on. Kelly looked afraid. She started to look around the room and made eye contact with Liz, who encouraged her to run away. With Liz's help, Kelly finally turned away from the perpetrator and walked away. A few of the other members rushed up to her in support. Some started to clap.

At this point, the cofacilitator called another freeze. She then asked Kelly how she felt at that moment. "OK," she said. "I feel OK now."

The cofacilitator then went on to heighten Kelly's awareness of how good it felt to get away and how scary it had been when she felt stuck. She then asked everyone to return to his or her seats, signaling an end to that role-play. The cofacilitator went on to question the members regarding their understanding of "what Kelly did that was good." Each member was asked to give this positive feedback to Kelly. Finally, each member was thanked individually and acknowledged for his or her specific efforts, whether this was participating in the role-play or giving time and attention to it.

Next, the cofacilitator asked Margaret if she would be willing to try the role of protagonist in the same role-play. Margaret agreed, and the scene was set up as before. We conducted the enactment in the same way, again freezing the action when Margaret was first approached by the perpetrator and doubling for her feelings.

Margaret was not able to get away immediately, and like Kelly, she needed a bit of coaching to run. When she finally did, her escape was met with cheers and clapping, and the emotional relief she experienced was clarified and reinforced, just as it had been with Kelly.

It is interesting to note that spontaneous cheers and clapping became common elements in many SAAT groups we conducted. It became evident that each of us present experienced considerable tension during the perpetrator's approach scenes and great relief or even joy when the protagonist ran to safety.

The enactment stage came to a close as we sat back down in our circle and had each of the members talk about what Margaret had done that was good. This transition brought us into the affirmation stage, the final stage of the session.

Stage Four: Affirmation

The affirmation stage is characterized by feeding back to each of the members the positive aspects of their group participation for that day. As we have described, affirmation is given throughout the sessions, often immediately following the observation of behaviors that represent individual progress. During the affirmation stage, however, the reviewing and affirming of progress is the sole focus of the group's energy. In other words, in this stage facilitators do not bring up new ideas to challenge members, nor do they accept new agenda items from the members. Members may attempt to bring up new material, such as ideas they have for a role-play, or questions about something that took place. These items should be respectfully validated as important issues, and members should be requested to bring these up at the beginning of the next session. It is important for facilitators to maintain the same atmosphere of consideration that they established from the beginning of the session. The reason for not delving into issues or questions at this point is because such involvement will keep the emotional level of the group too high. When the hour is up, members must return to their regular activities; what is needed is a closing down of the emotionally charged energy that was generated. Affirming each individual helps each member become aware of his or her own specific improvements; it encourages positive feelings of self-esteem and puts a frame or boundary around the session so that members feel an episode has truly come to a conclusion rather than simply stopping short because a certain time was reached on the clock.

THE LEARNING CURVE AND LIMITATIONS IN SELF-PROTECTION TRAINING

As the sessions progressed, we helped members learn that in addition to getting away quickly, that is, as soon as they felt fear, they could ensure their safety further by reporting what happened to a trusted adult. Sessions were devoted to helping members identify trusted people in their lives and having them practice telling what they had experienced in their own words. We even developed a saying that members learned to repeat to aid their memories: "*Say 'NO' and go, then tell someone you know*," echoing the school-based prevention programs for children developed in the 1980s (Berrick & Gilbert, 1991).

As could be seen in the example with Kelly and Margaret, initial role-plays are often unsuccessful for the protagonist. Over periods of weeks, we would work with repetitions of enactments such as the kissing closet, varying certain elements each time. With repeated exposure, Margaret, Kelly, and most other members learned how to get away from perpetrators in various types of encounters, without having to be cued. Ultimately, they learned to report the problem directly as well. We agree with the work of Miltenberger et al. (1999), cited in chapter 2, in which generalization of abuse avoidance training was enhanced via *in situ* training that incorporated novel staff in the role of perpetrator. Assessing and retraining in this manner, in a variety of settings, is clearly a powerful aid to generalization. The ideal training program would include such a component.

Although our methods may vary, the thrust of this work is similar to many of the prevention programs for children promoted in the 1980s. Earlier in this chapter we discussed the relative efficacy of prevention programs with emotional and behavioral components. A number of researchers have challenged the efficacy and feasibility of these programs, pointing out the limitations in children's abilities to protect themselves from adult perpetrators, even with specialized training. They assert that adult caregivers, specifically, parents and teachers, are children's "first line of defense" (Berrick & Gilbert, 1991). Parental and teacher education are being championed by some (Jensen, 2000) as the method of choice for child protection, and indeed, educated, alert, and sensitive adults, committed to children's protection, could never be replaced by the best efforts of an independent child. At the same time, however, a meta-analytic study of school-based child sexual abuse prevention programs has revealed positive behavior change as a result of these programs, similar to the results reported by Goleman (1995). Davis and Gidyez (2000) analyzed 27 evaluation studies, composed of 8,115 elementary and middle school children, and found significant gains in abuse-related skills and knowledge among children exposed to the prevention training groups. Furthermore, they found that programs that allowed active participation by the children, especially physical participation, produced the greatest gains. Program efficacy was greater in those programs that ran for more than three sessions and included behavioral skills training. Although any comparison between nondisabled children and adults with intellectual disabilities is tenuous, this research suggests that skills and knowledge related to abuse prevention can be learned and that such learning is maximized by the type of program that includes an active, behavioral component.

This finding lends support to the sociodramatic rationale at the core of IB/SAAT groups.

SUMMARY

Although there is still much more to learn about the extent to which adults with intellectual disabilities can be trained in self-protection, the reality remains that a great many adults with intellectual disabilities, many of whom are as vulnerable as young children, must function in unprotected work, community, and residential settings every day. Caregiver education is as important for the safety needs of severely disabled adults as it is for children. It does not seem reasonable to expect, however, that such protection will ever be fully in place for most adults with intellectual disabilities. In addition to educating caregivers, we believe that people with intellectual disabilities deserve to be taught self-protection to the best of their abilities. Even knowing how to report one instance of abuse can make the difference between care and treatment, versus repeated exposure to chronic, and possibly, psychologically damaging abuse.

To this end, we have made a point of attempting to incorporate a few pieces of learning that research suggests even young children seem to be capable of and that have value in improving one's ability to self-protect. These are (a) learning body awareness, including the correct names of body parts; (b) learning that it is good to talk about what one feels, physically and emotionally, with safe adults (identifying these adults is part of the process); (c) learning that one should seek help, and keep seeking it until someone does help; and (d) learning that anytime one is told to keep a secret about touching, something is wrong.

Empowering people with intellectual disabilities with some specific skills has, in our experience, improved their ability to function successfully and to feel good about themselves. We agree that the vulnerability caused by their cognitive impairments yields an ongoing reliance on supportive adults. However, our thinking is that we can maximize the safety of these vulnerable individuals by teaching them to do all that they can for themselves and to make maximum use of the support people available to them.

III

TREATMENT: MODALITIES, PROCESSES, INITIATION, AND TERMINATION

7

THE INITIAL INTERVIEW

The first duty of love is to listen.

—Paul Tillich

A number of difficulties frequently beset the clinician's first meeting with an individual with intellectual disabilities. Often, the individual is referred and brought in by a third party (a family member or staff member such as a group home manager or job coach). In many cases, the individual does not understand what the appointment is for and may be an unwilling or a fearful participant.

The usual responsibilities of an initial interview, such as setting the person at ease and formulating a preliminary diagnostic impression and tentative treatment plan, can be powerfully complicated when the would-be patient is confused or frightened, or has no frame of reference for understanding psychotherapy. Extra care must be taken to ensure that the individual understands the nature of the therapy process, as well as issues of confidentiality and voluntary consent. Fortunately, many people respond fairly quickly to a supportive, nonconfrontational approach. We detail some examples of initial interviews with different types of referrals in an effort to provide a framework that can guide the initial meeting for practitioners new to this work. In these examples, we refer to female survivors and male offenders, and, as elsewhere in this book, we use disguised versions of real-life cases to maximize their educational value. The gender of offenders and survivors used in this chapter and elsewhere in no way implies that all offenders are male or all survivors are female. Inevitably, clinicians will encounter male survivors, female offenders, and many people who are both. Good clinical skill, in the first meeting and beyond, will be needed to discern these and many other issues that plague our patients. Treatment of individuals with both cognitive and psychiatric disorders is complicated work indeed; conceptualizing the early stages of therapy as a lengthy period of assessment and retaining a willingness to reformulate clinical understanding as experience with the individual deepens can greatly assist this difficult undertaking.

A QUESTION OF ABUSE

The initial interview may or may not be the individual's first contact with a professional in which her abuse is the subject of discussion. It is essential, however, that the initial interview be conducted in a therapeutic manner when it is being done to determine the person's need for psychotherapy. This interview is likely to be the individual's first contact with a mental health professional.

Interviewing people about their abuse for clinical purposes is distinct from the investigative types of interviews done for forensic purposes. Unfortunately, however, pressure is sometimes brought to bear on clinicians by staff, families, attorneys, and other involved parties to go on a fact-finding mission that may be at odds with the nature of clinical work. It seems that such pressure is more likely to occur when the victim has an intellectual disability because those personnel involved in legal issues and prosecution often report feeling ill-equipped to interview people with such impairments. Despite even the best intentions of those trying to gain information and prosecute the case, however, it is generally a poor strategy to attempt to incorporate a forensic investigation into a clinical one. For those clinicians who plan to maintain an ongoing counseling or therapeutic relationship with the survivor, a better course of action is to leave the forensic questioning to the legal personnel, who can be assisted if necessary by a staff member familiar with the survivor. In this way, the clinical interview can be allowed to unfold toward therapeutic ends. Of course, the client may present previously undisclosed instances of abuse during the session. These would then have to be reported by the clinician in accord with the reporting procedures mandated by the state.

The hallmark of abuse is the invasion of an individual's boundaries. The abuse occurs because the abuser cannot or will not contain his needs or desires out of respect for the other person's limits. If the clinician then disrespects the individual's limits, even by simply pressing for information verbally, further harm may result. The individual may experience distress, become symptomatic, or withdraw into silence. The recommended interviewing strategies are aimed at providing the clinician with a frame for clinical interviewing toward the following objectives:

- to maximize the individual's comfort level with discussing the abuse;
- to help identify psychological issues associated with the abuse, such as defense mechanisms and impact on self-concept; and
- to enhance the rapport development that is essential to ongoing clinical work.

BEGINNING THE DISCUSSION

The recommendations concerning interviewing strategies with people who have intellectual disabilities have been informed by recommendations for general diagnostic interviewing (Othmer & Othmer, 1994), as well as by strategies recommended for women who have experienced sexual abuse (Walker, 1994), for children who have experienced sexual abuse (Shapiro, 1991), and by our own experience with abuse survivors who have intellectual disabilities. If the individual being referred is new to you, begin the discussion by introducing yourself and explaining your role. Experts in general diagnostic interviewing stress that putting the individual at ease is always the first order of business (Othmer & Othmer, 1994), and it is certainly no less important when the discussion may center on abuse. A generally helpful strategy, whether the referral issue concerns abuse or not, is to give a brief explanation to the individual of what the meeting will be about. For example, it can be helpful to say something like, "This meeting is a chance for us to talk about things that are important to you. You can talk about problems and things that bother you; you can also talk about good things, and things you like to do." Of course, the actual language you use should be tailored to the individual's comprehension as much as possible. It is then important to ask for the individual's consent, saying, for example, "Is that OK with you?" Even if the individual has a legal guardian who has already given written consent for treatment, it is important to begin right away to establish this contact as a therapeutic—and, therefore, respectful—one, one that is likely to be quite different from the types of contact the individual may be used to having with people in authority. For an individual who is her own guardian, it is important to address issues of confidentiality as well as consent. For many people with intellectual disabilities, a lifetime of compliance training has preceded your first meeting with them. It is often necessary to tell the person directly that, although you believe the session could be helpful to them, they do not have to stay and talk with you if they do not want to. Furthermore, you can make clear to them that they can change their mind later if they want to stop, even if they have signed a "consent for treatment" form.

If you are unsure whether the individual fully understands you, ask her to repeat back what she heard you say. It is often helpful to introduce the individual to this "checking back" as a regular part of the process. Be patient and praising of her efforts to feed back your communication. Similarly, check out your understanding of what was said to you, asking if you "got it right." For people whose communication is handicapped, this can help to enhance comprehension as well as to convey a sense of genuine interest in the individual.

If you have been informed through the referral that there has been some type of abuse, you can raise the issue, once you feel sufficient rapport has developed, by saying something such as, "I heard that something upsetting happened to you; that somebody did something to you that made you feel bad. Is that right?" If the person responds affirmatively, ask, "Can you tell me about it?"

Often we treat individuals who are referred for a problem other than abuse, who then disclose past experiences of abuse in a later session. In these cases, the disclosure is likely an outgrowth of the safety and respect felt in the counseling relationship, and so it is equally important to follow up on the disclosure with questions that encourage the individual to say more, but without feeling pressured. Abuse happens because the victim is, in one way or another, pressured without respect for her feelings; an overzealous drive to simply get information can do more harm than good in such a case. A good strategy is to say something like, "I'd like to hear about what happened to you. Can you tell me more about it?" If the individual is able to relate some of the experience, keep prompting disclosure with neutral, open-ended questions, such as, "And then what happened?" If the individual is silent or says "No," then switch gears and direct the discussion toward the person's *feelings* rather than the event. Use this strategy whether the person is a new referral and you raised the issue or whether the person has been in counseling with you for a while and disclosed the problem herself. After all, it is her feelings that are preventing discussion. The individual's perception of having her feelings understood and respected offers the best avenue for keeping the communication open.

FOLLOWING THE FEELINGS

In cases in which the individual "shuts down" after the issue is raised, follow up first with how she feels right at the moment. It is often helpful to convey a sense of understanding for the person's emotional state and then to ask questions about it. For example, you might say, "It looks like you feel pretty bad (or sad, or upset) when you remember what happened. Is that right?" If the person can respond by describing how she is feeling, acknowledge that it is good that she can talk about how she feels. If she is impeded by emotional or cognitive difficulties, say something such as the following: "Many people have bad feelings after going through what you went through. Sometimes they feel sad, sometimes they feel mad, and sometimes they feel scared or confused. Do you have any of those feelings?" Again, if the individual is able to respond, affirm the effort. If she remains silent, try to convey understanding of the silence by saying that right now this seems to be too hard to talk about. Then ask if that is right. Follow up with letting the individual know that many people have trouble talking about their bad experiences and that you know how hard it is to do. Also, let her know that it usually becomes easier to talk as time goes on and that you will help her try again. Even if the session ends with no new information regarding the abuse, affirm the individual for having made the effort to bear with you throughout the interview and listen to your questions. Verbalize respect for her, and explain your willingness to allow her to go at her own pace in learning how to talk about what happened. It is important that the individual feel good about her experience with you for her to be amenable to going on with some form of treatment.

With an individual who is able to express her current emotions, you can continue to clarify those emotions and to affirm the individual for being able to talk about them. Following this, you might move to a discussion of the feelings she had at the time of the abuse. If the person has difficulty, you can use a strategy similar to the one mentioned earlier in which you describe feelings people commonly have with abuse, and see if the individual is able to identify with any. Sometimes this attention to and support for the feelings leads to increased disclosure about the abusive event. If this happens, continue affirming the person's efforts at talking about it, and always follow the disclosure by checking on how the person feels at the moment. Care for the individual's feelings in the moment is essential to reducing her experience of distress in retelling the event and is also what therapy is really about. People who successfully complete therapy following traumatic experience are able to consciously think about and talk about the event, without experiencing overwhelmingly distressing emotions or symptoms. Along the way toward that ultimate goal, therapy should be aimed at helping the person learn to identify what she is feeling, as well as to develop a set of resources she can use when experiencing highly distressing feelings.

ASSESSING COPING AND DEFENSE MECHANISMS

Once the feelings have been identified, you can direct the discussion toward how the individual copes. ("What do you do when you start to feel bad about what happened?") Often the person has developed defensive styles in response to the abuse that leads to other problems, the remediation of which becomes a key feature of the therapy. For example, it is often so painful to acknowledge that one was completely at the mercy of the perpetrator that people distort the facts toward their own culpability. Rape and even childhood incest victims commonly report feelings of guilt over what they "allowed" to happen, citing things in hindsight they "should" have done differently (Walker, 1994). One woman with intellectual disabilities blamed herself for her rape because she did indeed want to "go out" with the man. She did not, however, want to have sex without a condom and was forcefully raped by the man once she told him she was leaving because he did not have a condom.

Sometimes, in answer to the question about coping, we find that the individual is quite unclear or may simply say she does "nothing" or that she just sits in her room or watches television. She may not be aware that these are ways of trying to cope. Quite often we see constriction of affect ("trying not to let yourself feel anything") and suppression ("trying not to think about it") in the people with whom we work. It can be helpful to feed back to the individual what she says, tying it together with the question. For example, you might say something like, "So when you start to think about what happened, you start to feel upset; then you try not to think about it and watch television. Is that right?" This not only helps clarify the individual's coping style for treatment planning purposes but increases her self-awareness as well.

Sometimes the individual displays self-abusive or aggressive behavior toward others. One woman with whom we worked was referred because of increasingly aggressive behavior toward other women, sometimes attempting to rub their hair and to hug them despite their protests. In some instances the "hug" turned into a full-throttle episode of pressing her body onto another woman's as she pushed her victim onto the floor. We learned that she had been raped on two prior occasions, and we were able to read the police reports. It could never be determined with certainty that her prior abuse was what led to these behaviors, yet helping her to think and talk about her abuse, albeit in a limited way due to her disability, did seem to greatly improve her behavior. It should be noted that when maladaptive coping strategies are identified, it is best not to rush in and pressure the individual to change. This can cause the individual to feel that once again they are dealing with an authority figure who is trying to tell them what to do. It tends to make for a poor relationship and to reinforce feelings of being misunderstood and not cared about. Affirm your understanding of the individual's feelings and behavior for now, and ask the person if she wants to learn how to change this behavior. Invariably people express a desire to change such behavior, having experienced negative consequences in response to it. Let the individual know that as she continues in therapy she will have the opportunity to learn how to make changes in her behavior.

In cases in which others or the individual herself stands to be hurt until the change is made, it may be necessary to consult with staff, family, or other support people in the person's life to ensure that a protective plan is in place. This should be done after the assessment session is finished. Allow this initial assessment to continue without presenting behavioral alternatives that may get in the way of the individual's presentation of her current mental status and functioning. In addition to making for a clearer assessment, fertile groundwork will be laid for ongoing therapy.

So far, we have looked at beginning discussions about abuse, establishing a frame for those discussions based on respect, getting a sense of the person's affective state at the time of the incident(s) and at present, and identifying coping and defense mechanisms. Identification of these factors helps to direct the therapy toward expanding the individual's own awareness of her feelings and coping behaviors. From here, we continue with questions about other symptoms the person may have, as well as with discussion aimed at clarifying self-concept and relationships with others.

INVESTIGATING SYMPTOMS

As the interview progresses, it is possible to gain a more complete understanding of the person's symptom complex by continuing the questioning as well as by observing the individual as she responds. It is important to bear in mind that sexual abuse, like exposure to other forms of trauma or extreme stress, can affect people across many dimensions: somatic, emotional, cognitive, behavioral, and characterological (Ursano, Grieger, & McCarrol, 1996). Similarly, as noted in earlier chapters, there is increasing support for the notion that traumatic exposure can lead to the development of a variety of disorders, including eating disorders, substance abuse, self-mutilation, dissociative disorders, and certain personality disorders, as well as posttraumatic stress disorder (PTSD), anxiety disorders, and depressive disorders (Ursano et al., 1996). Many factors are thought to influence the development of any particular disorder, and current thinking suggests that it is overly simplistic to assume that the development of a disorder is due solely to the experience of any one traumatic event. What we do know, however, is that exposure to extreme stress contributes to various forms of psychopathology. In particular, women with psychiatric disorders are much more likely to have experienced sexual abuse in their lifetimes than are women in the general population (Root, 1991; van der Kolk, 1996).

Begin addressing the individual's feelings directly after she tells you about the abuse. You might say, for example, "How does it feel to you to be talking about what happened?" For individuals who are able to verbalize their feelings, it is important to affirm them for doing so, saying something such as, "I'm glad you can tell me how you feel." If the person has indicated that they feel bad in some way about discussing or remembering the event, add, "I'm sure you do feel bad (or sad, or whatever word she used); these things are not easy to talk about."

When the individual is not able to tell you how she feels, it can be useful to check out with her your perception of her feeling state. For example, "I noticed you looked down at the floor just now and got quiet. It looks like you felt kind of sad. Is that right?"

In keeping with the focus on respect for the individual's limits, it is a good idea to ask permission to continue this line of questioning. It is important, however, to tell the individual your rationale for continued questioning, as this may help motivate her to go on with the process. You might say something like, "I know this isn't easy to talk about, but if it's all right with you, I'd like to ask you some more questions. I'd really like to understand what you went through, and how you feel about it. Also, if you and I look at what's been going on, we might be able to figure out what you can do to feel better. Is that okay with you?"

You can continue asking about depressive symptoms, asking if the person ever feels sad, down, or in a bad mood, grouchy, cranky, and so on. Use whatever language the individual uses, repeating back to her what she said, and checking out whether you have understood correctly. Remember it is better to go slowly and continue this checking process, repeating your understanding of what you have heard for verification. This demonstrates your interest in truly understanding the person, which is therapeutic in its own right, as well as being helpful for people who have speech or language difficulties.

In your assessment of depressive symptoms, bear in mind that people with intellectual disabilities may be more likely than nonimpaired adults to experience irritable rather than sad moods when depressed. Angry, aggressive, and self-injurious behaviors may also be displayed by depressed people with intellectual disabilities (Charlot, 1998). Many referral problems are initially presented by staff as "noncompliance," "temper tantrums," "self-abuse," or "going off with no provocation." Experience has taught that individuals with intellectual disabilities who exhibit such behaviors are often depressed and frequently, although not always, have histories of traumatic exposure.

Ask about symptoms of anxiety using words such as "jumpy," "nervous," or "scared." It can be helpful, when asking about any symptom experience, to clarify it with concrete, real-life examples. "Sometimes, after a bad thing happens, people feel kind of scared. Do you feel scared sometimes, like you're nervous inside and it's hard to calm down?" If she answers affirmatively, follow with increasingly concrete questions to assess the frequency and specificity of these experiences. For example, "Do you feel nervous when you lie down to go to sleep at night, or when you wake up in the morning? Do you feel nervous at work? Do you ever feel nervous at home? What happens at work that makes you feel nervous?" Continue in this fashion, regularly checking out your understanding. Note that the questions suggested in this paragraph are simply examples of the types of questions that might be used to encourage the individual to describe her symptoms. It is important not to barrage the individual with questions but rather to affirm and nurture the person along as she begins to respond.

As you are thinking about what, if any, symptoms of anxiety the person has, you may want to go on to see if the person has additional symptoms, such as those found in PTSD. This category includes symptoms seen in depression, such as loss of hope and loss of a sense of self-efficacy, as well as the hyperarousal and reactivity seen in anxiety disorders. In addition, it has unique features such as intrusive memories, flashbacks, or nightmares. It can be useful to ask the person if she has "bad dreams." You might also ask, "Do you ever feel like you can't stop thinking about what happened, even when you want to?" and "Do you have to try really hard not to think about what happened?"

A clinician working with individuals with intellectual disabilities may need to look for some unusual symptoms. The reexperiencing aspect of PTSD, which takes the form of intrusive memories, flashbacks, and nightmares, can also show up in what are known as "trauma-specific reenactments." Generally, these are only seen in children. In our work with people with intellectual disabilities, we have seen a few, relatively rare, cases of trauma-specific reenactments in adults. More often, we see limited, agitated, self-abusive states, in which the individual will head-bang, pick at his skin, or bite himself.

As opposed to reliving the *memory* of the trauma, which is primarily a mental phenomenon, the individual who exhibits trauma-specific reenactments acts out behaviorally the traumatic episode he experienced. It is common for children to reenact the episode with themselves, with toys, or with other children. In our work with one young woman with intellectual disabilities, initial symptoms of head-banging and agitation subsided as she progressed in treatment. We learned that her father had sexually abused her for quite some time, and he was removed from the home. After a fairly lengthy period of stability, the staff reported a new symptom pattern. The young woman would drop to her knees, motion with her hands toward various parts of her body, and cry and yell. She would seem to be in an almost trancelike state at these times and would need to come out of them on her own. In an adult, this behavior can appear psychotic, and close attention to assessment is needed. Ultimately, it became clear that this woman was not suddenly having unusual psychotic episodes but was demonstrating hand motions on her body, as she had experienced them during the abuse. She was displaying trauma-specific reenactments. People with PTSD will often regress to symptomatic states, even after long periods of stability, when faced with new stressors that evoke old fears and memories. In the case of this young woman, we learned that her father, now in failing health, had been moved back into the home.

In less cognitively impaired, and more verbal adults with intellectual disabilities, these reenactments are typically not seen. However, they are an important indicator of PTSD in adults whose cognitive limitations are severe.

Returning to the interview process, following the questions concerning intrusive memories and nightmares described earlier, it is possible to move into an assessment of eating disorders, addictions, and self-injurious behaviors. You might ask, "Do you ever try to do things to stop from thinking about it?" If the person is able to respond, affirm her for doing so. If the person cannot respond, you might say something such as, "Some people sometimes do things like smoke a cigarette or drink a beer to try to help them forget about what happened. Do you ever do things like that?" As long as the person is agreeable to responding, you can continue in this fashion.

People with intellectual disabilities are somewhat more likely than nonimpaired people to display certain response-style biases. A tendency to acquiesce or to want to get answers "right" may be observed. Some individuals habitually deny problems, fearing that anything problematic on their part may result in punishment or reprimands. To avoid the problems associated with the acquiescent style, make a point of phrasing similar questions in alternate ways. It is also important to say more than once that there are no wrong answers and to demonstrate affirmation for all efforts to respond. When people make the effort to give information that is obviously difficult for them, acknowledgment for that effort is essential.

ASSESSING SELF-CONCEPT

There is a good deal of evidence that victimizing experiences due to domestic violence, battering, rape, or incest contribute to a lowered sense of self-esteem as well as a sense of powerlessness (van der Kolk, 1996; Walker, 1994) among people in the general population. People with intellectual disabilities frequently have a lowered sense of self-esteem and personal power (often called *self-efficacy*) because of the experience of growing up with a significant disability. For these individuals, the experience of victimization often leads to the diminishment of an already compromised sense of self.

Careful assessment and treatment of this dimension are crucial to the healing process.

One way in which this diminished sense of self may manifest is through the victim's belief that what happened was in some way her own fault. This is a common theme among victims and may serve the secondary gain of allowing the person to believe that she had more power or control than she really did, but it can take a heavy toll on how she feels about herself. For instance, one adolescent girl with intellectual disabilities, referred after being raped, said that her mother kept asking her how she could have been "so stupid" as not to have yelled when the neighborhood boy first grabbed her on the street. She could barely understand the shock and terror she experienced and could not understand herself why she had been unable to scream. She decided she must indeed be "really stupid." Another woman felt she was to blame for her rape because she had agreed to date the man. And Martina, the woman with cerebral palsy introduced in chapter 1, believed for years that her childhood sexual abuse by her cousin was her fault because she was disabled and could not get away.

Needless to say, discussions regarding the person's sense of self and personal culpability must be entered into with great care. It can be helpful to say something like, "Often people who have been abused like you have feel it might have been their own fault, even though it wasn't. Do you sometimes feel like that?" If the individual indicates that it might have been even partly her fault, or she is unsure whether it was her fault, ask, "How does it make you feel to think that it might have been your fault?" The most important thing to look for is how the person really sees herself. For instance, Martina, as we saw, blamed herself for her abuse because she believed she was inherently flawed. The woman described earlier, who experienced the date-rape, suffered much less damage to her self-concept because she saw her blame as being in the fact that she broke a house rule by going out alone with a man whom she had not told the staff about. Although neither woman is actually to blame for her own abuse, there are important differences in their attributions of blame and self-concept, which will entail very different work in ongoing therapy.

It can be helpful to ask about the individual's attribution of blame toward the perpetrator. "What do you think the judge should do with (the perpetrator)?" might yield useful information in this regard. A conflicted response such as saying he should be locked up but only for a little while could suggest mixed feelings about the perpetrator or about the victim's own sense of self-blame (Shapiro, 1991).

To further explore these themes, you might ask, "Are you different in any way since the abuse, or are you just like you were before?" You might also ask, "Now that the abuse is over, is life pretty much the way it was before, or is it different somehow?"

RELATIONSHIPS WITH OTHERS

Good social support and secure attachment to key figures such as parents do much to buffer individuals against the destructive effects of trauma (Ursano et al., 1996; van der Kolk, 1996). It is important to determine whether the individual feels essentially isolated or has good-quality relationships with at least a few others in her life. If some good relationships appear to be present, you will want to look at the individual's ability to use those relationships in times of distress. This will be useful in planning the degree to which social skills development will need to be stressed in the therapy. You might ask, "Who can you tell if you have a really bad problem?" And also, "Is there anyone who would help you even if you made a really bad mistake?" If the answer is affirmative, always ask if there is anyone else who is also helpful. It is also useful to ask the person if they have friends and who they are, when they see each other, and so on.

For people who need more concrete examples, you might try something like, "If you had to go to the hospital to have an operation, who would you want to go with you?" You might follow this up with, "Would they go with you if you asked them to?" To get at the broader dimensions of their social world you might ask, "Who would you like to come visit you in the hospital?" And, "Who do you think would come?"

It is important to bear in mind that social support, in addition to its buffering effects against trauma, is equally important in protecting against depression. Research has found that for people with intellectual disabilities, just as for nondisabled people, depression tends to go hand in hand with insufficient levels of social support (Nezu et al., 1992). It will be important to pay close attention to this variable if the person has experienced a traumatic exposure or shows signs of depression, anger, or agitation.

For people who have experienced interpersonal violence such as sexual abuse, as opposed to the types of trauma not delivered by another human being (e.g., accidents, earthquakes), the construction of a safe social network is of great importance. Although social support is therapeutic in coping with all forms of trauma, for those whose traumatization was at the hands of another person, the creation of a safe social network can become a highly complicated event. Distrust of others and conflicted feelings, such as longing for companionship yet being afraid of people, can get in the way of much needed relationships. In addition, for those interpersonally traumatized people who also have intellectual disabilities, social skills deficits may further complicate the process. Specific help with how to create and use a social network is often necessary and may become a key focus of the ongoing therapy.

Finally, as we suggested previously, it is important to remember that assessment of the person need not begin and end with the first interview.

As the clinician, you will use the first meeting to begin (a) to develop a sense of the person, (b) to establish at least a tentative diagnostic impression, and (c) to propose an initial plan of treatment or intervention. People who appear to be in distress and who exhibit symptoms deserve the opportunity to receive treatment, even if clear information concerning the details of the trauma cannot be obtained. Unfortunately, there have been many cases in which treatment was delayed because of misguided efforts to simply determine whether or not abuse had actually taken place. Often, details regarding the abuse come forth in later sessions. In any case, if the individual is symptomatic, and there is reason to be concerned about her well-being, the best course of action is usually to begin her in therapy while continuing your observations and assessment during the initial stage of treatment.

INITIAL INTERVIEWS WITH PEOPLE WITH INTELLECTUAL DISABILITIES ACCUSED OF SEXUAL OFFENSE

The first meeting with a person with intellectual disabilities referred because of suspected, or known, sexual offense may find you seated across from a most reluctant and rather forlorn individual. Of course, the goals of the initial interview with an offender are the same as they are for a survivor. With some offenders, it is possible to conduct an in-depth clinical interview as described earlier. In every case, a genuine effort to do so should be made. In many cases, however, the individual's reluctance may pose a problem from the first meeting and may make it difficult, if not impossible, to obtain voluntary, informed consent. In our experience, although some offenders are court-ordered to obtain treatment, the majority of our referrals are under no legal constraints. Family members and support staff, such as job coaches and residential managers, are generally the impetus behind the referral. This pressure is often necessary and helpful to the offender with intellectual disabilities who does not understand the legal and emotional consequences of his behavior.

In cases in which the individual has a legal guardian, the guardian's permission and written consent should be obtained. However, it is also important to provide the individual with the same information that needs to be given to offenders who are self-guardians. That is, the therapist needs to review with the individual the reason he is being referred for therapy and make certain that the individual understands it. He should also be apprised of what therapy entails. As we have noted previously, it is helpful to ask the person to repeat back what he heard, using his own words. It may be necessary to reassure the individual that he is allowed to disagree with the reported problem and that his opinion, whether different or the same, is also important. It is crucial, however, that he understand both the referral problem and the nature of the counseling agreement as fully as is possible for him to secure consent for treatment.

The aim of the initial meeting with an offender can be thought of in two broad dimensions: (a) to clarify to the individual the nature of the referral problem and its consequences in his life and (b) to present therapy as a means of helping the individual avoid further negative consequences. As we discussed in chapter 5 on treating offenders with intellectual disabilities, if the therapist alone bears the burden of informing the individual about the nature of his problem, the individual will be very likely to want to avoid therapy. It is best that the individual be informed by the referring staff or family members so that he feels the consequences of his action in his own life, rather than solely in the therapy room.

Let us look at a particularly difficult case of a young man who, despite repeated efforts on the part of the clinician, could not be engaged in the interview process. He was in no way ready to respond to a clinical interview of the type described earlier in this chapter. Although his resistance was more active and directly oppositional than most of our referrals, his case is informative because it reflects the inherent difficulties found in approaching treatment with intellectually disabled offenders referred by third parties.

AN INITIAL INTERVIEW WITH A RESISTANT CLIENT

Ted was a 28-year-old man whose measured IQ placed him at the low end of the range of mild mental retardation. He was referred by his mother, with whom he lived. His mother reported that Ted had been suspended from his job because of inappropriate behavior with female coworkers. Ted and his mother came into the session together. The therapist introduced herself and explained to Ted that he was there to discuss the possibility of beginning counseling. Ted looked down at the floor and mumbled something about not needing any counseling. The therapist asked Ted if he could tell her why he had come in. Ted wriggled in his seat uncomfortably and said that he did not know. This angered his already agitated mother and she quickly began to relate the problems Ted had had at work. She was quite upset, stating that Ted had been employed for approximately seven years as a part-time stockperson at a large department store. His employer, who apparently had always been quite supportive of Ted, had reported that Ted's behavior around women had hit a breaking point. Ted had been following certain women around, touching them despite protests, and giving them gifts they did not want. A security guard also had reported to Ted's boss that he had seen him masturbating with his pants down, albeit in a room by himself. Ted's boss finally decided to suspend Ted indefinitely, adding that he would take Ted back if he got treatment and the treatment provider felt he was safe to return to work.

Ted appeared angry and uncomfortable but said little initially. At the first opportunity, the therapist asked Ted if he understood what his mother had said. Reluctantly, Ted admitted that he did. The therapist then invited Ted to share his concerns. Ted, however, had a different agenda. He began to deny and minimize the charges. He was particularly insistent that he never had his pants down. His mother seemed inclined to want to believe him but also stated that Ted's boss had been extremely kind to him all the years he had worked for him. She felt certain that his boss would not have ended Ted's job without good reason.

After thanking Ted's mother for the information, the therapist suggested that she next interview Ted alone to give him an opportunity to speak privately and to discuss counseling options with him. Ted and his mother agreed. After Ted's mother left the room, the therapist attempted to reduce Ted's apparent discomfort by supporting the feelings he seemed to be having. She stated, "I guess that must have felt pretty bad for you, listening to the mistakes you made at work." Ted looked up at her and said, "I just want my job back." The therapist responded by demonstrating that she heard Ted. "Yeah, I can see that you really want your job back. It sounds like your job means a lot to you." Ted was able to agree that it did. The therapist then made a few other attempts to demonstrate awareness and acceptance of Ted's feelings and to engage him in some discussion of his emotional state, but Ted remained unresponsive to these overtures. Instead, he restated many times his desire to simply return to work and bypass any talk or process, such as counseling, which he perceived as slowing up his return.

Because Ted could not engage in any discussion of feelings, the therapist restated her understanding that he wanted to go back to work. Ted was able to hear the therapist's demonstration of understanding, which brought down his growing agitation a bit. Because Ted had not been able to engage in any discussion regarding emotions, the therapist then attempted to bring up the issue of counseling by means of its connection to his return to work. She said, "So, Ted, you want to go back to work as soon as possible. What can you do to get back to your job?" Ted had been looking at her directly as she spoke the magic words ("get back to work"), but quickly looked down at the end of the question. "I don't know!" he said, too loudly. "I just want to go back!"

"You just want to go back," the therapist repeated. "But you don't know what to do about it. Is that right?"

"Yes!" said Ted, again almost shouting.

"Okay," continued the therapist. "Let's see if we can figure out what you can do to get back to work. Your mother said before that your boss would take you back if you completed counseling. Maybe we can talk about what that means."

Ted became more agitated on hearing this. In addition to reiterating his desire to return to work, he went on to deny that his boss had ever found fault with any of his behavior. As Ted's pressured speech continued, it became clear that Ted believed his job loss was actually his mother's doing. Through careful questioning, the therapist learned that the boss had never spoken directly to Ted, only to his mother. In addition, Ted had no job coach because he had been successfully employed for years. Therefore, the only person confronting Ted about his behavior was his mother. The absence of feedback from anyone else helped Ted support his denial. Ted saw his mother as the culprit, and all of his emotional energy was targeted at her. Therefore, the therapist decided to provide a clarifying summation to Ted of all that had been presented thus far and forgo further efforts at an interview. She said, "OK, Ted, you're saying that your mother pulled you out of work because she thinks you had some problems there. You don't agree with her. Nobody at work told you that you had any problems there, and you don't want any counseling or anything. You just want to go back to work." The therapist spoke each statement slowly and paused at the end of each to check for Ted's agreement. At the end of this summation, she asked if she had understood everything correctly. Ted affirmed that she had, yet persisted in repeating his desire to return to work. The therapist then said, "Ted, let's bring your mother back in and tell her these things." Ted agreed. The therapist told Ted's mother that Ted was unwilling to begin therapy and was, in fact, unwilling even to hear about the process of therapy. She explained Ted's perspective on the entire matter, continually checking with Ted that she was representing what he felt. Ted's mother began to tell Ted that he *had* to go to therapy, and both she and Ted started raising their voices. The therapist interrupted them and explained that Ted might better understand his need for treatment if he heard directly from his boss what his problems were, as well as what he needed to do to return to the job. She explained that therapy could not be enforced on Ted against his will: There was no legal order, and Ted was his own guardian. (Note that Ted, like so many people with intellectual disabilities, was a self-guardian by default; no own had ever challenged his guardianship. It was evident that Ted was completely dependent on his mother, who, in all likelihood, would have obtained at least partial legal guardianship over him had she applied for it.) The therapist offered Ted the opportunity to help him with his problems if he wanted help after checking things out with his boss. Ted's mother was annoyed that Ted's getting into therapy was being delayed by this step; Ted, on the other hand, seemed rather relieved that he was not being forced into therapy by the therapist and seemed to welcome the prospect of being able to talk to his boss. The therapist ended the interview by inviting Ted and his mother to recontact her if services were desired following discussion with Ted's boss.

The upshot of this intervention was that Ted's mother called the boss, who was kind enough to allow Ted to come in and meet with him briefly. The boss explained to Ted the problems with his behavior and stated his unwillingness to take Ted back without some assurances that he had completed a therapeutic program. He even drew Ted a picture, using stick figures, to show what he meant by "appropriate personal space" and explained that this was essential to learn for job success. Ted came back in for a therapy interview still unhappy about the prospect of therapy, but with a clear understanding that it was a necessary step to returning to work. He was willing to enter treatment because he understood that it could help him meet his goal. Ted has now been in a therapy group for over a year. Slowly, and with considerable difficulty in the early months, he has come to learn how to work in therapy. Ultimately, he has made a great deal of progress. In fact, he is able to admit to his problem behaviors and is working well in a job-training program that we recommended he attend while in therapy.

This case points out some of the difficulties involved in initial meetings with offenders with intellectual disabilities referred by third parties. Generally, the referring family or staff members are much more motivated to get the individual into treatment than the individual himself is. These third parties may be so motivated that they pressure the clinician to take on the case and "get through" to the individual. Some clinicians with whom we have consulted have reported succumbing to pressure to confront the individual's denial in the first interview and to take on the role of social gatekeeper. Often these clinicians identify with the plight of the distraught parent or caregiver, and they want to get the person into treatment as soon as possible to ease the caregiver's burden and prevent further offenses.

Unfortunately, confrontation by the therapist, a stranger whom the individual has just met and who is not a part of his life, has no productive impact on the individual's denial. Premature confrontation of this sort simply motivates the individual to avoid the therapist, and the therapy, so that he may avoid facing these problems. Moreover, the relationship between patient and therapist cannot be a therapeutic one if the patient feels he is being commanded by yet another authority figure in his life. The therapeutic relationship is different, and that difference needs to be consistently demonstrated by the therapist. The therapist is a tool that the patient can use to help himself with a problem, if he so desires. Similarly, therapy, whether group or individual, is a tool. Even when the individual is court-ordered, the therapist can maximize her efficacy with the client by maintaining consistent loyalty to her therapeutic role. Be clear with the patient that the *court* is requiring him to go to treatment, not you. You are simply obligated to report to his parole officer, or other legal monitor, on whether or not the individual attends. It may take a number of repetitions to clarify your role to the individual, but it is essential that you make clear to him that your interest is only in helping him if he would like your help, or, once in group, the group's help. You will not force him to attend sessions. If the individual complains about having to see you, demonstrate understanding of his feelings and remind him that you are not in charge of his court order; that is something he has to take up with court or his parole officer. In *Treating Intellectually Disabled Sex Offenders*, Haaven, Little, and Petre-Miller (1990) described a model treatment program for offenders with intellectual disabilities. They noted, "A frontal attack on denial has not been effective with intellectually disabled offenders" (p. 26). They supported an "incremental disclosure" approach, along with the use of peer and staff "tutoring" that bears similarities to the sharing that takes place in the group therapy process. Tough and Hingsburger (1999) similarly acknowledged the value of avoiding direct confrontation, and instead recommended engaging the offender with intellectual disabilities through the "therapeutic back door." Interestingly, new work in the treatment of nondisabled offenders (Marshall, Thornton, Marshall, Fernandez, & Mann, 2001) suggests that important therapeutic work, including behavioral and psychological change, can come about in a treatment that does not directly confront the patient's denial. In the research by Marshall et al., the offenders are already incarcerated but still in denial. The pressure to examine their behavior is brought to bear by the legal system, and, as we suggest for offenders with disabilities, is not impressed on them by the clinicians. The best thinking at this point seems to suggest that confrontation, or pressure to change, be presented by the individual's environment (boss, job coach, family, court, and so forth), and that the clinician present herself as a support to the individual as he goes about making these changes. Staff and family members who are highly motivated to get the individual into treatment may try to pressure the clinician into simply beginning therapy with the individual; however, the motivation of these third parties can best be put to use by having *them* clearly confront the individual's denial in his environment, and making clear to him that therapy can help him get out of his predicament, as ultimately took place with Ted. This allows the therapist to maintain an appropriate therapeutic stance, which is, in fact, what the individual needs from the therapist.

Note that this is not to say that there is no place for confrontation in the therapeutic relationship. Confrontation can be a useful therapeutic tool in the context of a well-established therapeutic alliance between the patient and his therapist, or the patient and his fellow group members. Lengthy discussion of confrontation as a therapy technique is beyond the scope of this chapter but, briefly stated, is most effective when the therapist, or another group member, confronts the individual on an inconsistency he himself has presented. For example, Nathan, whom we introduced earlier, often dressed in ill-fitting clothes he had outgrown and would carry small toys into group with him, making himself look quite childish. The other men in the group would often give him feedback on this behavior, but Nathan persisted in it. During one week, Nathan was complaining about how his mother still treated him like a child. He was angry about this, stating that he wanted to make his own decision about which workshop to attend. A few of the members quickly pointed out that he was not helping his case with his mother by dressing like a child and carrying toys and paper dolls around with him. This confronted Nathan's denial of his childlike behaviors in a way that was clear to him—all of the information was directly in front of him. In addition, the confrontation was delivered by a group of people he had come to trust and value.

Many individuals will warm up to the interview process as soon as they feel the therapist's genuine disinterest in pressuring them. The therapist is providing them with the very medicine they need: clear boundaries. A good therapist knows what her role is, and what it is not. A large number of the individuals we see are referred because of minor sexual offenses, with no legal charges, who initially deny or minimize their behaviors. They respond well to the respectful, nonpressuring climate created by the interview, however, and often end up disclosing clinically relevant information regarding their mood, level of self-esteem, and interpersonal problems. With these individuals, we can complete the interview process in much the same way as we described with survivors earlier in this chapter. Furthermore, having set a respectful atmosphere inclines the individual toward becoming fully engaged in the therapy process. Respect for the individual's boundaries is the foundation of a successful therapy, whether the patient has been referred for sexual victimization, sexual offense, or any other reason, and whether the patient can readily admit to his problems.

SUMMARY

In this chapter we looked at special concerns involved with the initial interview process with people with intellectual disabilities. We have stressed the importance of setting a therapeutic tone from the start of the first meeting so that the individual will experience the therapeutic relationship as something distinct, a relationship unlike those he or she is likely to have had with previous authority figures. We have reviewed how respect for the individual's boundaries is essential to establishing the therapeutic relationship with survivors as well as offenders—indeed for referrals of all types. Moreover, we have highlighted the need for the therapist to stay true to the role of clinician, that is, to avoid the sometimes compelling pull to take on roles such as social gatekeeper or forensic interviewer. Finally, we would like to end with a reminder to the clinician not to feel pressured to "have all the answers" by the end of the first interview. Rather, it is important to bear in mind that coming to a rich understanding of the person before you is a process that is unlikely to fit into a neat, scheduled hour; a willingness to revise and reformulate as the therapy proceeds can make for a very productive experience.

8

INDIVIDUAL TREATMENT: TECHNIQUES AND RATIONALE

Men do change, and change comes like a little wind that ruffles the curtains at dawn, and it comes like the stealthy perfume of wildflowers hidden in the grass.

—John Steinbeck

Throughout this book, we have expounded on the merits of group psychotherapy for people with intellectual disabilities and psychological disorders. In addition, we noted in chapter 3 that individuals with certain disorders are not likely to do well in group psychotherapy. Specifically, people with sociopathic personality organizations should not be included in groups of nonsociopaths, and people with severe paranoia, at the psychotic level of personality organization, tend not to do well in groups of any kind. We also pointed out that an individual should not be included in a group if he or she is deviant in key ways from the other members.

Furthermore, we realize that many clinicians may be interested in providing treatment to individuals with intellectual disabilities and may want to further develop their skills, but they may not have access to a large enough population to start treatment groups. For these reasons, we discuss individual treatment in some depth. In particular, we present ways in which action methods and psychodramatic techniques can engage people with cognitive impairments and facilitate healing and growth.

A BRIEF LOOK AT THE HISTORICAL CONTEXT
OF INDIVIDUAL TREATMENT

As we have previously mentioned, mental health treatment for people with intellectual disabilities is relatively new on the horizon. The 1980s saw the beginnings of a literature base on the process of psychotherapy with this population (Hurley, 1989; Hurley & Hurley, 1986, 1987; Reiss, Levitan, & McNally, 1982; Reiss, Levitan, & Szyszko, 1982; Szymanski, 1980). These initial attempts at carrying out and writing about such psychotherapeutic contact represented a giant step forward from a world in which "treatment" had thus far consisted almost entirely of behavior modification (Kroese, 1997). Essentially, behavioral change was sought in the absence of exploration of people's subjective, internal experience—their feelings, beliefs, unique set of life experiences, or preferences. In fact, a survey conducted in 1996 reported that 53% of mental health practitioners still believed that behavioral interventions were the most useful tool for treating individuals with dual diagnoses (mental retardation and psychiatric disorders). Only 24% of those surveyed felt it would be necessary to evaluate the needs of dually diagnosed patients against the full range of treatment options, including psychotherapy (Deutsch & DiMatteo, 1996, as cited in Nugent, 1997).

There is no doubt that behavioral interventions have contributed dramatically to the quality of life of many people with intellectual disabilities. Moreover, behavioral techniques continue to be an important part of the clinical armamentarium. Certainly, for people whose cognitive and verbal abilities are severely deficient, the use of behavioral interventions can mean the difference between endless suffering and genuine relief—for the patient as well as for those around the patient. Years of research documentation, as well as our own experience, attest to the power of behavioral methodologies for an extensive range of problems, including severe cases of self-injurious behavior, physical aggression, and compulsive behaviors. Additionally, behavioral procedures have been central to the acquisition of basic skills and adaptive behaviors in countless numbers of people with intellectual disabilities (Singh, Osborne, & Huguenin, 1996). Building on an extensive research base, behavioral techniques have continued to evolve into still more diversified and sophisticated applications (Gardner, 2000; Gardner, Graeber, & Cole, 1996).

The growing knowledge base in the field of intellectual disabilities has demonstrated, however, that simply because an individual has an intellectual disability does not necessarily mean he or she is best served by behavioral intervention. Assessing and understanding the nature of the referral problem can guide the clinician toward the best course of treatment (Hurley et al., 1996; Nugent, 1997; Schwartz & Ruedrich, 1996). For many individuals, behavioral procedures are the best course of action; for some they may be the only course. However, as we have already established, many people with intellectual disabilities are able to engage in a therapeutic relationship, and they benefit greatly from the opportunity to talk about and think about their own lives and play a conscious and active role in their own process of change.

TREATMENT MODIFICATIONS FOR PEOPLE WITH INTELLECTUAL DISABILITIES

Anne Hurley, cited earlier for her pioneering work in establishing the first journal aimed exclusively at understanding and treating mental health problems in people with intellectual disabilities, made some of the seminal contributions to the literature base (Hurley & Hurley, 1986, 1987). Hurley and Hurley described the use of modified cognitive–behavioral techniques, along with a Rogerian demonstration of acceptance and genuine interest in the individual. Specific accommodations were recommended, such as using a directive, as opposed to unstructured approach; asking the client regularly to feed back what he or she has heard to assess comprehension; and concretizing the work to aid understanding. In this regard, Hurley and Hurley suggested the use of audiotaping or videotaping portions of the session for clients to use at home. In addition, they put forth the idea of constructing a *lifebook,* which the client creates by assembling pictures and other memorabilia of significance to the client and that frames the narrative of his or her life in a meaningful way.

More recently, in a collaborative effort, Hurley et al. (1996) elaborated on the theme of individualizing treatment based on the client's unique set of needs and developmental level. These authors clarify specific ways in which therapy can be successfully tailored to facilitate treatment with people who have intellectual disabilities. We review these recommendations and provide working examples of each because they serve as important guideposts to clinicians beginning work in this field. Briefly stated, the therapeutic modifications consist of the following:

- simplifying/concretizing abstract concepts
- incorporating visual and tactile activities into sessions
- incorporating active and interactive techniques into sessions
- using language familiar to the patient and continually assessing comprehension
- structuring sessions and using a directive style
- involving caregivers
- and finally, being flexible! Duration and frequency of sessions, as well as therapeutic goals and approaches, may need ongoing—and inventive—revisions.

Let us look at the process of simplifying or concretizing the complicated, abstract concepts discussed in therapy. For example, to help an individual develop a better sense of self-esteem, the therapist might begin to identify specific, clear-cut behaviors and qualities the patient has. The patient might be able to acknowledge that she is a good dancer, is responsible about keeping her room clean, and go on to identify other such specifics throughout the course of therapy. Ultimately, such things as learning to speak up or gaining control of physical outbursts can be represented in some concrete form. They may be written up in a list for patients who read or they may be represented by pictures to foster the individual's conscious awareness of her positive qualities.

The process of simplifying and concretizing the therapy overlaps with the idea of incorporating visual and tactile activities into the sessions. In the previous example, the creation of a photo album depicting qualities in which the patient can feel a sense of pride demonstrates such an activity. Using art therapy and clay sculpting to express and clarify emotion, and using elements of play therapy, can also be helpful.

There is a growing awareness of the benefits of nonverbal techniques for treating the general patient population, both children and adults. An edited work by Wiener (1999) presented dramatic and psychodramatic techniques, music, dance, movement therapy, and other related modalities that have successfully enhanced the therapeutic process in both individual and group treatments. As we have noted previously, many traumatized patients can be better helped to access, express, and ultimately transform their experiences when the treatment includes alternatives to purely verbal methods.

We have discussed throughout this book the value of using active and interactive techniques and described examples of these techniques in group therapy settings. Such techniques can also be used in individual work. For example, the patient can be asked to portray a particularly salient scene, bringing to life in the session his own behavior, actions, and words at the time. He can then be doubled for by the therapist, as we have detailed in previous chapters, to help him with identifying his emotions and feeling understood. Action techniques can also be used to help the patient try out new ways of responding to difficult people, as well as to gain a better understanding of another person's role. Later in this chapter, we detail the individual therapy of Carrie, a young woman with mild mental retardation. We highlight specific examples of action techniques from her treatment that the clinician can incorporate into individual work.

It is important for the therapist to gear her language to the patient's understanding. Frequently pausing and asking the patient to repeat back what she has heard helps to clarify the individual's understanding, and it gives the therapist a chance to reword or break down confusing concepts.

It also provides an opportunity for the therapist to demonstrate her genuine concern that the patient understand and communicate with her. In addition, it is a good idea for the therapist to repeat back to the patient her understanding of what the patient said, and ask the patient if her understanding is correct. This further emphasizes the concern for communication and genuine understanding.

Hurley et al. (1996) stressed the need for structuring sessions, noting that simply leaving the initial moments open, for the client to begin in any way she wants, may be too ambiguous for most people with intellectual disabilities. Asking specific questions and explaining what the therapeutic process entails, as we have noted in previous chapters, help orient the client toward productive use of the session. It is important to say to the client that there are no right or wrong answers in therapy, and that even though you will be asking a lot of questions, it is okay for the client not to answer if she does not want to. In addition, she should be told that she may always bring up another topic if she would like.

Hurley et al. (1996) further indicated that such structuring does not preclude the use of a supportive or psychodynamic orientation to the treatment and reported that these approaches have been successfully used. (The interested reader is referred to Szymanski, 1980, and Levitas & Gilson, 2000.)

Caregivers, such as family members and staff members from vocational or residential settings, can enhance treatment efficacy. Hurley et al. (1996) noted, however, that caregivers must be assessed as to their abilities to carry out their roles respectfully and consistently before any collaboration is attempted. It should be pointed out that even though caregiver intervention can be an important support to the process of behavior change, it is not always helpful or desirable. Some individuals are capable of working in therapy without caregiver involvement, and others do not want caregivers involved, sometimes for good reason. Keller (2000) and Levitas and Gilson (1997) have found that the referring caregiver and the client may often have different goals for therapy. Keller discussed the sometimes problematic nature of caregiver involvement in that the referring caregiver is frequently the deciding party on such key issues as whether the therapy appears to be useful and if it should be continued. This can be particularly thorny in cases in which the client's sense of self-efficacy needs to be developed through learning to exercise greater control regarding personal decisions, and the caregiver's goal is to achieve greater compliance with rules.

For individuals who are self-guardians, every effort to respect their wishes needs to be made. Of course, in cases in which it becomes apparent that the patient is in some way at risk because caregivers are lacking in information or involvement, the therapist needs to discuss these risks with the individual in the hope of his making a well-informed decision regarding caregiver involvement. For example, in one case, a therapist working with a young woman came to realize that the woman was not capable of taking her medication correctly. The medication was prescribed by a psychiatrist at the same clinic. The patient had repeatedly told both the therapist and the psychiatrist that she did not trust her mother and that her mother would forbid her to come to treatment or to take medication if she knew about it. The patient, highly depressed and quite disorganized in her thinking, was having tremendous difficulty on her job. Her concerns regarding her mother were corroborated by her job coach, who had referred her for treatment. Eventually, however, the patient had to be told by the treatment team that the risks of her monitoring her own medications were too great to continue and that her mother's help was needed. She agreed and allowed a team member to contact her mother. The mother was invited in for a meeting and was informed of the seriousness of her daughter's depression, as well as her need for psychotherapy, medication, and medication monitoring. The mother agreed to assist her daughter with the medication and did not object to the therapy as long as sessions did not conflict with the daughter's job schedule. Problems continued to arise on occasion. However, having the opportunity to work with the mother and involve her in the daughter's treatment still reduced the risk of the patient's medication errors.

Unfortunately, not every individual who needs assistance at home will have a willing or capable caregiver. It may be necessary in some cases for the therapist to talk with the individual about her need for supports and to help the individual to get residential or other social service support through public agencies.

In our work with offenders we make a special effort to involve all parties—family members, job coaches, vocational program staff, residential staff, and so on—in the patient's treatment. We inform the patient directly that, because their problem hurts other people, we would like to have a team meeting prior to beginning therapy, to make sure the patient has the support and supervision of everyone on his team. Generally, this does not surprise the patient, who has typically been referred to treatment by one or more of these involved parties. At the meeting, we clarify each person's role as to supervision and monitoring. Finally, once we are working with the patient in therapy, we limit our contact and discussions with the team members so that the patient comes to feel safe in discussing a great depth of material in session. We do not disclose to the other parties the multitude of issues that are discussed, and almost all of the clients come to understand this. For most of the members, their behavior in session suggests that they feel safe in presenting vulnerable material. We use our contact with team members to take reports of problem behaviors and to offer support to the staff and family members responsible for monitoring the individual's behavior. When we attend meetings, we always make a point of presenting and affirming the patient's positive efforts to the rest of the team. Finally, we aim to be flexible to each patient's needs throughout the therapy and encourage students and trainees to adopt a flexible, open-minded approach to treatment as well.

It is important to mention that the modifications we have outlined cut across theoretical orientations. As we noted, Hurley et al. (1996) reported that a range of theoretical orientations, including psychodynamic, have been used successfully in treating people with intellectual disabilities. Additional contributions by Hurley and others have described the successful use of cognitive–behavioral techniques in treating anxiety and depression in people with intellectual disabilities (Hurley & Silka, 1998; Hurley & Sovner, 1991). In a recent keynote address at an international conference, Gaus (2002) presented a detailed discussion of cognitive–behavioral therapy with people who have intellectual disabilities, noting the successful use of modifications similar to those of Hurley et al. with such cognitive–behavioral techniques as problem solving, assertiveness training, relaxation training, cognitive restructuring, and disputing irrational beliefs. British clinicians Kroese et al. (1997) have contributed an entire edited volume on the use of cognitive–behavioral therapy approaches tailored to the specific needs of people who have intellectual disabilities. Additional edited volumes by Fletcher (2000) and Strohmer and Prout (1994) describe a range of individual approaches (and devote chapters to group and family interventions as well). A chapter in Strohmer and Prout's book (Prout & Cale, 1994) discusses published modifications of a range of therapeutic approaches that have been used with clients who have intellectual disabilities, including rational emotive therapy, person-centered (Rogerian) therapy, reality therapy, psychoanalytic/ psychodynamic approaches, and crisis intervention counseling. In addition, Levitas and Gilson (1997), who have made numerous contributions to the field of dual diagnosis, presented a succinct discussion of individual psychotherapy. Each of these works will be informative to the interested reader. Like Hurley et al., these authors stress similar needs, across the various approaches, for structuring and directing the treatment, incorporating action, modifying verbal discussion, and, always, being flexible in response to the particular needs of the client.

INDIVIDUAL TREATMENT: CARRIE, SESSION ONE

At this point we would like to present a detailed case study, so that the reader may walk through the individual therapy process in such a way that, we hope, will give a feel for the subtle, intangible, moments that make the process a therapeutic one—a process of true change. Carrie's case allows us to look closely at each of the therapy modifications described by Hurley et al. (1996) and exemplifies the spirit of flexibility, incorporating a range of strategies to address her unique needs.

Carrie was referred to the outpatient mental health clinic of a local hospital for psychotherapy. Her mother made the call at the insistence of her sister, Carrie's aunt. Carrie had been raped approximately two weeks earlier by an adolescent in her neighborhood. Carrie had her 17th birthday during the period between the rape and the call to the clinic.

The clinic staff were reluctant to take on the case. One of the therapists recognized the family name and reported that the family was known to the clinic because Carrie's older sister had been in treatment there. The sister had been referred by the New Jersey Division of Youth and Family Services (DYFS) because of the seriousness of her problems and the family's negligence and suspected abuse. In addition to oppositional behavior and school truancy, the sister had made highly dramatic suicide attempts. The therapist reported that the mother was very resistant to coming in and working conjointly in treatment. As if the family history was not enough, Carrie was reported to have mental retardation.

Despite the staff's misgivings, Carrie was given an appointment. There were no mental health services for people with intellectual disabilities to refer her to at the time.

Carrie had a rough-and-tumble look. She wore jeans and a T-shirt and looked quite a bit younger than 17. She had a distinct body odor. Nevertheless, she had very even, pretty features and did not have the stigmatizing appearance many people with intellectual disabilities have. Her speech was slow, with an obvious southern drawl.

Carrie was accompanied by her mother and younger sister, approximately age 10. Carrie's mother spoke slowly as well. She was extremely overweight and unkempt. Her affect was flat through most of the session, although she demonstrated a few expressions of annoyance and disgust. The little sister did not appear stigmatized at all. She quietly entertained herself drawing and coloring.

The mother described what she knew about the rape and about her sister's pressure to get Carrie into treatment. Apparently Carrie had been taken to the emergency room just after the rape, and the staff had recommended follow-up counseling.

"But what I don't understand is why she didn't holler." Carrie's mother pressed this point at me in the middle of my questions about the attack. She stared at me, unflinching. I met her eyes and nodded, reluctant to offer an explanation that was premature and, probably, unwanted. Her mother then turned her heavy gaze onto Carrie.

"Why didn't you *holler*? It just makes no sense. Anybody would give a good yell, being grabbed on the street like that. You should have hollered. What's *wrong* with you?"

Carrie watched the bland industrial rug at her feet. She remained motionless for a long minute after her mother spoke. Then, without warning, she swung her head toward her mother.

"I told you I *don't know*! I just don't know why I didn't yell. I just, . . . I don't know." She started out in a blaze of anger, but dwindled down to a sigh.

"I don't know what's wrong with me."

All three of us just sat in the heavy silence that ensued. I came to learn that some form of this dialogue, and little else, had been the chief discussion since the rape. My focus had been on acquiring the details of the episode and Carrie's resulting symptoms. What Carrie and her mother were showing me, however, was another source of pain, a very significant one, that went far beyond the rape.

After obliging me with a few more bits of information, the mother lobbed a last, quick volley at Carrie.

"And you *know* you did the wrong thing, going to that lady first. You should turn to your home, before anything. I don't know why you would go to that lady before your Gran."

I thanked Carrie's mother for her input, and she left the room with Carrie's sister to wait down the hall. Carrie looked up at me, then dropped her gaze again to the rug.

"It sounds like things have been pretty awful," I ventured.

As she had done when her mother addressed her, Carrie remained motionless, giving the impression that she was not going to respond. Another long moment passed.

"I just can't stop thinking about it. I just didn't know what to do."

I nodded. "I know." I waited a bit, then said, "Maybe you could tell me the things you can't stop thinking about."

Carrie rose to this response a little more quickly. "It was like, as soon as he grabbed my arm, why didn't I yell? But I couldn't."

"And then what happened?"

"He dragged me into his house, and pushed me down real hard. I told him to get the f— off me!"

Carrie went on to describe the rape. She said that when it was over, the rapist, a boy of only 14, told her to get into the tub. When she did, he threw tomato sauce on her.

When Carrie was able to leave the house, she went straight to the home of another neighbor close by, whom she felt would help her. The neighbor called the police, who came and brought Carrie to the emergency room. The hospital staff called her grandmother, with whom she was living, and her aunt, who lived roughly an hour away. Her parents and five siblings were in a rural part of Virginia at the time.

We talked about what she could expect from therapy in some detail, providing the beginnings of a structure for Carrie's expectations and an orientation toward the therapy process. Moreover, we talked about what Carrie wanted. Carrie stated firmly that she wanted to be able to talk about what happened by herself; she did not want her family involved. She was tremendously angry at her family's reaction to her rape. Moreover, she already had been at odds with them, which was why she had not been in Virginia with them at the time.

To start closing down the initial session, I thanked Carrie for being able to tell me so much about her experience. I expressed my sorrow that she had to go through such pain and affirmed her for having gotten help right away.

Before we ended, and after feeling a sense that Carrie was comfortable with the process so far, I offered a normalizing frame for her failure to scream. I explained that it is very common for people in a state of terror to be speechless. Carrie seemed to understand but clearly had doubts about herself that went beyond her reaction in a moment of terror. I assured her we could talk more about this in future sessions.

We ended the session by again affirming Carrie's efforts to help herself, highlighting both what she did following the rape and the efforts she made in that first session to discuss painful material. Because she was a minor and would need parental permission as well as help with transportation to continue sessions, I asked Carrie if we could bring her mother back in, tell her about the plan for her therapy, and also tell her about the common reaction of being speechless in response to terror.

Carrie agreed. In discussing the plan, Carrie's mother had some concerns about getting Carrie in each week but felt her husband would probably be able to drive her. I affirmed her efforts to help her daughter in this way. Finally, I offered a normalizing understanding of Carrie's behavior at the time of the rape. She sustained a deadpan stare. "Anybody would holler," she said.

CASE CONCEPTUALIZATION AND
THERAPEUTIC PROCESS

Carrie was the fourth of six children, with the oldest sibling, a 22-year-old sister, married and out of the house. Her second oldest sister, Alice, had been the sister previously in treatment at the clinic. Next was Carrie's brother, just a year and a half older than she. Carrie was followed by a brother approximately two years younger, who, like Carrie, was identified as having an intellectual disability. Finally, there was the youngest sister who came along to the first session.

Carrie's parents were married and living together; all six children were the products of this marriage. The family had been living in New Jersey for roughly the past three years, staying at the maternal grandmother's home. Prior to this they had lived in a rural section of southwestern Virginia. Carrie's mother reported that her sister, Carrie's Aunt Jean, had convinced them to move to New Jersey because there were better educational opportunities. They could not afford a home of their own and so stayed with the grandmother. Carrie's mother had never worked, nor did she drive. Her father was working as a gas station attendant, apparently unofficially. The family received food stamps. The father was able to drive, using the grandmother's car. The family would return to Virginia for a few weeks each summer, staying with other relatives there. Carrie had asked to stay in New Jersey with her grandmother during their last trip, which was when the rape took place. She reported that there was "lots of drinking and fighting" in Virginia, and she preferred to stay in New Jersey. Indeed, she had made some friends here and enjoyed the break from her family.

Carrie was in special education high school classes two days per week and in a specialized vocational training program the other three days. Through contact with the school personnel, it was clear that the parents were seen as very limited. Apparently the mother's sister, Carrie's Aunt Jean, felt a sense of responsibility for the family and often advised the mother. The school reported that Carrie was generally cooperative, although during the school year following the rape she had an increase in complaints about other students hitting her. School personnel were frequently at a loss as to whether these acts had actually occurred. In any case, assuming she could overcome her chronic hygiene problems, the school felt Carrie would be able to work part time at a routine job after graduation.

Carrie had not been involved in any services outside of school, and most of her nonschool hours were unstructured. Child study team assessments showed that Carrie had a measured IQ in the mid-range of mild mental retardation, with little scatter among the various subtests.

The chief symptoms Carrie exhibited during the early period of her treatment were a moderate degree of emotional lability, intrusive recollections of the rape, and guilt and self-doubt regarding her role in the rape. She denied sleep problems and reported occasional appetite loss, often skipping lunch at school. Her weight, which was average, remained stable.

Carrie was able to describe events and to put feelings into words with only moderate difficulty. She could listen to and understand my questions and feedback as long as I avoided abstract concepts and lengthy discourses. Interestingly, although her verbal ability was reasonably good, she had a very limited fund of information. Facts such as her address, ages of her siblings, her phone number, or where her school was located were completely unknown to her. I would sometimes find myself surprised at things she did not know as the course of her therapy went on. In addition, Carrie had very poorly developed reading and writing skills. She could recognize only a few simple words commonly seen on signs. Moreover, she was anxious about any tasks related to reading and writing and consistently wanted to avoid them. Her fund of information and reading limitations were lower than that of many people we have seen over the years with intellectual functioning in the same range and may have been adversely affected by environmental deprivation.

In the early months of treatment, Carrie often began her sessions with complaints of having been punched in the stomach by a certain boy at school and not having been able to eat lunch. We discussed actions she could take, such as how and to whom to report this problem, focusing on *her* role in coping to increase her sense of self-efficacy. Also during this early period, Carrie had some involvement with lawyers, social workers, and court, which she handled without a great deal of distress, and which created additional opportunities to affirm her coping and sense of self-efficacy. Carrie was happy that something was being done about the boy who raped her. Before long, the boy was sent to a residential program for juveniles. Carrie was glad he was out of the area but angry that he did not go to jail. She felt his young age was no excuse.

As time went on, Carrie talked more about the distress she experienced at home with her family. She described her father as alcoholic, with sudden temper outbursts that sometimes included throwing things, such as plates of food at mealtime. She would occasionally report that she or someone else was struck during one of these rages. Often she would describe fights, sometimes physical, with her siblings.

Carrie was angry toward her mother because she felt her mother was mad at her for having been raped. For quite some time after, her mother continued to reprimand Carrie for not having yelled for help and for having gone to the neighbor afterward. It seemed that Carrie had not felt very close to her mother even before the attack, but she had not felt particularly angry with her either. Each time Carrie or her mother brought up the issue of the rape, an argument would ensue. Although these discussions always ended badly, Carrie frequently instigated them in a doomed effort to alter her mother's judgment of her.

With respect to the guidelines for treatment to which we referred earlier, in Carrie's case it was relatively easy to structure the sessions into the traditional 50-minute, weekly meetings, setting an agenda together at the beginning of each session. Carrie sometimes liked to ask questions about my life. I generally gave brief bits of information, along with an explanation of why I did not want to talk too much about myself. We often spent the last 10 or 15 minutes talking about light subjects, such as activities Carrie enjoyed. We used this as a way of winding down the emotion of the session and of allowing Carrie a chance to relax her focus. Twenty minutes or so on the deeper issues, after a few minutes to warm up, seemed plenty.

The format we recommend for individual sessions is essentially the same as for group sessions. The chief difference is that, except for severely impaired patients, the orientation phase can usually be bypassed after the first few meetings. The warm-up and sharing phase is generally a sufficient start for follow-up sessions, although some of the structure normally provided in the orientation phase may be needed. For example, sometimes patients get to a key awareness in a previous session that needs ongoing follow-up. If the patient fails to make mention of the issue from the previous session, the therapist should inquire about it during the warm-up and sharing, reviewing what was done last time.

In Carrie's case, she was able to develop goals for her treatment, which we could refer to periodically and revise as needed. In addition, we were able to use language we could each understand. Carrie eschewed any idea of using clay or the dolls I had in the room, threatened that such materials implied she was a child. She had a similar dislike for any kind of artwork or pictures, which seemed amplified by a sense of not being good at putting anything at all on paper. Any attempts at writing, such as affirmations or journaling, were very distressing to her.

Continuing with the guidelines recommended by Hurley et al. (1996), let us consider the role of caregiver involvement in Carrie's case. For the most part we conducted sessions individually, although at one point later in treatment, we asked Carrie's mother to come for a session. She was somewhat more positive and accepting of input since Carrie's arguing had diminished; we were able to use this session to review Carrie's accomplishments and acknowledge some of the supportive things the family had done. (To her father's credit, he drove her to sessions fairly regularly. After a time, we were able to arrange transportation by taxi, which Medicaid paid for.) With respect to Carrie's extended network, we had a fair amount of contact with the school, especially early on, to gain background information, get test reports, and follow up on problems with schoolmates and on the general status of her functioning there. We had some contact with authorities involved with the court case, which provided us with information about Carrie's role as a "witness" and gave us the opportunity to support her in that regard. We had no contact with DYFS as the family no longer had an active case. There had been no new reports since the sister involved had turned 18.

We did not refer Carrie for a medication evaluation because her symptoms did not warrant one, although we always kept an eye out for exacerbations. We did refer her to the Arc of Monmouth for recreational services, in an effort to add structure and social support. Carrie came to enjoy this involvement tremendously, and her brother, apparently quite disabled with language and communication deficits, became productively involved as well.

AN ENACTMENT

Carrie continued to agonize over her inability to have screamed when first grabbed on the street, and she remained frustrated with both her mother and herself in coming to terms with this. The same unproductive arguments continued at home, and presentations of these episodes regularly found their way into sessions. Even as Carrie coped successfully with the court case, managed conflicts better at school, and had positive social experiences with recreation at the Arc of Monmouth—where she was well-liked and benefited from a good deal of positive feedback—she remained stalemated on this point.

"I guess I'm just stupid," Carrie would say sometimes. When she did, she always looked defeated, yet peaceful, too. Concluding that she was simply stupid seemed to be the one explanation that made sense to Carrie. It put a stop to the nagging self-doubts that just did not let up any other way. But she could not stay with it long.

"I wish I kicked him in the balls right there on the street!" Carrie would then go off in this angry vein, fantasizing about how she might have fought off her perpetrator, hurt him, and sent him home crying, with his tail between his legs. Indeed, Carrie had always considered herself a tomboy and a good fighter. She was her older brother's most frequent target and prided herself on knowing how to fight back. She did not fight "like a girl." She had also had plenty of opportunities to scrimmage with her two older sisters over the years. What's more, she generally took on the role of protector toward her younger, intellectually disabled brother, Billy. As Billy's shield, she had taken, and thrown, many a punch. She was truly anything but a sissy. In fact, she had initially been reluctant to make any reports about the boy who hit her at school because, as she put it, "I could take the pain."

Carrie rarely showed sadness, nor did she allow her self to consciously experience it often, even regarding the rape. Her tough-guy persona was extremely thorough. The experience of the rape was a serious threat to this important self-image.

One time, after Carrie described her angry thoughts, I asked her if I could double for her. She agreed. We moved her chair away from the wall so I could stand behind her, in the position of the double. I began by voicing some of the feelings she was most aware of.

"I'm so mad! That kid just grabbed me when I didn't even know he was coming. It isn't fair. I have all this anger; I don't even know what to do with it. Sometimes I think about hurting that kid who did this to me. I get angry at kids at school, too. I have so much anger I even get mad at myself."

Carrie was nodding through all of this. I tested out each statement with her, asking her to repeat each one out loud to see if each felt right to her as she said them. I then repeated the statement about being "mad at myself," making sure this resonated with her. I continued.

"I'm so mad at myself that I think I must be stupid. Sometimes I think I must be a real jerk because I let this happen. I didn't even scream. Even my mother thinks I was stupid because I didn't scream." I continued the checking process with Carrie, who was clearly engrossed in the moment. I went on.

"I *hate* to feel stupid. I HATE IT! It sucks, and it isn't fair!"

"It's no fair," Carrie echoed.

"I felt stupid so many times, with reading and writing. I hate that stuff. But even more than that, I hate to *feel* stupid. That really brings me down. So I don't think about it much. Anyway, I'm pretty good at taking care of myself. I'm tough. I like being tough. Plus, I can take care of Billy, who is really handicapped."

Carrie was still in sync with this, even though I had said a great deal. Continuing from the double role, I began a leap from Carrie's usual thinking.

"I get scared sometimes that I'm really stupid. But, I know I'm not really stupid. There are just some things I'm not good at, and other things I am good at."

I paused to make sure Carrie was following this. I had said each statement slowly. Carrie repeated them, somewhat tentatively.

"I'm usually good at fighting, and I've been wondering why I didn't yell on the street." I paused, then said very slowly, " Maybe I didn't yell because I'm not one to yell for help. I don't go crying to other people for help; I fight my own fights."

Carrie was thinking hard about these words, and repeated them slowly.

"I *do* fight my own fights," she said, thoughtfully. "I do."

I repeated her words, then added, "I fought my own fight that day, and didn't cry to anybody. I have nothing to be ashamed of."

Carrie repeated these words. I thanked her for working at this for so long with me. Then I asked her to think about the last thing she wanted to say for now.

Carrie wrestled with her thoughts for quite a while, shaking her head a few times in frustration, unable to come up with what she wanted to say. Finally, very softly, she spoke.

"I don't know what happened, but it weren't fair. It weren't nothin' I did wrong."

"It was nothin' I did wrong," I echoed.

THE FINAL PHASE

After the enactment, we moved to the affirmation stage, just as we do in group treatment. I reviewed and highlighted each of the efforts Carrie had made that day, facing up to painful, even shameful feelings and also trying on new ways of thinking.

As the next few sessions went by, we further developed the understanding of Carrie's emotions and self-concept brought out in the enactment. Carrie's chief defense against feeling bad about herself, that is, against feeling "stupid," had come from feeling tough and unafraid of physical threats. Her failure to prevent the rape cut right through her tough-guy defense and exposed her shame over feeling stupid, making her feel that shame again, raw, in a way she generally managed to avoid pretty well. Through the enactment, Carrie was made ready to try on a new interpretation of her behavior at the time of the rape, one that preserved and was consistent with her conscious identity of being tough and handling her own problems.

In time, we added the idea that she could now expand her thinking to allow that *sometimes* it is okay to ask for help. It may even be the best thing to do. Everyone needs help sometimes, even very strong people. In the same way, everyone needs to ask questions sometimes and learn new things, even very smart people. Carrie could understand and accept these ideas. She could accept that she was a tough person who was so much in the habit of always taking care of herself that she did not call for help when she needed it.

After establishing this idea firmly, we used some sessions to carry out an enactment in which Carrie faced her mother with all of the shameful feelings that had haunted her, as well as with her new understanding. In addition, Carrie played out her mother's role. After expressing her mother's usual lines, I then asked Carrie to double for her mother. Standing behind the chair that represented her mother, Carrie was able to say some of the painful things she believed her mother was thinking about her. Following this, Carrie returned to her own seat. I helped her return to her own role by asking her how it felt to play her mother and get in touch with her feelings about her. I then affirmed her own reactions and her efforts. Ultimately, Carrie was able to have a different kind of dialogue with her mother at home, one that was somewhat less painful for her.

We affirmed Carrie's ability to have asked for help right after the rape. There was still work to be done concerning the conflict between her effort in that regard and her mother's message that one should not go outside the family for help. At any rate, Carrie evolved to where she could think about the rape and not fault herself for her behavior. Eventually we used her mother's "*don't go outside the family*" message to further diminish her self-blame and reframe her interpretations about herself. Part of the reason she did not have the habit of asking for help is because she had already been taught that to do so is wrong, especially when it is outside the family. Now she could learn a new way of protecting herself that included asking for help sometimes. Asking the neighbor for help after the rape marked her first successful effort in that regard. She had not cried to anybody, but she had been brave enough to ask for the help she knew she needed at that point, even though it was different from what her mother had taught her. Even using her therapy to help herself get better was a way of asking for and receiving help that was appropriate and good for her.

It had become clear that Carrie did not have well-developed assertiveness skills. She was used to fighting, or dodging hits, and derived a sense of self-efficacy from these skills. She had much to learn when it came to verbalizing needs and boundaries assertively, which apparently interfered with her reporting ability at school in the early phase of treatment. We did some work to reframe "complaining and tattling" into "speaking up for myself." Accomplishing this change in her beliefs about these behaviors went a long way toward helping her develop new skills. We did many enactments practicing scenes assertively and helping Carrie become aware of how she felt when she played the scenes in their original form versus how she felt when playing them with assertive language.

After approximately one year, we were able to start a women's group at the Arc of Monmouth. Carrie was able to tell her story without self-blame. Moreover, she was a great support to some of the other women who had been sexually abused. Interestingly, each time a new woman joined the group, Carrie would voluntarily recount her story. It seemed to have become an important new part of her identity.

As Carrie worked in group, she came to an even deeper understanding of her experience—that sometimes things happen that we just cannot control. And that even strong people, and smart people, have bad things happen to them that they cannot control and are not their fault. It is just an inevitable part of life. Carrie was firm in this position when supporting other women, and it continued to bolster her own sense of self.

A few years later, Carrie's grandmother died and the family made plans to move back to Virginia. Carrie decided she wanted to stay in New Jersey and applied for residential services. She lived in a sponsor home for the first few years, and eventually got an agency-supervised apartment. During this time period she "graduated" from group, having achieved considerable emotional stability, a lengthy period of reduced distress, an improved sense of self-efficacy, and a good connection to social supports. She got a part-time job in the community with the help of a job coach. She visited her family a few times, flying to Virginia by herself, and has stayed in regular phone contact. After a long period of stable years, she was referred by her apartment staff back to group. She again had become emotionally labile ("angry and moody"). Much of her distress was, and is, related to disapproval and criticism from family members. She is in the process of coming to terms with her family and her emotions in new ways and works actively at making her life better.

Carrie's therapy gives us one example of a real-life application of the therapeutic guidelines delineated in this chapter. There are as many variations on these guidelines as there are individuals in need of treatment. We hope that Carrie's experience will inspire others to attempt this important work.

TRANSITIONING FROM INDIVIDUAL TO GROUP THERAPY

For the patient who has been engaged in individual treatment for a length of time, care needs to be taken to ensure a successful transition. In some cases, as with Martina in chapter 1, or with Carrie, whose case was just discussed, individual therapy was all that was available at the time each started treatment. However, as time went on, we had sufficient referrals to form a group that would be a good fit for both. Patients may become very attached to their therapists and feel threatened by the prospect of group treatment, as was initially the case with both Martina and Carrie. They perceive the change as representing a loss of the relationship with the therapist and have no way of truly knowing the benefits they stand to gain.

The transition process begins with the therapist explaining to the patient the rationale for the change. For example, the patient can be told something such as, "I would like you to have the chance to talk with other women (or men) who have been through what you have been through. You will be able to get help from other people who have been through some of the same things, and who really know how it feels. Also, you will have the chance to help other people. You will be able to share your progress with them, and help them get better."

In addition to working with the patient to make sure she understands the rationale, it is important to encourage the patient to express her feelings about the prospect. Validate the patient's fears and concerns, letting her know that you understand how she might feel the way she does and affirming her for telling you her feelings.

When the patient will be entering a group run by therapists other than the individual therapist, the next step is to ask the patient to attend two meetings and come back to see the individual therapist after that. The individual therapist should inform the patient that she would like to be in contact with the group leaders to discuss the transition. It is necessary to get the patient's consent for this contact. Following the patient's attendance at two group sessions, the individual therapist and group leaders can talk. Then, the individual therapist will be in a position to validate the patient's efforts during the follow-up session, stressing the *positive* feedback from the group leaders. For example, "They said you really did a good job of listening to the other members and looking at them while they spoke. And you didn't interrupt anybody. You made a really good start!" If the patient said very little about herself, this should not be pointed out and criticized.

The patient will also be getting positive feedback in the group sessions that will help warm her up to the process. Assuming all is going well, and the patient is beginning to feel safe in the group, the therapist and patient can decide on setting a final session for the individual treatment. Some members may want to terminate at the first follow-up; others may want to schedule a second follow-up a few weeks later. At the termination session, the therapist and patient should review the positive gains the patient made in therapy and the goals she is working on in group. The move into group treatment should be framed emphatically as a step that marks progress and that reflects the patient's continuing efforts to improve her life.

When the patient will be entering a group run by the same therapist who has provided the individual treatment, the initial transition is often somewhat easier. The same process, however, of having an individual follow-up session, and sometimes a second session a few weeks later, is still recommended. For these patients, group sessions sometimes stir feelings of jealousy over having to "share" the therapist. If the therapist senses that the patient may be having, but not verbalizing, some uncomfortable feelings, the therapist should take the initiative in bringing them up. This should be done in an understanding way, and one that normalizes these feelings. Helping the client to label and normalize what he or she is feeling takes some of the intensity out of the discomfort. Furthermore, the therapist can inform the patient that these feelings will transform over time. The discomfort will die down, and their relationship will evolve as they continue to work in group together.

Finally, we suggest that conjoint individual and group therapy be avoided, beyond what is needed for purposes of transitioning. In our experience, involving a patient in both at once encourages the patient to selectively present certain topics only in one setting or the other. Patients are often inclined to bring the most threatening issues only into individual treatment, or to use the individual session to vent ill feelings regarding other members. In both cases, these feelings need to be brought into the group. The patient will gain much more psychological mileage from facing his or her fears honestly with others; some of whom, inevitably, will share that they have some of the same shameful secrets. Regarding the patient's interpersonal reactions stirred by other members, bringing them up in group will allow the patient an opportunity to learn new, more productive ways to cope with interpersonal difficulties.

SUMMARY

In this chapter we described in detail the recommendations of Hurley et al. (1996) for adapting psychotherapeutic techniques to the needs of people with cognitive limitations. Along these lines we looked at how psychodramatic techniques and action methods can empower individual treatment. We draw on many of the techniques we use in group psychotherapy. For example, in the work with Carrie, we used supportive doubling by the therapist for Carrie's feelings; we used the empty chair to help Carrie begin to talk to her mother and express her feelings more freely; we used role reversal, so that Carrie could demonstrate her mother's behavior; and we used doubling as a technique to get at what Carrie believes her mother is thinking and feeling but maybe not saying. (To accomplish this, we had Carrie stand behind the chair that represents her mother after she finished portraying her mother in that chair.) We staged many enactments in which Carrie portrayed a boy at school who aggressed against her and then demonstrated her own response. We also staged enactments in which Carrie could practice new responses. Finally, we used doubling to move from supporting Carrie to helping her to try on and reframe key self-beliefs.

The stages of an individual session follow the same format as group sessions do. This format provides a comfortable structure for the therapist as well as the patient. The orientation stage is used to help the patient understand what to expect, to explain confidentiality, and to teach needed skills such as listening and checking back, making eye contact, and so on. Next, in the warm-up and sharing stage, the patient is encouraged to discuss emotionally meaningful material, with the help of questions from the therapist. Note that this may include painful as well as joyful experiences, problems as well as progress. Some individuals may need considerable questioning to accomplish this even after several sessions, whereas others will come in almost bursting with what they have to say. The emotional material can then be expressed through action, in the enactment stage. This stage is a good vehicle for the provision of emotional support and for testing out alternative behaviors and beliefs. Lastly, we close the session down with the affirmation stage, in which the therapist provides affirmation to the patient for good work done in the session and for the patient's progress overall.

9

GROUP PROCESS IN DEPTH: INEVITABLE TROUBLE SPOTS AND OPPORTUNITIES FOR GROWTH

If you shut the door to all errors, truth will be shut out.
—Rabindranath Tagore

A number of problems have surfaced during the course of our interactive–behavioral therapy (IBT) groups, some with predictable regularity. We share our experiences with these problems in the hope that beginning clinicians might be better prepared to recognize and manage these hurdles along the way. Although the informed clinician may be able to prevent certain difficulties—and we offer our recommendations toward that end—many other problems are an outgrowth of the process itself. Some of the problems, such as interpersonal conflict and confidentiality breaks, unfailingly arise when people are grouped together. Other problems, such as the presence of a monopolist or a disruptive member, are simply demonstrations of the very pathology for which the individual needs treatment. In every case, however, working through these problems leads to new growth. There is a powerful truth to the adage that everything is "grist for the mill."

THE FOUNDATION: SAFETY AND CONFIDENTIALITY

We begin by looking at what happens when a member breaks one of the fundamental group rules. Recall that at the foundation of any IBT group are two important rules: safety and confidentiality. Failure to honor either rule can result in termination of membership. Safety refers to the idea that all members are entitled to feel safe with their fellow members. This means that no member can subject another member to violence or threats of violence in the group session or in any other context in which they might meet. If a member is violent or threatening to a *non*member, he can work on this problem in group. However, if his aggression is directed at a fellow member, then his group membership is in jeopardy.

Confidentiality refers to the agreement that each member makes to refrain from discussing any other members' business outside of group. We instruct our members not to mention any other member's name outside the session as a way of making this requirement concrete.

Breaking the Safety Rule and Managing Interpersonal Conflict

Martin was a long-time group member with poor impulse control and poor judgment. He came to group faithfully, however, and although angry and withdrawn for his first few months, evolved to the point where he readily disclosed his problems each week. Martin had a long history of touching women inappropriately and, despite some initial improvement, maintained an ongoing struggle with self-control. Some of Martin's problems came about because he enjoyed teasing people, especially people he liked. Martin was also prone to taking things impulsively and to making repetitive phone calls. Again, these behaviors were connected to people he liked and whose attention he wanted. After we had worked with Martin in group for some time, we referred him to a psychiatrist to determine if his problems were in part the result of attention-deficit hyperactivity disorder (ADHD). Following some resistance on the part of Martin's family, Martin was started on a medication for the treatment of ADHD, which resulted in a moderate degree of improvement.

As might be expected, Martin required a high degree of structure and supervision. If his transportation brought him to our building too early for his meeting, Martin would frequently use this time to get himself into trouble. Instead of sitting in the waiting area adjoining the receptionist's office as the members were all asked to do, Martin would roam the halls looking for someone to talk to, tease, or take things from.

One week Martin entered the reception area and began to tease Don, a fellow group member who had also arrived early for the session. Martin made a few silly but annoying comments to Don and then took Don's hat and began to throw it around. Don became angry and punched Martin in the arm. No staff members or therapists were in the area when the interaction took place; however, their story quickly unfolded upon entering the group room.

When the two entered the session, Don was red-faced and agitated. Martin appeared downcast. The other members, some of whom had observed the interaction, were also concerned. Don asked to speak first. He explained the incident, admitting that he had hit Martin. He was very anxious and stated that he feared being "thrown out" of the group; he knew he had broken a cardinal rule. He attempted to justify his aggression by blaming Martin's irritating behavior. Martin began to grow angry as Don spoke, not wanting to accept all the blame. Although the two began to argue, they responded well to the facilitator's intervention, which was twofold: The first part consisted of repeating back to both Martin and Don what they had stated, reassuring them that they had each been heard; the second part was a request to both Martin and Don that they give the other members a chance to share their feelings about the incident.

The other men were first acknowledged for their patience in allowing Don and Martin to use the initial group time to address their difficulties. Then the men were asked to share their feelings regarding what happened. As the members engaged in this discussion, they spontaneously began to offer ideas regarding appropriate "punishment" for the breaking of group rules. Having been through the process over previous infringements, the members were ready to have input into the "sentencing."

Unfortunately, group opinion was very much against Martin. Martin's behavior was so often problematic and bothersome that, even though he did not directly break the safety rule, many of the members wanted him to have a lengthy suspension from group. Furthermore, despite Don's having clearly broken the safety rule, most of the members felt that he should be given only a one-week suspension. Most of the members identified with Don's anger toward Martin and recognized that Don had done something they themselves had harbored a desire to do.

The unbalanced sentiment among the members presented a problem for the facilitators to manage. Certainly it was positive that the members felt sufficiently empowered in the group to voice their opinions; it would not be good for them to have the facilitators simply override their opinions or fail to demonstrate to them that their opinions were being taken into account. On the other hand, it was clear that the members' emotions, led by anger toward Martin for his chronically irritating behavior, could not be the sole basis for a fair resolution. Leadership from the facilitators was needed to provide balance and fairness, yet it was essential to lead in a democratic manner, showing respect for the men's opinions and feelings.

The cofacilitators thanked the men for sharing their feelings and opinions and made a special point of acknowledging both Don and Martin for their honesty and their self-control in discussing the issue during session. Then, the primary facilitator asked if the session could continue with the regular group format and return to the suspension issue at the session's end. The members were agreeable to this. The thinking behind this move was that it would allow for a further cooling down of the emotional intensity. In addition, of course, it would allow group members time to work on whatever issues each of them may have needed to address that day. The group members all knew that they had been heard; yet the group facilitators did not abandon all responsibility for the solution by leaving the group members completely in charge. Although the members may have presented as though they wanted such responsibility, members generally feel safer and more supported when leadership rests on the shoulders of the facilitators, while respecting and incorporating their viewpoints.

As the session drew to a close, the primary facilitator returned to the dilemma posed by Martin's and Don's infractions. She reiterated her understanding of each member's input, stressing that she agreed with the men that Don and Martin ought to be suspended rather than terminated. She acknowledged the anger generated by Martin's behavior and noted that the group would continue to work further on this, pointing out that many members could benefit from practicing ways to express anger nonviolently. She also noted that Don had come to group to learn alternatives to his violent outbursts and had been making good progress up to this point. She suggested that to treat Don's aggression as something less serious would not aid his progress; what's more, Don's behavior represented the breaking of a serious group rule. She added that Martin's behavior of teasing and annoying others was something that he was attempting to change through his work in group. Even though he did not technically break either the safety or the confidentiality rule, it would be good for him to have a serious consequence also. For these reasons, the facilitator suggested that both Don and Martin receive one week's suspension from group, pointing out that this had been the "usual" consequence for such infractions previously. She then asked the members if they would be agreeable to this proposal. All of the members agreed, and even seemed rather relieved. The process and the facilitation had demonstrated concern for their feelings. Moreover, it had provided a reasonable balance between their emotions and their needs to learn new behaviors. Ultimately, it put a safe frame around the entire experience. In fact, the sessions that followed reflected a renewed sense of mutual respect and cohesiveness among the members.

You will note that a fallback consequence (one week's suspension) for infractions had been previously established in the group described. Generally, we do end up imposing a one-session suspension on a member who breaks one of the two primary rules. We do this following the same sort of group process just described, provided that we deem this to be in the best interest of all involved. It is certainly possible to terminate a member, however, even after his first breach of one of these rules. In groups with nondisabled members, termination is often the result. In groups with members with intellectual disabilities, however, we have found that a working comprehension of the group rules often comes only through experience—and experience entails making mistakes. Certainly, if the infraction were deemed to be so hurtful that the perpetrator's continuation in the group could be damaging, we reserve the right to terminate the member immediately. Note that immediate termination could result from breaking either the safety or the confidentiality rule.

Group Safety and Sociopathic Individuals

One further thought concerning issues of group safety and termination of membership is the problem of sociopathic personalities in a group setting. The organization of the sociopathic personality is such that there is a complete absence of feelings such as guilt, remorse, or shame; a failure to develop attachment to others; and a drive to "get over on" others (McWilliams, 1994). Those who show empathy are "weak" in the mind of the sociopath. Therapists and group members who make efforts to bend rules, whether to foster learning opportunities or to demonstrate empathy, are "asking" to be taken advantage of, according to the sociopath.

Clinicians who treat sociopaths stress that unfailing integrity and rigid rule- and boundary-keeping are essential to the treatment of these individuals. As we noted previously, a sociopathic individual should not be placed in a group with nonsociopaths. If an individual's sociopathic dynamic is not recognized during the initial interview and he ends up in group, it is best to terminate his membership as soon as he violates any group rule. It will not serve him to demonstrate empathy or provide "learning opportunities" that may run the risk of harming vulnerable members. The sociopath should be referred for individual therapy or to a group for sociopaths.

Nonviolent Interpersonal Conflict

Many interpersonal conflicts occur in the group setting that never escalate to the point of breaking the safety rule but that require judicious intervention nonetheless. Two members sometimes become polarized on a certain point and go back and forth unproductively, intensifying the emotion with each successive volley.

For example, in one group, Daniel talked about having gotten into a special dinner for free. The dinner was sponsored by his temple for a religious holiday. The involved personnel waived the normal contribution for him. Another group member, Helene, had also attended the dinner. She became angry at Daniel, accusing him of having cheated the temple. Daniel became angry at her in turn, and the two escalated in intensity, locked in an unproductive round of reproaches. In a different group, with more impaired members, Gwen chided C.J. for talking about death. She did not want to hear about death. C.J. made an immediate retort about her rights. A few more rounds followed with increasing intensity.

In situations such as these, it is tempting for the facilitator to take a direct approach to end the feuding. The facilitator's mission, however, is, as always, to maximize the psychological functioning of all of the group members. As in the earlier example with Martin and Don, the facilitator needs to begin by freezing the action between the two antagonists long enough to connect with the other members. This freezing of the action is more than a move to create a ceasefire. It creates the opportunity for the rest of the group members to share what they are feeling. Group members have feelings about witnessing their fellow members' conflicts that are no less important than the feelings of the two antagonists. The facilitator should verbalize this point clearly to the members and check in with each of them. The facilitator may need to make a number of efforts to clarify to the members that it is their personal feelings that are being sought, not their opinions regarding the conflict. Each member should be encouraged in turn to describe his present feelings. Finally, the facilitator should affirm the group for the time they gave to the antagonists.

The next step consists of demonstrating support for each of the antagonists' feelings. This can be done by one or both of the facilitators, or by various group members, depending on how much "sociometric pull" the issue has. By sociometric pull, we mean how strongly connected each of the members is to the issue. In the example with Gwen and C.J., conflicts arise from time to time and are relatively brief. In facilitating these interactions, we have found that both antagonists respond well to short verbalizations from one of the facilitators demonstrating understanding of their feelings. For example, "Gwen, it sounds like you are saying that hearing about death makes you upset. Is that right?" Gwen always agrees to this readily. We then ask Gwen to express her feelings to C.J. in this manner rather than telling C.J. what to do.

"I get upset when you talk about death," Gwen says to C.J. She is then affirmed for this effort, as is C.J. for listening. We ask C.J. to repeat what Gwen said. Then, we help C.J. clarify her feelings to Gwen in a similar fashion.

This process moves relatively quickly and ends with affirmations for the antagonists as well as the observing members. In cases in which the issue and the antagonists seem to have greater sociometric pull, the facilitator may move the interaction into an enactment. This "pull" can be noted in the body language and verbalizations of the other members. The more members who spontaneously voice opinions or feelings about the dilemma, the more pull the issue has. This may be the result of members' feeling toward the particular individuals or toward the nature of the issue. When C.J. and Gwen would get into a scrimmage, the other members would demonstrate a desire to put a quick end to it and get on to important business. In the case of Helene and Daniel, however, other members showed interest and began to comment.

To tackle the standoff, the facilitator had each of the two choose a double who understood their respective feelings. This process can be aided by having the two antagonists' chairs moved so that the two chairs face the *same* direction. In other words, both members can be seated next to each other, facing the group rather than facing or opposing each other. One double stands behind each chair. The doubles then take turns verbalizing the feelings and checking with their respective protagonists. The experience of having one's feelings understood and not diminished, as well as of feeling safely connected to the group as a whole, does much to bring down the hostility and fear. Once the doubling is accomplished, the drama can be drawn to a close by returning the chairs to the circle and having the participating members go back to their seats. The observing members can then be asked to describe "what was good" about what the antagonists and the doubles did. The facilitator can make a process comment that highlights the entire membership's growing ability to engage in productive group interactions. The facilitator can also comment that the group is showing the ability to tolerate different feelings in healthy ways, that is, by discussion rather than conflict. The facilitator can then finish with an affirmation to the group members for their patience and support, and to the antagonists for having enough self-control to stop fighting and for instead helping the group with the important task of truly understanding their feelings. Note that the conflict does not have to be resolved in the sense that one antagonist's feelings prevail; rather, the point of the experience is to help members learn to value being heard, understood, and respected, and giving the same respect to the opinions of others, even when different. Having everyone agree on every issue is not a reasonable goal; having everyone strive to express their own opinions and learn to tolerate the opinions of others is a valuable, ongoing, interpersonal process.

In future groups, the facilitators should stay alert for different types of interactions the two antagonists may have. There will likely be a time when the two former antagonists are on the same side concerning a particular issue or are both able to give support to a third member. These observations should be stated directly to help each member see his growing ability to work with people with whom he may not always agree.

Breaking the Confidentiality Rule

Earlier we described an example in which a group member in one of our women's groups broke the confidentiality of another member by disclosing something to the member's boyfriend (see chap. 4, this volume). The offended member reported this infraction to the group, and the perpetrator admitted her wrongdoing. As she spoke it became clear that she had not realized the significance of her actions at the time. She apologized readily. The offended member and the other members felt comfortable with keeping her in the group, without even imposing a one-session suspension. Unfortunately, the same woman re-offended by teasing certain other members on the bus about problems they were addressing in the group. This resulted in the woman's termination from the group.

Following a termination of this sort, it is important to have an individual meeting with the terminated member. Two key objectives should be addressed: making certain that the individual is clear on the reason for termination from group and determining what the individual's therapeutic needs are at this point. Referral for individual treatment can then be made.

In one of our men's groups, many breaks in confidentiality have occurred. These were successfully resolved by group discussion and one-session suspensions. A confidentiality break we have often encountered is that of one member's discussing another member's group business with a mutual job coach. Often, the job coach had asked how the other person was doing in group. We have had to make a point to members that, even when well-intentioned staff may ask about fellow group members, it is not permissible to give any information. We have found the need to do a fair amount of coaching and practicing with our members to resist an appeal for disclosure by people in authority. In fact, the issue has allowed for much useful training in assertiveness skills. In addition, we make ongoing efforts to sensitize staff members to patient confidentiality, although keeping up with staff changes because of high turnover rates has made this daunting.

Another area in which members have shown greater vulnerability to inappropriate disclosure is in the area of social contact that occurs outside of session. As we described earlier in this book, the restricted social network in which most of our members live and work means that it is quite likely that members will run into each other in settings outside of session. Furthermore, many of our members develop friendships with each other because of their group connection. For the most part, our observation is that more good than harm comes from these friendships. Most members have very little in the way of true peer friendship and benefit greatly from the social skill development and enhancement of intimacy gained from experiences in the group. The drawback, however, is that when members see each other outside of group, they sometimes inadvertently disclose confidential information in front of third parties. The case with the two women in chapter 4, in which one said something to the other's boyfriend, is one such example. In another example, one of the men called a fellow group member. The member was out and his mother took the call. The man ended up sharing information with the other member's mother. In another example, one man was visiting another member at his supported apartment and continued speaking to the member about a confidential matter in front of the member's staff person. Yet another breach in confidentiality occurred when one member ran into another member at a job site, and, happy to see him, innocently introduced him to a coworker as a fellow group member.

These infractions have become the basis for a great deal of productive discussion and consciousness-raising. Issues concerning assertiveness with authority figures, such as staff and parents, have been addressed, as well as the need for awareness of others' needs for privacy. A great many breaks in confidentiality occur innocently, suggesting that members need continued feedback and group experience to learn the rules, and to learn how to be good members. Happily, such learning often takes place. Simply terminating membership would eclipse that important opportunity.

In one very problematic case, we had a loud, irate father come into our center screaming that another member had disclosed confidential information regarding his son, Isaac, to others at their sheltered workshop. The father's behavior was aggressive and threatening, and, unfortunately, the two of us who cofacilitated the group became quite intimidated. The father, who was the legal guardian of the member, was deeply ashamed of his son's pedophilic behavior. Isaac was in serious legal trouble, and the father, elderly and a recent widower, was financially and emotionally burdened as a result. The fact was, however, that there were few people at Isaac's workshop who had *not* already known what he had done. Gossip had gotten around well before we received the referral; the young man had committed an offense on a group outing with many peers and staff nearby. Nevertheless, the father insisted that a particular member was responsible for talking about his son in front of others at the workshop. He demanded we terminate the member because we had explained at both the initial interview and team meeting that breaking confidentiality could lead to termination.

Swept up in the sudden, angry tirade presented by Isaac's father, neither the cofacilitator nor I realized that Isaac had also broken confidentiality by identifying another group member to his father. Of course, there is a dilemma regarding the son's telling his father because his father is his legal guardian. It might be argued that communications between an individual and the individual's legal guardian are not constrained by ordinary limits of confidentiality. Nevertheless, that communication cannot defensibly include confidential information regarding *other* group members when the problem could have been resolved without breaking another member's confidentiality.

Specifically, Isaac's responsibility was to have brought this problem directly into the group, where it would have been immediately addressed. In addition, we make all members aware of how to call us and leave voicemail messages at any time if a problem arises during the week, so that they may contact us immediately if they feel distressed. Unfortunately, Isaac was new to group and had a long-standing habit of reporting all of his problems to his father, who would then champion his cause. This habit was not influenced by one brief experience with our group and its rules.

We told the father that we would follow up with the identified member. When we did so, the member admitted to teasing the young man but not to disclosing information to other parties. We decided to move the member who did the teasing to a different men's group to appease the father. Sadly, the father withdrew his son from treatment a few months later for reasons unrelated to our treatment. He terminated Isaac from group after learning that he was legally obligated to notify neighbors of his son's pedophilic crime. The father was experiencing a tremendous amount of shame and was extremely motivated to avoid situations that would further label his son as an offender.

For our part, we failed to identify the son's breech of confidentiality in reporting the other individual by name to his father. This failure on our part has sensitized us to the impact of hostile behavior on our problem-solving ability, and, we hope, has increased our attentiveness to the multi-faceted nature of confidentiality.

MANAGING MONOPOLISTS

It is not unusual to find a monopolist in the therapy group setting (or other group settings!). The individual who talks on at length, seemingly unaware of how others might feel about the verbiage, can cause discomfort and even annoyance to members and facilitators alike. Moreover, if not managed effectively, monopolizing behavior can eclipse the therapeutic value of the group.

Yalom (1995), whose research in group psychotherapy we have referred to at length, reminds us that the monopolist does not operate in a vacuum. A group member can only monopolize for as long as no other members attempt to speak. Yalom's research with the nondisabled patient population suggests that members who monopolize are indeed unaware of the degree to which their volume of speech exceeds that of their fellow members. He theorized that for many monopolists, silence is anxiety-provoking; lengthy discourses are a means of avoiding increased anxiety. Moreover, Yalom suggested that much of the monopolist's presentation avoids the heart of his issues. Talking is often done around, rather than about, the most painful matters.

In our experience, monopolists in groups in which members have intellectual disabilities pose particularly difficult problems in that few members are assertive enough to address the monopolizing member directly—although many, through much group work, have learned. Many people with intellectual disabilities demonstrate greater passivity than do people in the general population, leaving the burden of addressing the monopolist essentially in the laps of the facilitators. Although there are steps facilitators can and should take to address the monopolist directly, the facilitator's chief function is, as always, to encourage the maximal psychological functioning of each member. In that regard, the facilitator needs to help members identify their own feelings about what is going on, and to develop a means of expressing those feelings. Some characterologically passive members, for example, feel angry toward the facilitators for "allowing" the monopolist to go on. At the same time, they take no action of their own. In contrast, timid members, reluctant to speak, may be relieved by the presence of a monopolist whose command of the group's attention allows them to hide on the sidelines.

Monopolists in Groups With More Impaired Members

In new groups, especially those with more severely impaired members, the facilitator had best take a fairly directive role in helping members curtail run-on, unproductive presentations. The facilitator can ask the member to stop and check in with other members to see who has heard what he said. It is a good idea to ask the monopolizing member if he can tell who was paying attention to him. If he chooses a member who can, in fact, repeat the message, both the monopolist and the listener should be acknowledged for their respective roles in the communication process. If, on the other hand, no one can repeat the message, the monopolist should be asked to say "one important thing" to the group to see if someone can understand him. In this way, the monopolist is being helped to actually communicate to his peers. He should be affirmed for this effort and helped to frame it into a workable construct. For example, if George had been going on and on about all the problems with his job coach, the first step would be to help him deliver a simple statement about his feelings. He might say, "I'm mad at my job coach."

"Good," the facilitator should immediately say, preventing further discussion. "That *is* important! Now ask one of the members if he heard you."

George might then ask Eric if he heard him. The facilitator can ask Eric to repeat what George said. Once this is accomplished, both members can be affirmed for their efforts. The facilitator can then ask if anyone else has been through similar problems with job coaches and encourage a process of offering support for George. This moves the group into an interactive mode. Then, if the facilitator feels this issue has enough group support to be moved into an enactment, the stage can be set for a psychodramatic role-play, or even a simple scene in which members double for George. If such support is not present, George should be acknowledged for his efforts at communicating his feelings clearly, and then asked to pass the turn and check in with someone who has not shared yet.

Monopolists in Groups With Mildly Impaired Members

Carol, a group member we introduced in earlier chapters, is infamous among the various cofacilitators who have led the women's group for her monopolizing behavior. Highly verbal and highly anxious, Carol circles round and round what truly threatens her, discussing repeated instances of the same hurtful treatment she experiences at home: Her freedom is restricted, her outings and even phone calls are questioned, her time is burdened by unpaid hours spent babysitting her sister's kids.

When Carol's relationship with her boyfriend is on the rocks, her complaints about her home life intensify. Similarly, the closer she gets to taking steps to change her situation, the more anxious she becomes, and the more she goes on about the original set of complaints.

At the same time, Carol wants very much to be liked and to be seen as a good group member. She is attentive to others when they speak and makes frequent efforts to offer support to others, often sharing from her own experience. She has a tendency to lapse into too much self-disclosure when giving support, but she does respond to reminders to allow the presenting member to continue.

In groups with members who do not have intellectual disabilities, and in groups with members who have mild to moderate disabilities and a fair amount of group experience, the facilitator might address the monopolist, after sensing too much unproductive time has gone by, and ask her to check in with the rest of the group. Using the example of Carol, the facilitator might say something to the effect of, "Carol, I can see that you are quite upset and need to talk. Clearly the other women see this too, and are giving you their time and attention without interruption. I'm thinking, also, that some of the other members may feel a need for some time to speak as well. I'm wondering if you would be willing to ask each of them about their needs, so everyone can decide as a group how we should proceed."

This technique allows the monopolist to feel the chief responsibility for her behavior and fosters member-to-member interaction, which, of course, is the heart of the group process. If the monopolist tries to avoid interaction through the use of a "poor me" response ("Oh, never mind! I'll just pass the turn!"), it is best not to give way to such an easy out. No new learning will have taken place. Remind the monopolist that these members have just given her the gift of their time and attention; their interest in her deserves to be reciprocated.

Once the checking process starts, especially in groups with intellectually disabled members, it is important to affirm both the monopolist and each successive member with whom she speaks. ("Carol, you did a nice job of looking right at Trish and asking her directly. And, Trish, you were able to tell Carol you need some time to speak, too.") A member who appears to be genuinely comfortable with allowing the monopolist extra time, and is able to say so, should be similarly affirmed.

Make a point to encourage each member to be honest and to address fears that she may be having. If a member appears uncomfortable and avoids responding, it is best for the facilitator to intervene. For example, it may be helpful to say to the member, "Erin, I noticed you looked down when Carol asked you if you wanted time to talk. I'm thinking that maybe it's hard for you to tell Carol that you would like some time to talk. Is that right?" If Erin agrees, encourage her to tell Carol these things in her own words. If she disagrees, ask her to explain what she is feeling using her own words.

As is, no doubt, obvious at this point, this intermember checking is a belabored and time-consuming process. Lest the reader be overly frustrated at the thought of such a lengthy process, we would like to offer the following reminder: The process *is* the therapy. If the facilitator simply directs traffic so that each member gets an equal share of the time, none of the members will experience any new interpersonal learning—a major, and unique, gift group therapy has to offer. Interpersonal difficulties are chief among referral issues. An individual whose history is replete with abusive experiences and with symptoms such as depression or acting-out behavior inevitably experiences interpersonal difficulties in day-to-day life; members are distressed by their failures to communicate feelings to caregivers, to make friends with coworkers, to cope with criticism, and so on. A person who experienced abuse, especially repeated abuse, is likely to have a diminished sense of efficacy and assertiveness in interpersonal relationships. As we saw in looking at the theoretical underpinnings of group psychotherapy, interpersonal difficulties go hand-in-hand with psychological distress. Moreover, learning good interpersonal skills is even more difficult for people with intellectual disabilities. Once learned, however, these skills powerfully enhance one's sense of self and ability to enjoy life. Without this effort, Carol, in this case, would have lost the benefit of having to come face-to-face with her peers and seeing the effects of her self-absorption on them. Erin would have lost an opportunity to learn that she has the right to want to speak and be listened to, and that she has the right to state that need. And each of them, as well as the others, would have missed an opportunity to learn how to negotiate uncomfortable situations such as this. These opportunities give members a chance to learn and rehearse ways of asserting themselves, so that they are less vulnerable to abuse of all kinds, including the subtle, insidious verbal abuses of everyday life. In addition, each member has the chance to learn how her particular style of relating contributes to the treatment she receives in turn. These are hard-won lessons. People will relate to others in the group in some of the same, unsuccessful ways they relate to others in their lives. Becoming aware of these patterns, and trying out ways of changing them, are essential components of their therapy.

Continuing with Carol's example, she knows only how to vent, at length, and without resolution, and she knows how to "clam up," as she says, at all other times. She knows nothing of the flow, the reciprocity, the back-and-forth movement of enjoyable relationships. In addition, her pent up feelings leek out in angry looks and hostile, under-her-breath comments that cause her problems with peers, coworkers, supervisors, and customers. They add to her bad feelings about herself and have cost her jobs and friendships. *How* she talks is every bit as important as *what* she talks about.

THE ATTENTION THIEF

In consulting with other professionals who have begun therapy groups for people with intellectual disabilities, we have received frequent complaints about attention thieves, members who steal the group's attention through nonproductive behaviors. One staff member told us about a women's group she formed in which one of the women would regularly jangle her bracelets, rummage through her bag, and get up to complain that she needed a drink of water, or to go to the bathroom, during other members' presentations. The staff member reported that she, and most of the members, were highly annoyed by the woman's antics and frustrated because she had not decreased these behaviors despite many clear verbal requests to do so. The staff member was also concerned because, although she felt tempted to throw the woman out, she was keenly aware of the woman's troubled history and feelings of distress. She wanted to help her.

Particularly in new groups, in which the norms for behavior have not yet been established, such disruptive behavior can be difficult to reshape. Yet, if the disruptive individual is truly interested in drawing attention to herself, the facilitator and the group hold the trump card. A person who wants attention, but steals the attention through disruptive behaviors, is a person who wants what the group has to give. She simply has to be taught how to work for it legitimately.

We have had great success by remembering behavioral principles and using them in the session. As soon as the attention thief presents a disruptive behavior, one of the therapists should directly praise another member, perhaps starting with the member who was speaking at the time. "Teri, you stayed calm, and kept talking, even during that noise. Good for you!" The therapist might next turn to another member, especially if the attention thief is still disrupting, and say, "Lynn, you kept looking at Teri the whole time she was talking. That was the right thing. I'm glad you stayed calm and kept listening, even though there was some noise in here." Note that the attention thief is not named. Avoid making any reference to the attention thief because it is likely to be reinforcing.

Even though most of us in facilitator roles are familiar with behavioral principles, it can be a challenge to keep them in mind and resist the pull to respond to the disruptive member with some words or even a look that might, unintentionally, be reinforcing. When delivering the pointed praise to the cooperative member, make every effort to resist glancing in the direction of the disruptor. As soon as the disruptive individual presents a disruptive behavior, that is the facilitator's cue to look at and praise a *different* member, one exemplifying prosocial behavior.

It is equally important to remember the old behavioral adage, "Catch them being good!" Be on the lookout for moments when the attention thief is quiet, and emphatically affirm her. (In behavioral terms, this represents a DRO—differential reinforcement of other behavior.) For example, if Lynn is speaking and the attention thief, Mia, is sitting still, one of the facilitators should say, "Mia, you're doing a great job letting Lynn speak. You're really learning how to be a good group member." As difficult as Mia might be, there are inevitably moments when she is simply sitting there. These can be caught and reinforced. As her behavior evolves, she can be reinforced for actually looking at the member who is speaking, and, ultimately, for being able to repeat what the speaker said. (In behavioral terms, we can conceptualize these as DRA strategies—differential reinforcement of adaptive behaviors.)

ADDITIONAL DISRUPTIVE BEHAVIOR PROBLEMS

Some members, in addition to a reinforcement history that unwittingly rewarded disruptive behaviors, have other complications that contribute to their disruptiveness. We have observed that people with impulse control problems and ADHD are particularly challenging. Some of the disruptive behavior seems to be very difficult for them to inhibit, even once they have made considerable improvement. Such individuals are often very reactive to any changes in the setting, such as someone walking in late or a loud noise in the hall. We have found, however, that while such an individual may continue to have some degree of disruptive behavior, the overall rate goes down over time and the person becomes much more workable.

We have also found that some individuals with autistic features can be disruptive in ways that, initially, are independent of the group's attention toward them. Such individuals have been known to say things out loud while others were speaking because what they heard triggered some association for them. Usually these statements are directed at no one in particular, and the individual does not seek a response. With these individuals, the goal is to help them increase their awareness of their own behavior and to relate more directly and consciously to other members of the group. If the individual makes a completely bizarre and idiosyncratic comment while another speaks, it is best not to give attention to it directly. If, however, the comment has some potential to connect with what the presenting member was saying, it can be helpful to address the autistic member as soon as the presenting member finishes his thought. In chapter 5 we described one of the offenders named Nathan. In addition to the offense problems we discussed, Nathan has autistic features and tends to make idiosyncratic remarks, addressed to the rug, while others speak. In facilitating this, we have found it helpful to say, "Nathan, I heard you say something when Ben was talking. Would you look right at him and say it to him?" Then, of course, Nathan should be affirmed for his effort, as should Ben for listening. With members such as Nathan, we have made a point of discussing in the affirmation stage each measure of progress in communicating with others. As a footnote, we would like to add that, even though Nathan still has this problematic tendency, his rate of erratic verbalizations has gone down considerably, and his eye contact, listening, and direct communication have vastly improved.

In groups that have been meeting for some time, the norms for group behavior become well established. Members have learned to look at and listen to each other, from repeated experiences of reinforcement by the facilitators for this behavior, and in time, from experiences of reinforcement from other members as well. Introducing a new member with disruptive behaviors into an established group makes for a fairly quick reshaping of that behavior. However, in new groups, in which none of the members have group experience to draw on, even one member with a long history of disruptive, attention-stealing behaviors can take considerable time to adapt. In any case, it is important not to lose heart. Remember the phenomenon behaviorists refer to as the "extinction burst": The disruptive behaviors may get worse before they get better.

BEHAVIORAL STRATEGIES: SOCIOMETRIC CONCERNS

Remember, also, to pay attention to the group's sociometry. Typically, members who defy group norms through disruptive behaviors and fail to attend to and support other members are not well liked. This will be evident in selection processes. For example, during the warm-up and sharing stage, each member presents an issue to work on and then asks another member what he would like to work on. This continues until each of the members has presented a topic. The disruptive member is likely to be the last one chosen. Similarly, if a member moves his issue into an enactment, the disruptive member is unlikely to be chosen by the protagonist for an auxiliary role. As a facilitator, you will know when the disruptive member has made real improvements in his behavior by increases in the rate in which he is chosen to speak or play roles by other members.

As the disruptive member begins to make improvements through the behavioral strategies we described, you can add to his repertoire of prosocial behaviors and bolster his sociometric standing as well. One way to do this is to invite him to double for another member. Previously, we have described the use of multiple doubles, in which more than one member doubles the emotional experiences of the protagonist. As the facilitator, you can invite members to stand up and double for a protagonist. Invite the disruptive member when you sense that he has a reasonably good chance of being able to verbalize the protagonist's feelings. If the disruptive member cannot yet respond to the question, for example, "Jeff just got in trouble at work. How do you think he is feeling?" you can assist the disruptive member (or any other member, for that matter) by directing him to try on the role the protagonist is in. For example, with our disruptive member, Mia, we might invite her to stand behind Lynn, a protagonist, who is upset that her job coach called her father and complained about her. To warm her up to the role, we might say, "Mia, pretend your job coach just called your parents and complained about you. How would you feel?" As she makes an effort to verbalize feelings, affirm these efforts, and have her ask the protagonist if they are the same as she feels. As the other members begin to experience the disruptive member as being interested in and understanding of their feelings, their sense of connection to her will grow.

Most important, you can be certain that if the disruptive member is not well liked by her fellow group members, she is similarly disliked in her interpersonal world outside of group. The opportunity to learn behaviors that improve others' feelings and connection toward her is a valuable gift for such a person. She will ultimately gain attention in ways that feel much better than she ever knew was possible.

SUMMARY

In this chapter we have endeavored to share problematic experiences that we, and some of our trainees, have had in running therapy groups with people with intellectual disabilities. We spent time on problems resulting from infractions related to the group rules of safety and confidentiality, as these occur with some frequency in our experience and touch on the very foundation of a group. We also identified common pathological patterns, such as people who monopolize and those who disrupt, and discussed ways in which the group process can be used to promote growth in these targeted individuals as well as the rest of the membership. We reviewed examples of conflict between two members of a group and ways in which the feuding members and the observing members can be helped to learn new interpersonal skills from these experiences.

Along these lines, we would like to return to the notion that "everything is grist for the mill." This is not merely a euphemism; it is the essence of the group experience. Every problem one has in the group represents an area in that person that is in need of growth. Problems displayed by individuals in the group are examples of the problems they experience in other aspects of their lives. These problems are the raw materials, brought into the group room, for us to work with. They tell us in no uncertain terms where to direct our attention. An individual may report on or describe experiences he has had and these certainly need to be addressed; but the difficulties he displays, which we can observe in live action, let us see exactly where his interpersonal style gets him into trouble and allows for active practice and remediation, as well as the acquisition of new skills and experiences.

Finally, we encourage clinicians to try to maintain a forgiving attitude toward themselves for their own mistakes, a recommendation that is easier for us to write about than to adhere to in our own lives. Whether we like it or not, we learn from our mistakes, too, and become better clinicians for them.

10

TERMINATION

I don't punch holes no more; I'm doing good.
                                        —Tom S., group member

For the most part, members of our treatment groups tend to have fairly long lengths of stay, often remaining in treatment for several years. This is true of trauma survivors as well as offenders.

These may be unpopular words in today's insurance-driven world. We believe, however, that as we strive to evolve a long-overdue treatment model for people with intellectual disabilities, our goal can be nothing less than the best of which we are capable. Moreover, we contend that long-term group therapy for this population is, in fact, pragmatic. The per-person rates are low, and we generally have eight members in each group, making for a tremendous cost advantage over individual therapy.

Moreover, many people with intellectual disabilities are in full-time day programs, or they are in program part time and work in the community part time. Group therapy lends itself well into incorporation into day programs. One caveat in this regard, however, is that many staff are misinformed regarding group psychotherapy and think that any assembly of individuals in a circle is "group." As we have taken great pains to present, group psychotherapy, following the treatment format and rationale we have outlined, is entirely different from social skills training groups. Social skills groups of the various sorts commonly used in day programs serve an important purpose as well, but they are no substitute for therapy for those with serious psychological symptoms.

Whatever the costs of group therapy, and they are minimal, they must be weighed against the costs of *not* providing adequate treatment. In our experience, many of the patients we have taken into treatment had previous histories that were highly costly—financially, emotionally, and socially. Some members had multiple hospital stays, many had multiple job losses, and many had symptoms that caused disruption in the family and with roommates, including physical fighting and property destruction. Many others had episodes of sexual offending, some of which were minor, some of which were quite serious. Some were incarcerated. Some simply suffered, having symptoms that distressed only themselves and did not command the attention of caregivers. Others had intermittent visits to psychiatrists or psychologists who would be willing to see them for a time or to prescribe medication. The symptoms would subside, and treatment would be discontinued, often because it was burdensome for the caregiver in terms of costs and transportation. The symptoms would later resume, leading to new searches for new professionals, because the previous treatment was seen as having "failed."

In the vast majority of cases, long-term group therapy has led to decreased problematic behaviors and symptoms, as well as gains in self-control, self-efficacy, and self-esteem. As we have noted previously, we typically maintain individuals in treatment long after their initial symptom level has subsided. This practice serves two important goals. First, members are able to go beyond symptom reduction, continuing their psychological development toward enhanced self-efficacy and self-esteem, as just noted. This psychological development leads to a greater sense of well-being and allows for extended opportunities to evolve prosocial coping methods, thus reducing the likelihood of regressing to old patterns. Second, veteran members who are functioning at improved levels offer hope and provide actual, lived experience with the process of change for new members. They are role models no nondisabled therapist can match.

LENGTH OF STAY FOR THE GENERAL POPULATION

Once again we would do well to turn to the expertise of Irvin Yalom (1995). Yalom stated that only very general conclusions can be drawn concerning length of group treatment, because, of course, individuals are unique and have unique needs that demand to be addressed, despite the presence of a common diagnostic label such as depression. Reporting very broad averages, Yalom found that most patients require a minimum of approximately 12 to 24 months of treatment. These patients, of course, are not impaired by intellectual disabilities. Certainly impaired individuals cannot be expected to require less.

Yalom (1995) acknowledged the dilemma posed by managed care's insistence on treatment that is brief and problem-oriented, geared toward short-term symptom relief. He stated unequivocally that true characterological change does not result from such treatment, and that change of this magnitude requires the lengthier time frames just mentioned. Group therapy may well be the most practical way of allowing for this level of change for those patients who want and need it.

Nancy McWilliams (1999), who has authored several professional training works and teaches at the Graduate School of Applied and Professional Psychology at Rutgers University, asked us to look closely at the self-serving research cited by insurance companies. Symptom relief, the lone outcome measure in studies with single-diagnosis patients (those with no compounding, characterological Axis II conditions), is studied exclusively. In real practice, many patients require more. McWilliams cited the work of Martin Seligman, a living historical figure in psychology, famous for his pioneering understanding of depression through *learned helplessness,* and recent president of the American Psychological Association. Seligman (1996) argued the implausibility of extrapolating from controlled, single-outcome research to the realities of practice with patients, with whom we have ongoing relationships and who present us with multifaceted needs we cannot ignore. In fact, a recent study headed by a researcher at the Yale University School of Medicine found that more treatment is indeed better (Hansen, Lambert, & Forman, 2002). Hansen et al. reviewed 28 published studies, summarizing the outcomes of 2,109 patients in 89 psychotherapeutic treatment conditions, including cognitive–behavioral, behavioral, interpersonal, and group. Even a very modest level of improvement, such as 50%, appears to require as many as 18 sessions for the average patient to reach. Also, the authors noted that, of the many sites studied, the site with the best response rate was also the site that had the most sessions delivered per patient and the highest median treatment length. They acknowledged studies that have found that improvement hits a plateau following symptom reduction, and that there may be diminishing returns to continuing treatment beyond a certain point. This plateau, however, may simply be a function of the particular outcomes that are measured. Hansen et al. noted that some domains, such as interpersonal problems, continue to show improvement after other domains, such as symptoms of distress, have leveled off. Overall, the results suggest that mental health managers might more reasonably require justification for early termination rather than for continuing treatment. In addition, in thinking about the needs of trauma survivors with intellectual disabilities, we might look at the treatment of combat survivors with posttraumatic stress disorder in the general population, who often require combinations of long-term group and individual psychotherapy over periods of many years (Ford & Stewart, 1999).

Haaven et al. (1990), whose residential treatment program for sex offenders with intellectual disabilities we presented in chapter 2, provided data on length of stay and recidivism for their patients. Reviewing data collected from 1979 through 1988, they found that recidivism, defined as "committing a new sexual offense," occurred at a rate of 25% for patients who completed 365 days or less of treatment and 21% for patients who completed more than 365 days. Haaven et al. also found in studying recidivism in its broadest definition, that is, looking not only at sexual offense but at all forms of criminal activity (including such things as driving on a suspended license and trespassing), the longer the length of stay in their full-time, residential program, the lower the recidivism. The lowest broad-definition recidivism rate across the study's 9-year span was 39% for those patients who completed more than 545 days of inpatient treatment and 29% for those who participated in some form of after-care treatment following discharge.

PLANNING FOR TERMINATION

We can conceptualize a member's readiness for termination in terms of three broad criteria: significantly reduced symptomatology, a moderate sense of self-efficacy (especially with respect to one's improvement), and a reasonably well-functioning support network.

When our members begin group, we strive to make sure that they have at least a rudimentary awareness of a behavior or symptom that they need to change. As they progress through treatment, we attempt to help members become aware of a more complete and clear set of changes they need to make. Generally, people make uneven progress, with longer and longer periods of stability, marked by less frequent and shorter periods of instability. When a member has had a prolonged period of stability and can consciously identify changes he has made that account for his improvement, we begin to think about termination from treatment.

In most cases, our experience has been that group members with intellectual disabilities are less likely than nondisabled therapy patients to initiate termination from treatment. Of course, there are some patients with intellectual disabilities who do initiate plans for their own termination. Some are individuals who have truly progressed and are thinking constructively about moving on. Others have less noble reasons for desiring departure. Often, however, we as facilitators see the individual's readiness and initiate the discussion of termination.

For example, Joanna was in our women's group for about four years. She was initially referred by her workshop staff because she would frequently seek staff members out complaining about troubles she was having at home. She was moderately depressed, with occasional periods of crying. These would sometimes occur at work, apparently unprovoked. Furthermore, in her irritable state, Joanna readily misinterpreted and overreacted to comments from coworkers, frequently getting into verbal skirmishes as a result.

Joanna's depressive affect began to improve within the early months of treatment. Helping her learn how to cope successfully with peers took considerably longer. During the last year or so of her treatment, however, Joanna was relatively symptom-free and in good spirits. She did not initiate complaints at her workshop. In fact, she rarely brought in problems to work on in group. She continued to enjoy coming to group, however, and took obvious pleasure in supporting the other women. We began to speak to Joanna about ending her treatment, which we refer to as "graduation" to emphasize the effort and achievement of the individual in getting to this point.

PRESENTING TERMINATION TO THE MEMBERS: IT'S *THEIR* SUCCESS, NOT YOURS

With successful group members such as Joanna, who show no inclination to end treatment, we facilitate the termination process by reviewing the member's accomplishments. We do this in much the same way that we do in the affirmation stage of each session. We verbally present the member's achievements and affirm the member for her efforts in bringing about these changes. It is essential that the member feel a sense of self-efficacy with regard to her improvement. If the member attributes her improvement to the group or to the facilitators, she will forever feel dependent on these others. Frequently during the course of therapy, patients will come in and thank the group for helping them so much. The facilitator must always reframe this statement.

For example, in discussing her "graduation," Joanna stated, "The group helped me a lot." We responded immediately by saying, "Yes, the group did give you lots of help. But the reason you're doing better is because you *used* the help. We aren't there when you have to deal with Brenda at work, or during all the times you are upset with your stepfather and have to calm yourself down. You made good changes in the way you deal with problems, and that's helped you a lot." In addition, we highlight the ways in which the graduating member has helped the group, such as by having offered support to others and having taken on roles during enactments.

As we have stressed throughout this book, fostering each member's sense of self-efficacy is a critical part of the ongoing group process; it is not something that is first addressed as the member is preparing to leave. It is essential, however, that the member's sense of self-efficacy be securely in place for success to continue beyond termination. This is a crucial part of anyone's therapy but is arguably of heightened significance in the lives of people whose self-concept has been shaped by an intellectual disability that encourages a passive, dependent role in life.

Carol, for example, a patient we have described at length, is capable of becoming quite angry with us at times ("you help the others more") and highly grateful to us at other times (for "all your help. I don't know what I'd do without you"). Both stances come from the same emotional place within her: a deep sense of dependency. She blames others for her troubles but also credits others with her achievements. Many other patients also come in and thank us, crediting us with their improvement. This is flattering, of course, and as facilitators we can be tempted to bask in the praise. But the patient's gratitude is a cue to kick into action, especially if the gratitude is directed primarily at the facilitators rather than the group as a whole. It is as important for Carol to feel ownership over her successful efforts as it is for the offender to feel ownership over his abusive behavior. To Carol we have said, "Carol, it's true the group has given you lots of support, just as you have given support to the other women. We can't take the credit for your success, though. All of our support only helps when people use it. You have made good use of the support. We are not there when you are struggling to cope with difficult customers at work, or when you were brave enough to speak up to your boyfriend about how he was treating you. We did not get you off social security or keep you from quitting your job. You did. *You* have done some difficult things, and the credit is yours."

We present these types of interpretations unfailingly with our members. In fact, in our women's group, some of the members, such as Carol and Martina, have been exposed to this type of thinking so much that they rarely thank us in the same way anymore. Moreover, they can increasingly credit themselves. Interestingly, we have observed what is probably a male–female difference in the expression of gratitude, noting that the men in our groups much less often say thank you or express gratitude. This does not necessarily reflect a greater sense of self-efficacy, however. These men often relate to and discuss key others in their lives in ways that project a sense that certain others are the decision makers, the powerful figures, while they themselves are relatively small. Accordingly, we make the same effort to frame each man's achievements in terms of the individual effort put forth toward those ends.

COLLATERAL CONTACT AND SOCIAL SUPPORT

Generally, as we approach termination, and with the individual's permission, we touch base with significant others, such as parents or group home managers, job coaches, or social service staff who may have referred the individual. We ask for their feedback about the individual's behavior to determine if there are concerns about which we were unaware. (The support and supervision of significant others is particularly crucial when ending treatment with offenders, and we discuss that next.)

In addition to making certain that there are no other problems or symptoms of which we have been unaware, we consider the social system's ability to maintain support, and the individual's ability to make use of his or her system. For example, very often members will tell us in group about problems in their workplace that they have not disclosed to their job coaches. Often, we use the group process to help the member identify which problems to bring to a job coach, or to overcome fears or assertiveness deficits that get in the way of directing problems to appropriate sources for help. Similar sorts of dynamics are frequently addressed regarding how to direct problems to other key supports, such as state case managers or residential sponsors.

Often, the social network is lacking with respect to peer involvement, which becomes a thrust of the treatment, and which needs a plan for maintenance. Not infrequently, some of the men who have offended children are socially isolated from peers. As members gain social skill, we often encourage involvement in structured recreational programs. We use the group process to help them evolve their interpersonal skills, so that they might have enjoyable experiences with peers and be encouraged to continue.

With almost all individuals, disabled and nondisabled, who are in distress and seeking psychotherapy, the natural support system will in some way be lacking. If it were sufficient, the individual would be using it to relieve his distress. In some cases, a relatively good system is overwhelmed by the stressor's severity (e.g., a young girl, previously asymptomatic, is violently raped and the entire family is in turmoil). In some cases, the members of the support system are themselves causing the distress (such as in abusive or alcoholic families, or with abusive caretakers of people with intellectual disabilities). In some cases, the system is deficient (as in a home with a single mother and no additional adult supports, or an intellectually disabled adult living with an elderly parent and not involved with any social activity). Finally, a potentially helpful support network may exist, but the individual may fail to use it, as in the case of the woman whose family must look good at all costs and as a result will not seek the confidence of a friend for support, or of the intellectually disabled person who is afraid to tell his job coach that he is being reprimanded regularly on the job; he is ultimately fired before his job coach can intervene.

It is often the case that, for people without intellectual disabilities, learning to make changes in their social network is a key ingredient of their therapy. The individual brings an end to the one-sided relationship that only depletes her or risks sharing confidences with a friend. People with intellectual disabilities often lack the freedom to meet others and to choose friends that nondisabled individuals enjoy. Their social world tends to be smaller and is often dependent on caretakers. Moreover, people with intellectual disabilities are often shunned by nondisabled people in the community, which greatly restricts their capacity for developing satisfying relationships. What may seem like a simple referral for recreational programs may play a critical role in developing a sense of relationship and belonging that is essential for mental health.

THE FINAL SESSION

When all the pieces appear to be in place, and the member understands and agrees with graduation, we decide on a date for the last session. (Note that we use the term *graduation* in discussions with the members, capitalizing on the sense of accomplishment associated with that word.) We often use a simple enactment to give a sense of ceremony to the important day. We run our session as usual and conduct the graduation either after or instead of another enactment. We put an empty chair in front of the graduating member. Then we each take a turn sitting in that chair, facing the member directly, and saying our goodbyes. Usually one of the facilitators goes first to provide a model for the members. The facilitator once again affirms the graduate for her specific efforts and progress, and usually offers one or two other bits of positive feedback. Then the facilitator gets up and stands *behind* the empty chair. As she does so, she invites the members to take turns *sitting* in the chair and saying goodbye. The facilitator need not direct members to participate in any particular order. Generally, members respond well to an open invitation and can self-select their turns, although reluctant members who fail to step up should be directly encouraged. The facilitator can remain behind the empty chair in a position of support for each of the members. As each member takes her turn in the chair, the facilitator simply asks her to say whatever she would like to say to the graduating member. The graduating member then, of course, can respond. The facilitator thanks each member for her effort, and then asks that another member come to the chair until each member, as well as the other facilitator, has had a turn. At the end of this enactment, one of the facilitators presents the graduating member with a certificate of accomplishment. Such a tangible artifact, while a departure from traditional therapy practice, seems to reinforce a sense of pride in the individual for her achievement.

ADDITIONAL CONSIDERATIONS IN TERMINATING OFFENDERS

Generally, we maintain the men in our offender groups for as long as they are willing to come. Men who have not re-offended in many years continue to come to group in much the same way that recovering alcoholics with many years of sobriety continue in Alcoholics Anonymous. As we have noted previously, the involvement supports their continuing recovery, and their presence provides an invaluable support for newcomers.

Some offenders from the general population who are committed to maintaining their recovery voluntarily continue in weekly support groups for many years. Although much of their initial treatment may have occurred in a specialized, intensive program, the minimal time commitment of a weekly therapy group is easy for the offender to maintain even once reengaged in full-time employment. In an article on offender treatment in the *Family Therapy Networker*, Wylie (1998) described the "continual, nagging fear that keeps them coming back to group sessions, even when no longer legally required to do so" (p. 41). She quoted one member who has been in group for 15 years: "I would like to be able to drop out of the group, but I'm not ready. I will be sitting in a group like this for the rest of my life" (p. 41).

Our aim is to provide a supportive group experience to offenders with intellectual disabilities for as long they need it. We stress the need for continued treatment, especially when the member's improvement leads to significant life changes. We have sometimes had the experience of members being helped to get new jobs following a good period of stability, with caregivers and support staff thinking the member is well enough to end treatment and go on with his employment. We encourage support staff and family to help the member find employment and, at the same time, continue in treatment. The stress of a life change, such as a new job, often leads to a period of instability, which can mean the return of symptoms, including re-offending. The group can be a great source of support as the offender goes on to make important life changes.

Sometimes, an offender becomes intent on ending his treatment. We support this desire if we feel he has made significant progress as defined by the three parameters noted earlier. For those who do not yet meet the three indicators, we share with them our specific concerns. We present a rationale for their continued involvement, along with clear, specific behaviors that would suggest readiness for graduation. The majority of our members are not legally obligated to stay in treatment, and we acknowledge their right to make their own decision, while also making certain they understand what they may risk by leaving. We have found that only a small percentage actually terminate prematurely once they have been well integrated into the group and have the support of their caregivers or staff behind them. Premature terminations have more often resulted when significant others had reasons for ending the patient's group memberships. We discuss these next. In any case, we typically call a meeting together, to make sure all parties involved with the individual are apprised of the potential risks and of our recommendations.

UNPLANNED TERMINATIONS

In chapter 9, we discussed the case of a young man who was removed from one of our treatment groups by his father, who was angry and over-whelmed by the fallout from his son's sexual offense. A more common reason for premature termination is a move to a new location. In any case, we attempt to set up a meeting in which the patient, one of the facilitators, and the caregivers can plan for continuing treatment and monitoring of the patient's behaviors. We document this meeting in the patient's file. If the involved parties are not willing or able to attend a meeting, we write a letter with our recommendations. This letter can be given to the patient with copies to the legal guardian and other key individuals with the permission of the patient or his legal guardian.

When members leave a group, especially if the departure was abrupt, the remaining members should be given ample opportunity to discuss their feelings about the matter. Facilitators cannot disclose confidential information to the other members, who may have numerous questions about the departure. Facilitators need to be clear and direct in telling members that they are constrained from sharing details. At the same time, however, facilitators can share that they understand the remaining members' frustration. They can create a safe place for members to discuss their reactions. Members will often share feelings and fears in the wake of terminations that prove valuable for their own therapy.

RETURNS TO TREATMENT

Sometimes members are referred back to treatment because symptoms have reemerged. In some cases, members are stable for a number of years before this occurs. As in Martina's case, described at the beginning of this book, we always welcome such returns. When members leave, whether through planned or unplanned terminations, we make a point of explaining that the member is always welcome to come back.

Usually, the second round of treatment is characterized by a quick reintegration into the group process. In addition, members are often functioning at relatively improved levels and can more easily make changes. We frame the return to group as an additional growth step representing the member's motivation to further improve his life. A returning member who voices the belief that he is in some way a failure meets with a vigorous challenge to this belief. Certainly for individuals with depression, who are loaded with self-blame, "failures" need to be construed as symptoms of the depression. The individual is then helped to understand what factors (experiences and beliefs) lead to her depression and what changes she can make. This is much of the work of therapy. The sense of self as failure must be tackled with unswerving force. With an offender who may view himself as a failure, similar challenges to his self-concept must be made. Steadfast attention must be given to demonstrate respect for the individual, while at the same time maintaining his responsibility for his behavior, both offensive and prosocial.

Some members independently ask to come back to group. For example, Joanna, whom we described earlier in the chapter, told her mother and her staff that she would like to return to group approximately five years after her graduation. She had been feeling a great deal of subjective distress following a serious surgery and lengthy recovery. Also, both her mother and stepfather were ill with cancer and receiving chemotherapy. In reaction to these new stressors Joanna was experiencing the same sort of depressive symptoms as she had some years earlier. To her credit, she was able to acknowledge the need for help and to ask for it. We affirmed her for doing so, and she easily integrated herself into a group with mostly new members. And in case you think Joanna is unusually capable for having had the awareness to ask for treatment, you should know that her IQ, measured at various points throughout her 50-plus years, hovers around 50–55, placing her at the high end of moderate mental retardation to the low end of mild; there are reports that categorize her at each. And, although living with her family now, Joanna spent a number of her younger years at the notorious Willowbrook before its well-publicized close.

SUMMARY

In this chapter we have discussed matters pertaining to the ending of treatment, including how to determine readiness to terminate, as well as how to prepare for the termination of individuals whose behavior has been known to harm others. In addition, we have discussed ways in which to approach termination with members who are ready but do not seek to leave voluntarily. Perhaps the single-most unique factor related to the termination of individuals with intellectual disabilities is their relative lack of self-initiation in this regard, compared with patients from the general population. This phenomenon is likely to be related to the overall higher levels of passivity common to people with intellectual disabilities, as we noted in earlier chapters. It also appears to be related to the relative lack of a supportive and enjoyable social network. Many members find their most reliable sense of social support and meaningful connection in their therapy group. Of course, this often happens with nondisabled people as well. However, the focus of treatment then takes a turn toward helping that individual navigate the process of developing sustaining connections outside the group.

People with intellectual disabilities need considerable assistance to accomplish these connections. Often, professional systems must become involved. Referring the individual to recreational services and helping them negotiate relationships with peers can be a crucial aspect of his therapy. Similarly, helping an individual cope with a new living arrangement, or initiate a move, or take steps to find a job when he has been isolated at home for years, can be key elements of his therapy. These processes, although similar to the processes of many nondisabled individuals who need to develop new social connections, often require the involvement of others: family members, sponsors, group home or apartment staff, or professional recreation program staff. Note that this is not simply a matter of making a referral. It is analogous to helping the nondisabled patient build and utilize social relationships, but with the added assistance of systems intervention. Once these connections are in place and the individual is able to make use of them, his readiness to end treatment can be addressed.

Termination from treatment, of course, is the beginning of a new phase in the individual's life. We have stressed the importance of helping the individual to leave with a cognitive understanding of her gains, as well as a felt sense of self-efficacy in her own ability to go about her life. We make a point of a creating a ceremony that affirms the individual and that conveys an unequivocal sense of support; no matter where she may go from here, she will take the feeling of this group with her. A group of people stand behind her who believe in her, accept her mistakes or difficulties, and admire her progress. She goes forward on a foundation of caring.

11

ENDINGS AND BEGINNINGS

Whatever you can do or dream you can, begin it.
Boldness has genius, magic and power in it.

—Goethe

The Centers for Disease Control and Prevention (1996, sect. 1) reported that "Mental retardation is the most common developmental disability and ranks first among chronic conditions causing major activity limitations among persons in the United States." Yet, people with mental retardation constitute approximately 3% of the population, for children and adults, in the United States and throughout the world (World Health Organization, 2001), a fact of which we have been reminded on numerous occasions. Most often, this statistic is supplied in the form of a rationale for the absence of treatment initiatives. In this book, we have looked long and hard at the numerous historical reasons for the lack of mental health treatment for people with intellectual disabilities. And, as we noted in chapter 2, there is clearly a growing interest in providing treatment for this long-underserved group, as evidenced in the literature and in the growth of supporting organizations. Unfortunately, some mainstream clinical publications and conferences still deem treatment issues for people with intellectual disabilities too peripheral to merit consideration (personal communication, R. Simon [Ed.], *The Psychotherapy Networker*, October 14, 2003). Even for those of us without disabilities, the process of change can be a slow one.

In discussing prevalence rates, we might do well to consider the prevalence of other disorders in the population. The U.S. Department of Health and Human Services reports the following statistics (National Institute of Mental Health, 2003): In the United States, bipolar disorder affects approximately 1.2% of the population; schizophrenia affects roughly 1.1%. A major depressive disorder, which is one of the more common disorders, is found in approximately 5% of the adult population; dysthymic disorder is reported to affect 5.4% of adults. Some of the more prevalent anxiety disorders have the following rates of occurrence in adults: panic disorder, 1.7%; obsessive–compulsive disorder, 2.3%; generalized anxiety disorder, 2.8%; and, agoraphobia, 2.2%. We might contend that these, too, are small percentages of the population. However, while data are important, they are not the whole story. What quantifiers do we attach to the young woman who cannot seem to stop cutting her own arm, or to the child whose father's functioning has been lost to an intractable depression? What numbers might give meaning to their pain?

Even posttraumatic stress disorder (PTSD), which has garnered so much research interest and public attention in recent years, affects only about 3.6% of the population during a given year. Roughly 30% of Vietnam veterans meet the criteria for PTSD, however—a sizable number. It is noteworthy that it was the advocacy of these veterans, angry and wounded heroes from a war their own country devalued, that propelled PTSD to center stage. Their trauma led to the recognition that certain experiences are so far outside the range of normal human encounters that no one can be unaffected. PTSD acknowledges the vulnerability of the human condition, without implicating the individual as deficient in some way. The call to attention begun by these veterans was joined by feminist advocates, and recognition was given to the universal effects of trauma, now documented in rape and sexual assault survivors, as well as combat veterans and numerous other trauma survivors (McFarlane & van der Kolk, 1996). Countless women who have suffered, and will suffer, sexual abuse in isolation have been powerfully benefited by the momentum spurred by veteran groups who, already banded together by their military experience, demanded attention, understanding, and help.

Mental retardation, like PTSD, reminds us of the vulnerability of the human condition, an uncomfortable piece of reality many of us prefer not to think about. Nevertheless, a reliable percentage of the human population will be born with congenital or trauma-induced or illness-induced damage to the brain. Still other infants and children, through illness or accidents, will sustain enough brain damage to prevent normative developmental growth. It is a fact of existence: Not every human being will have the same opportunities to develop. Some will sustain damage severe enough to cast them into the bottom 3%.

It is unlikely that formidable ex-military groups will ever be in a position to rally for the rights of people with intellectual disabilities. Arguably, that is not for them to do. But, perhaps, those of us who do clinical work, who have experience to bring to this profound need, can direct ourselves toward this end. Having heightened our awareness, we can now begin to expand our skills. We can begin our process of change.

A circle is both the form we use for group sessions and the symbol for continuity. Who can say where the circle ends? Each end point is also a beginning. If you will allow the analogy, we hope that the same will be the case for the ending of this book, that it will be a beginning for each of you who reads it.

Mental health treatment for people with intellectual disabilities remains unavailable in many areas. In traveling to conferences and trainings throughout the United States and abroad, we hear over and over about the difficulties in finding clinicians who can treat people with intellectual disabilities. Those of you who have read this book are among the instrumental people preparing to do more.

We urge you to begin.

REFERENCES

American Psychiatric Association. (1994). *Diagnostic and statistical manual of mental disorders* (4th ed.). Washington, DC: Author.

Baroff, G. (1996). The mentally retarded offender. In J. Jacobson & J. Mulick (Eds.), *Manual of diagnosis and professional practice in mental retardation* (pp. 311–321). Washington, DC: American Psychological Association.

Bateson, M. C. (1994). *Peripheral visions: Learning along the way*. New York: Harper Collins.

Berger, K. S. (2001). *The developing person through the life span*. New York: Worth Publishers.

Berrick, J., & Gilbert, N. (1991). *With the best of intentions: The child sexual abuse prevention movement*. New York: Guilford Press.

Blaine, C. (1993). *Interpersonal learning in short-term integrated group psychotherapy*. Unpublished master's thesis, University of Alberta, Alberta, Canada.

Blatner, A., & Blatner, A. (1988). *Foundations of psychodrama history: Theory and practice*. New York: Springer.

Bloch, S., & Crouch, E. (1985). *Therapeutic factors in group psychotherapy*. New York: Oxford University Press.

Browning, P. L. (Ed.). (1974). *Mental retardation: Rehabilitation and counseling*. Springfield, IL: Charles C Thomas.

Burke, L., & Bedard, C. (1995). A preliminary study of the association between self-injury and sexual abuse in persons with developmental handicaps. *Sexuality and Disability, 13,* 327–330.

Burton, D. (2000). Were adolescent sexual offenders children with sexual behavior problems? *Sexual Abuse: A Journal of Research and Treatment, 12*(1), 37–48.

Butz, M., Bowling, J., & Bliss, C. (2000). Psychotherapy with the mentally retarded: A review of the literature and the implications. *Professional Psychology: Research and Practice, 31,* 42–47.

Caine, A., & Hatton, C. (1998). Working with people with mental health problems. In E. Emerson, C. Hatton, J. Bromley, & A. Caine (Eds.), *Clinical psychology and people with intellectual disabilities* (pp. 210–230). Chichester, England: Wiley.

Carey, A. (1997). Survivor revictimization: Object relations dynamics and treatment implications. *Journal of Counseling and Development, 75,* 357–365.

Carlin, M. (1998). *Death, bereavement, and grieving: A group intervention for bereaved individuals with cerebral palsy*. Unpublished doctoral dissertation, Long Island University, C.W. Post Campus.

Carlson, B. E. (1998). Domestic violence in adults with mental retardation: Reports from victims and key informants. *Mental Health Aspects of Developmental Disabilities, 1*(4), 102–112.

Centers for Disease Control and Prevention. (1996, January 26). State-specific rates of mental retardation, United States, 1993. *Morbidity and Mortality Weekly Report, 45*(3), 61–65. Retrieved November 19, 2003, from http://www.cdc.gov/mmwr/preview/mmwrhtml/00040023.htm#00001471.htm

Charlot, L. (1998). Developmental effects on mental health disorders in persons with developmental disabilities. *Mental Health Aspects of Developmental Disabilities, 1*(2), 29–38.

Charlot, L., Doucette, A., & Mezzacappa, E. (1993). Affective symptoms of institutionalized adults with mental retardation. *American Journal on Mental Retardation, 98,* 408–416.

Cox-Lindenbaum, D. (2001). Group therapy for mentally retarded sex offenders. In A. Dosen & K. Day (Eds.), *Treating mental illness and behavior disorders in children and adults with mental retardation* (pp. 343–357). Washington, DC: American Psychiatric Press.

Cox-Lindenbaum, D., & Lindenbaum, L. (1996). The parallel process in the clinical treatment of persons with developmental disabilities and the supervision of mental health professionals: Supporting the therapist in abuse focused treatment. *The NADD Newsletter, 13*(2), 1–4.

Daniels, L. (1998). A group cognitive–behavioral and process-oriented approach to treating the social impairment and negative symptoms associated with chronic mental illness. *Journal of Psychotherapy Research and Practice, 7,* 167–176.

Davis, M. K., & Gidyez, C. A. (2000). Child sexual assault prevention programs: A meta-analysis. *Journal of Clinical Child Psychology, 29,* 257–265.

Day, K. (1997). Clinical features and offense behavior of mentally retarded sex offenders: A review of research. *The NADD Newsletter, 14*(6), 86–90.

Day, K. (2001). Treatment: An integrative approach. In A. Dosen & K. Day (Eds.), *Treating mental illness and behavior disorders in children and adults with mental retardation* (pp. 519–528). Washington, DC: American Psychiatric Press.

Emerson, E., Hatton, C., Bromley, J., & Caine, A. (Eds.). (1998). *Clinical psychology and people with intellectual disabilities.* Chichester, England: Wiley.

Fago, D. (1999). Co-morbidity of attention deficit hyperactivity disorder in sexually aggressive children and adolescents. *The Forum* (A publication of ATSA: The Association for the Treatment of Sexual Abusers), *XI*(1), 3–4.

Fletcher, R. J. (Ed.). (2000). *Therapy approaches for persons with mental retardation.* Kingston, NY: NADD Press.

Fletcher, R. J., & Dosen, A. (Eds.). (1993). *Mental health aspects of mental retardation.* New York: Lexington Books/Macmillan.

Ford, J. D., & Stewart, J. (1999). Group psychotherapy for war-related PTSD with military veterans. In B. Young & D. Blake (Eds.), *Group treatments for posttraumatic stress disorder* (pp. 75–100). Philadelphia: Brunner/Mazel, Taylor & Francis Group.

Friedman, S. H., Festinger, D. S., Nezu, C. M., McGuffin, P. W., & Nezu, A. M. (1999). Group therapy for mentally retarded sex offenders: A behavioral approach. *Behavior Therapist, 22*(2), 32–33.

Furey, E. (1994). Sexual abuse of adults who have mental retardation: Who and where. *Mental Retardation, 32,* 173–180.

Gardner, W. (2000). Behavioral therapies: Using diagnostic formulation to individualize treatment for persons with developmental disabilities. In R. Fletcher (Ed.), *Effective therapy approaches for persons with mental retardation* (pp. 1–25). Kingston, NY: NADD Press.

Gardner, W., Graeber, J., & Cole, C. (1996). Behavior therapies: A multimodal diagnostic and intervention model. In J. Jacobson & J. Mulick (Eds.), *Manual of diagnosis and professional practice in mental retardation* (pp. 355–369). Washington, DC: American Psychological Association.

Gardner, W., Graeber, J., & Machkovitz, S. (1998). Treatment of offenders with mental retardation. In R. Wettstein (Ed.), *Treatment of offenders with mental disorders* (pp. 329–364). New York: Guilford Press.

Gaus, V. (2002, October). *What is cognitive–behavioral therapy and can it help people with mental retardation/developmental disabilities?* Keynote address presented at the First International Congress on Psychotherapy for People With Mild/Moderate Intellectual Disabilities (Symposium Hoeve Boschoord: Psychotherapie Bij Mensen met een Lichte Verstandelijke Handicap), Zwolle, The Netherlands.

Goleman, D. (1995). *Emotional intelligence.* New York: Bantam Books.

Groth, A. N., & Oliveri, F. (1989). Understanding sexual offense behavior and differentiating among sexual abusers: Basic conceptual issues. In S. Sgroi (Ed.), *Vulnerable populations: Vol. 2. Sexual abuse treatment for children, adult survivors, offenders, and persons with mental retardation* (pp. 309–327). Lexington, MA: Lexington Books.

Haaven, L., Little, R., & Petre-Miller, D. (1990). *Treating intellectually disabled offenders: A model residential program.* Orwell, VT: Safer Society Press.

Halpern, A. S., & Berard, W. R. (1974). Counseling the mentally retarded: A review for practice. In P. L. Browning (Ed.), *Mental retardation: Rehabilitation and counseling* (pp. 269–289). Springfield, IL: Charles C Thomas.

Hansen, N. B., Lambert, M. J., & Forman, E. M. (2002). The psychotherapy dose–response effect and its implications for treatment delivery services. *Clinical Psychology Science and Practice, 9,* 329–343.

Harney, P. A., & Harvey, M. R. (1999). Group psychotherapy: An overview. In B. Young & D. Blake (Eds.), *Group treatments for post-traumatic stress disorder* (pp. 1–14). Philadelphia: Brunner/Mazel, Taylor & Francis Group.

Haseltine, B., & Miltenberger, R. (1990). Teaching self-protection skills to persons with mental retardation. *American Journal on Mental Retardation, 95,* 188–197.

Herman, J. (1992a). Complex PTSD: A syndrome in survivors of prolonged and repeated trauma. *Journal of Traumatic Stress, 5,* 377–391.

Herman, J. (1992b). *Trauma and recovery*. New York: Basic Books.

Herman, J. (1995). Crime and memory. *Bulletin of the American Academy of Psychiatry and the Law, 23*(1), 5–17.

Hingsburger, D. (1995). *Just say know: Understanding and reducing the risk of sexual victimization of people with developmental disabilities*. Eastman, Quebec, Canada: Diverse City Press.

Hodges, S. (2003). *Counselling adults with learning disabilities*. Basingstoke, England: Palgrave.

Hudgins, M. K., & Drucker, K. (1998). The containing double as part of the therapeutic spiral model for treating trauma survivors. *International Journal of Action Methods: Psychodrama, Skill Training, and Role Playing, 51*(2), 63–74.

Hudgins, M. K., & Kipper, D. A. (1998). Introduction: Action methods in the treatment of trauma survivors. *International Journal of Action Methods: Psychodrama, Skill Training, and Role Playing, 51*(2), 43–46.

Hunsberger, M. (1999). No more secrets. *People With Disabilities, 9*(2), 28–30.

Hurley, A. D. (1989). Individual psychotherapy with mentally retarded individuals: A review and call for research. *Research in Developmental Disabilities, 10*, 261–275.

Hurley, A. D., & Hurley, F. J. (1986). Counseling and psychotherapy with mentally retarded clients: I. The initial interview. *Psychiatric Aspects of Mental Retardation Reviews, 5*(5), 22–26.

Hurley, A. D., & Hurley, F. J. (1987). Psychotherapy and counseling: II. Establishing a therapeutic relationship. *Psychiatric Aspects of Mental Retardation Reviews, 4*(4), 15–20.

Hurley, A. D., Pfadt, A., Tomasulo, D., & Gardner, W. (1996). Counseling and psychotherapy. In J. Jacobson & J. Mulick (Eds.), *Manual of diagnosis and professional practice in mental retardation* (pp. 371–378). Washington, DC: American Psychological Association.

Hurley, A. D., & Silka, V. R. (1998). Cognitive–behavioral treatment for panic disorder. *Mental Health Aspects of Developmental Disabilities, 1*(4), 119–123.

Hurley, A. D., & Sovner, R. (1991). Cognitive behavior therapy for depression in individuals with developmental disabilities. *Habilitative Mental Healthcare Newsletter, 10*, 41–47.

Hurley, A. D., Tomasulo, D., & Pfadt, A. (1998). Individual and group psychotherapy approaches for persons with mental retardation and developmental disabilities. *Journal of Developmental and Physical Disabilities, 10*, 365–386.

Jacobson, J., & Mulick, J. (Eds.). (1996). *Manual of diagnosis and professional practice in mental retardation*. Washington, DC: American Psychological Association.

Jensen, C. J. (2000). Challenging the ATSA membership to really "make society safer." *The Forum* (A publication of ATSA: The Association for the Treatment of Sexual Abusers), *XII*(3), 1–3.

Kaminer, Y., Feinstein, C., & Barrett, R. P. (1987). Suicidal behavior in mentally retarded adolescents: An overlooked problem. *Child Psychiatry and Human Development, 18,* 90–94.

Keller, E. (1993). *Process and outcomes in interactive–behavioral groups with adults who have both mental illness and mental retardation.* Unpublished doctoral dissertation, Long Island University, C. W. Post Campus.

Keller, E. (2000). Points of intervention: Facilitating the process of psychotherapy with people who have developmental disabilities. In R. Fletcher (Ed.), *Therapy approaches for persons with mental retardation* (pp. 27–47). Kingston, NY: NADD Press.

Kirchner, L., & Mueth, M. (2000). Suicide in individuals with developmental disabilities. In R. Fletcher (Ed.), *Therapy approaches for persons with mental retardation* (pp. 127–150). Kingston, NY: NADD Press.

Kroese, B. S. (1997). Cognitive–behaviour therapy for people with learning disabilities: Conceptual and contextual issues. In B. S. Kroese, D. Dagnan, & K. Loumidis (Eds.), *Cognitive–behaviour therapy for people with learning disabilities* (pp. 1–15). London: Routledge.

Kroese, B. S., Dagnan, D., & Loumidis, K. (Eds.). (1997). *Cognitive–behaviour therapy for people with learning disabilities.* London: Routledge.

Levitas, A. S., & Gilson, S. F. (1997). Individual psychotherapy for persons with mild and moderate mental retardation. *NADD Newsletter, 13*(4), 34–38.

Levitas, A. S., & Gilson, S. F. (2000). Transference/countertransference in individual psychotherapy. In R. Fletcher (Ed.), *Therapy approaches for persons with mental retardation* (pp. 49–64). Kingston, NY: NADD Press.

Levitas, A. S., & Gilson, S. F. (2001). Predictable crises in the lives of people with mental retardation. *Mental Health Aspects of Developmental Disabilities, 4*(3), 89–100.

Lewis, T., Amini, F., & Lannon, R. (2000). *A general theory of love.* New York: Vintage Books/Random House.

Luiselli, J. (2000). Introduction to the special issue. *Mental Health Aspects of Developmental Disabilities, 3*(2), 41–42.

Lumley, V., & Miltenberger, R. (1997). Sexual abuse prevention for persons with mental retardation. *American Journal on Mental Retardation, 101,* 459–472.

Lumley, V., & Miltenberger, R. (1998). Evaluation of a sexual abuse prevention program for adults with mental retardation. *Journal of Applied Behavior Analysis, 31,* 91–101.

Macklin, M. L., Metzger, L. J., Litz, B. T., McNally, R. J., Lasko, N. B., Orr, S. P., et al. (1998). Lower precombat intelligence is a risk factor for posttraumatic stress disorder. *Journal of Consulting and Clinical Psychology, 66,* 323–326.

Mansell, S., & Sobsey, D. (2001). *The Aurora Project: Counseling people with developmental disabilities who have been sexually abused.* Kingston, NY: NADD Press.

Mansell, S., Sobsey, D., & Calder, P. (1992). Sexual abuse treatment for persons with developmental disabilities. *Professional Psychology: Research and Practice, 23*, 404–409.

Mansell, S., Sobsey, D., & Moskal, R. (1998). Clinical findings among sexually abused children with and without developmental disabilities. *Mental Retardation, 36*, 12–22.

Marineau, R. F. (1989). *Jacob Levy Moreno, 1889–1974*. London: Routledge.

Marshall, R. D., Olfson, M., Hellman, F., Blanco, C., Guardino, M., & Struening, E. L. (2001). Comorbidity, impairment, and suicidality in subthreshold PTSD. *American Journal of Psychiatry, 158*, 1467–1473.

Marshall, W. L., & Mazzucco, A. (1995). Self-esteem and parental attachments in child molesters. *Sexual Abuse: A Journal of Research and Treatment, 7*, 279–285.

Marshall, W. L., Thornton, D., Marshall, L. E., Fernandez, Y. M., & Mann, R. E. (2001). Treatment of sexual offenders who are in categorical denial: A pilot project. *Sexual Abuse: A Journal of Research and Treatment, 13*, 205–215.

Matich-Maroney, J. (2003). Mental health implications for sexually abused adults with mental retardation: Some clinical research findings. *Mental Health Aspects of Developmental Disabilities, 6*(1), 11–20.

Mayou, R. (2001). Prediction of psychological outcomes one year after a motor vehicle accident. *American Journal of Psychiatry, 158*, 1231–1238.

McDermut, W., Miller, I. W., & Brown, R. (2001). The efficacy of group psychotherapy for depression: A meta-analysis and review of the empirical research. *Clinical Psychology: Science and Practice, 8*, 98–116.

McFarlane, A. C., & De Girolamo, G. (1996). The nature of traumatic stressors and the epidemiology of posttraumatic reactions. In B. A. van der Kolk, A. C. McFarlane, & L. Weisaeth (Eds.), *Traumatic stress: The effects of overwhelming experience on mind, body, and society* (pp. 129–154). New York: Guilford Press.

McFarlane, A. C., & van der Kolk, B. A. (1996). Conclusions and future directions. In B. A. van der Kolk, A. C. McFarlane, & L. Weisaeth (Eds.), *Traumatic stress: The effects of overwhelming experience on mind, body, and society* (pp. 559–575). New York: Guilford Press.

McWilliams, N. (1994). *Psychoanalytic diagnosis: Understanding personality structure in the clinical process*. New York: Guilford Press.

McWilliams, N. (1999). *Psychoanalytic case formulation*. New York: Guilford Press.

Miltenberger, R., Roberts, J., Ellingson, S., Galensky, T., Rapp, J., Long, E., et al. (1999). Training and generalization of sexual abuse prevention skills for women with mental retardation. *Journal of Applied Behavior Analysis, 32*, 385–388.

Monat-Haller, R. (1992). *Understanding and expressing sexuality: Responsible choices for people with developmental disabilities*. Baltimore: Paul H. Brooks.

Monday Morning: A newsletter of the New Jersey Developmental Disabilities Council. (2002). Surgeon General releases report on health disparities and mental retardation. *Copy Editor, 8*(6).

Morgan, R. D., & Flora, D. B. (2002). Group psychotherapy with incarcerated offenders: A research synthesis. *Group Dynamics: Theory, Research, and Practice, 6*, 203–218.

Moss, S. (2001). Psychiatric disorders in adults with mental retardation. In L. M. Glidden (Ed.), *International review of research in mental retardation* (pp. 211–243). San Diego, CA: Academic Press.

Murphy, L., & Razza, N. (1998). Domestic violence against women with mental retardation. In A. Roberts (Ed.), *Battered women and their families* (pp. 271–290). New York: Springer.

National Institute of Mental Health. (2003, May). *The numbers count: Mental disorders in America.* Retrieved November 8, 2003, from http://www.nimh.nih.gov

Nezu, C. M., & Nezu, A. M. (1994). Outpatient psychotherapy for adults with mental retardation and concomitant psychopathology: Research and clinical imperatives. *Journal of Consulting and Clinical Psychology, 62*, 34–42.

Nezu, C. M., Nezu, A. M., & Gill-Weiss, M. J. (1992). *Psychopathology in persons with mental retardation: Clinical guidelines for assessment and treatment.* Champaign, IL: Research Press.

Nugent, J. (1997). *Handbook on dual diagnosis: Supporting people with a developmental disability and a mental health problem.* Evergreen, CO: Mariah Management.

Oliver-Brannon, G. (2000). Counseling and psychotherapy in group treatment with the dually diagnosed (mental retardation and mental illness—MR/MI) (Doctoral dissertation, The Union Institute, 2000). *Dissertation Abstracts International, 60*(10-B), 5230.

Othmer, E., & Othmer, S. (1994). *The clinical interview using DSM–IV.* Washington, DC: American Psychiatric Press.

Perlman, N., & Ericson, K. (1992). Issues related to sexual abuse of persons with developmental disabilities: An overview. *Journal on Developmental Disabilities, 1*(1), 19–23.

Pfadt, A. (1991). Group psychotherapy with mentally retarded adults: Issues related to design, implementation, and evaluation. *Research in Developmental Disabilities, 12*, 261–285.

Prescott, D. (2002). Book review: Developmentally delayed persons with sexual behavior problems: Treatment, management, supervision, and program manual and forms. *The Forum* (A publication of ATSA: The Association for the Treatment of Sexual Abusers), *XIV*(1), 10.

Prout, H. T., & Cale, R. L. (1994). Individual counseling approaches. In D. C. Strohmer & H. T. Prout (Eds.), *Counseling and psychotherapy with persons with mental retardation and borderline intelligence* (pp. 103–141). Brandon, VT: Clinical Psychology Publishing.

Prout, H. T., & Strohmer, D. C. (1994). Issues in counseling and psychotherapy. In D. C. Strohmer & H. T. Prout (Eds.), *Counseling and psychotherapy with persons with mental retardation and borderline intelligence* (pp. 1–19). Brandon, VT: Clinical Psychology Publishing.

Prout, H. T., & Strohmer, D. C. (1995). Counseling with persons with mental retardation. *Journal of Applied Rehabilitation Counseling, 26*(3), 49–54.

Ragg, D., Mark, L. B., & Rowe, W. (1991). The effective use of group in sex education with people diagnosed as mildly developmentally disabled. *Sexuality and Disability, 9,* 337–352.

Raphael, B., Wilson, J., Meldrum, L., & McFarlane, A. C. (1996). Acute preventive interventions. In B. A. van der Kolk, A. C. McFarlane, & L. Weisaeth (Eds.), *Traumatic stress: The effects of overwhelming experience on mind, body, and society* (pp. 463–479). New York: Guilford Press.

Raymond, N., Coleman, E., Ohler King, F., Christenson, G., & Miner, M. (1999). Psychiatric comorbidity in pedophilic sex offenders. *American Journal of Psychiatry, 156,* 786–788.

Razza, N., & Tomasulo, D. (1996a). The sexual abuse continuum: Therapeutic interventions with individuals with mental retardation. *Habilitative Mental Healthcare Newsletter, 15,* 84–86.

Razza, N., & Tomasulo, D. (1996b). The sexual abuse continuum: Part 2. Therapeutic interventions with individuals with mental retardation. *Habilitative Mental Healthcare Newsletter, 15,* 84–86.

Razza, N., & Tomasulo, D. (1996c). The sexual abuse continuum: Part 3. Therapeutic interventions with individuals with mental retardation. *Habilitative Mental Healthcare Newsletter, 15,* 116–119.

Reiss, S., Levitan, G., & McNally, R. (1982). Emotionally disturbed mentally retarded people: An underserved population. *American Psychologist, 37,* 361–367.

Reiss, S., Levitan, G., & Szyszko, J. (1982). Emotional disturbance and mental retardation: Diagnostic overshadowing. *American Journal of Mental Deficiency, 86,* 567–574.

Root, M. P. (1991). Persistent, disordered eating as a gender-specific, post-traumatic stress response to sexual assault. *Psychotherapy, 28,* 96–102.

Rose, J. U., Jenkins, R., O'Connor, C., Jones, C., & Felce, D. (2002). A group treatment for men with intellectual disabilities who sexually offend or abuse. *Journal of Applied Research in Intellectual Disabilities, 15,* 138–150.

Ryan, R. (1994). Posttraumatic stress disorder in persons with developmental disabilities. *Community Mental Health Journal, 30,* 1.

Sawyer, S. (2000). Some thoughts about why we believe group therapy is the preferred modality for treating sex offenders. *The Forum* (A publication of ATSA: The Association for the Treatment of Sexual Abusers), *XII*(2), 11–12.

Schneider, N. (1986). Treatment and group therapy with dually diagnosed populations. *Journal for Specialists in Group Work, 11,* 151–156.

Schwartz, S. A., & Ruedrich, S. (1996). Psychopathology update: On the distinction between mental illness and behavior problems in persons with mental retardation. *Psychiatric Aspects of Mental Retardation Review, 15*(3), 60–63.

Seghorn, T., & Ball, C. (2000). Assessment of sexual deviance in adults with developmental disabilities. *Mental Health Aspects of Developmental Disabilities, 3*(2), 47–53.

Seligman, M. (1996). Science as the ally of practice. *American Psychologist, 51,* 1072–1079.

Sgroi, S. (1989). Evaluation and treatment of sexual offense behavior in persons with mental retardation. In S. Sgroi (Ed.), *Vulnerable populations: Vol. 2. Sexual abuse treatment for children, adult survivors, offenders, and persons with mental retardation* (pp. 245–284). Lexington, MA: Lexington Books.

Sgroi, S., Carey, J., & Wheaton, A. (1989). Sexual abuse avoidance training for adults with mental retardation. In S. Sgroi (Ed.), *Vulnerable populations: Vol. 2. Sexual abuse treatment for children, adult survivors, offenders, and persons with mental retardation* (pp. 203–216). Lexington, MA: Lexington Books.

Shalev, A. Y. (1996). Stress versus traumatic stress: From acute homeostatic reactions to chronic psychopathology. In B. A. van der Kolk, A. C. McFarlane, & L. Weisaeth (Eds.), *Traumatic stress: The effects of overwhelming experience on mind, body, and society* (pp. 77–101). New York: Guilford Press.

Shapiro, J. P. (1991). Interviewing children about psychological issues associated with sexual abuse. *Psychotherapy, 28,* 55–66.

Sinason, V. (1997). The learning disabled (mentally handicapped) offender. In E. Welldon & C. Van Velsen (Eds.), *A practical guide to forensic psychotherapy* (pp. 56–61). London: Kingsley.

Singh, N. N., Osborne, J. G., & Huguenin, N. H. (1996). Applied behavioral interventions. In J. Jacobson & J. Mulick (Eds.), *Manual of diagnosis and professional practice in mental retardation* (pp. 341–353). Washington, DC: American Psychological Association.

Smallbone, S. W., & Dadds, M. R. (2000). Attachment and coercive behavior. *Sexual Abuse: A Journal of Research and Treatment, 12,* 3–15.

Sternberg, P., & Garcia, A. (2000). *Sociodrama: Who's in your shoes?* (2nd ed.). Westport, CT: Praeger.

Strohmer, D. C., & Prout, H. T. (Eds.). (1994). *Counseling and psychotherapy with persons with mental retardation and borderline intelligence.* Brandon, VT: Clinical Psychology Publishing.

Szymanski, L. S. (1980). Individual psychotherapy with retarded persons. In L. S. Szymanski & P. S. Tanguay (Eds.), *Emotional disorders of mentally retarded persons* (pp. 131–147). Baltimore: University Park Press.

Tomasulo, D. (1992). *Group counseling for people with mild to moderate mental retardation and developmental disabilities: An interactive–behavioral model* [Video]. New York: Young Adult Institute.

Tomasulo, D. (1994). Action techniques in group counseling: The double. *Habilitative Mental Healthcare Newsletter, 13*(3), 41–45.

Tomasulo, D. (1997). Beginning and maintaining a group. *Habilitative Mental Healthcare Newsletter, 16*(3), 41–48.

Tomasulo, D. (1998a). *Action methods in group psychotherapy: Practical aspects*. Philadelphia: Taylor & Francis.

Tomasulo, D. (1998b). Substance abuse: Who will do it? *Mental Health Aspects of Developmental Disabilities, 1*, 20–22.

Tomasulo, D. (1999). Group therapy for people with mental retardation: The interactive–behavioral therapy model. In D. Wiener (Ed.), *Beyond talk therapy: Using movement and expressive techniques in clinical practice* (pp. 145–164). Washington, DC: American Psychological Association.

Tomasulo, D. (2000). Group therapy for people with mental retardation. In R. Fletcher (Ed.), *Therapy approaches for persons with mental retardation*. Kingston, NY: NADD Press.

Tomasulo, D., Keller, E., & Pfadt, A. (1995). The healing crowd. *Habilitative Mental Healthcare Newsletter, 14*(3), 43–50.

Tough, S., & Hingsburger, D. (1999). Counseling sex offenders with developmental disabilities who deny. *Mental Health Aspects of Developmental Disabilities, 2*, 103–107.

Turner, S. W., McFarlane, A. C., & van der Kolk, B. A. (1996). The therapeutic environment and new explorations in the treatment of posttraumatic stress disorder. In B. A. van der Kolk, A. C. McFarlane, & L. Weisaeth (Eds.), *Traumatic stress: The effects of overwhelming experience on mind, body, and society* (pp. 537–558). New York: Guilford Press.

Ursano, R. J., Grieger, T. A., & McCarrol, J. E. (1996). Prevention of posttraumatic stress: Consultation, training, and early intervention. In B. A. van der Kolk, A. C. McFarlane, & L. Weisaeth (Eds.), *Traumatic stress: The effects of overwhelming experience on mind, body, and society* (pp. 441–462). New York: Guilford Press.

van der Kolk, B. A. (1996). The complexity of adaptation to trauma: Self-regulation, stimulus discrimination, and characterological development. In B. A. van der Kolk, A. C. McFarlane, & L. Weisaeth (Eds.), *Traumatic stress: The effects of overwhelming experience on mind, body, and society* (pp. 182–213). New York: Guilford Press.

van der Kolk, B. A., McFarlane, A. C., & van der Hart, O. (1996). A general approach to treatment of posttraumatic stress disorder. In B. A. van der Kolk, A. C. McFarlane, & L. Weisaeth (Eds.), *Traumatic stress: The effects of overwhelming experience on mind, body, and society* (pp. 417–440). New York: Guilford Press.

Walker, L. E. A. (1994). *Abused women and survivor therapy*. Washington, DC: American Psychological Association.

Walker-Hirsch, L. (1983). *Circles*. Santa Barbara, CA: James Stanfield.

Walker-Hirsch, L. (1986). *Circles: Stop abuse* [Video/multimedia]. Santa Barbara, CA: James Stanfield.

Walker-Hirsch, L. (1988). *Circles: Safer ways* [Video/multimedia]. Santa Barbara, CA: James Stanfield.

Walker-Hirsch, L. (1993). *Circles: Intimacy and relationships* [Video/multimedia]. Santa Barbara, CA: James Stanfield.

Ward, T., Hudson, S. M., & Marshall, W. L. (1996). Attachment style in sex offenders: A preliminary study. *Journal of Sex Research, 33,* 17–26.

Ward, T., Hudson, S. M., Marshall, W. L., & Siegert, R. (1995). Attachment style and intimacy deficits in sexual offenders: A theoretical framework. *Sexual Abuse: A Journal of Research and Treatment, 7,* 317–335.

Wiener, D. J. (1999). *Beyond talk therapy: Using movement and expressive techniques in clinical practice.* Washington, DC: American Psychological Association.

Wisconsin Council on Developmental Disabilities. (1991). *At greater risk: Legal issues in sexual abuse of adults with developmental disabilities (A training guide for caregivers).* Madison, WI: Author.

World Health Organization. (2001). *Mental retardation: Fact Sheet No. 265.* Retrieved November 19, 2003, from http://www.who.int/inf-fs/en/fact265.html

Wylie, M. S. (1998). Secret lives. *The Family Therapy Networker, 22*(6), 38–47, 56–59.

Yalom, I. (1995). *The theory and practice of group psychotherapy* (4th ed.). New York: Basic Books.

Young, B. H., & Blake, D. D. (1999). *Group treatments for post-traumatic stress disorder.* Philadelphia: Brunner/Mazel.

INDEX

Guidance, 56
Guilt, 92, 136, 141, 166–167
    admission of, as treatment
        condition, 94
    See also Denial of guilt

Home care, 4
Hope as therapeutic factor, 55–56
Horizontal self-disclosure, 48, 59
Hurley, A., 153

IBT. *See* Interactive–behavioral therapy
    model
Individual psychotherapy, 64–66, 67–68,
    170
    affirmation stage, 166
    caregiver participation, 155–156,
        163
    case study, 157–168
    communication style, 154–155
    conjoint group therapy, 169–170
    enactment in, 164–166
    indications, 151
    modifications of therapy models for
        people with disabilities, 153–157,
        170
    sexual abuse avoidance training and,
        115, 117
    structure, 155, 170
    transition to group therapy, 168–170
    treatment modalities, 157
    treatment team, 156–157
Informed consent
    for accused offender assessment,
        143–144
    for initial interview, 133
    for sexual abuse avoidance training,
        116–117
    transition from individual psycho-
        therapy to group therapy,
        168–169
Initial interview, 6–7, 149–150
    of accused sexual abuse offender,
        143–144
    assessment of client coping and
        defenses, 135–137
    beginning, 133–134
    challenges in, 131–132
    client consent, 133

client with acquiescent response
    style, 140
confidentiality issues, 133
eliciting disclosure of abuse, 134
forensic issues, 132, 147–148
goals, 132–133, 143
individual psychotherapy case
    example, 160
interpersonal relationships assess-
    ment, 142–143
investigating symptoms, 137–140
resistant client, 144–149
self-concept assessment, 140–142
sensitivity to client emotions in,
    134–135, 137–138
Intellectual disabilities, people with
    ability to generalize learning,
        100–107
    access to care, 12, 21
    advocacy for, 202–203
    assessment considerations, 6–7, 22
    benefits of group therapy, 41–42
    benefits of psychotherapy, 41
    capacity for healing, 18–19, 153
    clinical conceptualization, 4, 11, 42
    depression manifestations, 138
    mental health care trends for, 21–
        23, 152, 201
    modifications of therapy models for,
        153–157
    prevalence, 201
    prevalence of psychopathology
        among, 22, 23–24, 27
    preventive intervention rationale,
        128
    psychopathology risk factors among,
        24–25, 73–74
    sexual abuse complications, 25–27
    sexual abuse risk, 17, 25, 27, 28, 71
    sexual offense behavior by, 29–31
    traumatization risk, 72–75
    understanding of confidentiality
        issues in therapy, 77–78
    whole-person treatment approach,
        108–109
Interactive–behavioral therapy (IBT)
    model
    for abuse avoidance training, 6
    affirmation stage, 45, 52–53, 69,
        100
    applications, 5, 43–44

group therapy efficacy in treatment
for effects of, 67
group therapy rationale, 36
as risk factor for subsequent offense
behavior, 30–31
risk of, for people with intellectual
disabilities, 72–75
as therapy topic, 81
types of, 71, 74–75
See also Sexual abuse
Trauma-specific reenactments, 139–140
Treatment planning, 64–68
for termination, 192–193

Universality, 54–55

Vertical self-disclosure, 48, 49, 59
Videotaping, 153
Vietnam veterans, 202
Violent behavior. *See* Aggressive
behavior
Vocational counselors, 4

Warm-up and sharing, 45–46, 49,
69
in sexual abuse avoidance
training, 117–121

Yalom, I., 53, 79, 180–181, 190–
191

ABOUT THE AUTHORS

Nancy J. Razza, PhD, CGP, is a licensed clinical psychologist and certified group psychotherapist. She maintains a private practice in Holmdel, New Jersey. A corresponding focus includes a 25-year commitment to individuals with intellectual disabilities. She has designed and implemented mental health treatment programs for this population and supervises the training of mental health professionals in this specialized area. She has authored articles and chapters on dual diagnosis, trauma, sexual offense, sexual victimization, and psychological assessment. Dr. Razza serves on the editorial board for the journal *Mental Health Aspects of Developmental Disabilities*.

Daniel J. Tomasulo, PhD, TEP, MFA, is a psychologist, psychodrama trainer, and writer recently appointed to the faculty of New Jersey City University and formerly a visiting faculty member on fellowship at Princeton University. Together with his wife, Dr. Nancy J. Razza, he has gained international recognition for development of the interactive–behavioral therapy (IBT) model of group psychotherapy for people with intellectual and psychiatric disabilities. He is a consultant for YAI/National Institute for People With Disabilities in New York City and is on the editorial board for the journal *Mental Health Aspects of Developmental Disabilities*. He is also a consulting editor for *The Journal of Group Psychotherapy, Psychodrama, and Sociometry* and recipient of their Innovator's Award for development of the IBT model.

Dr. Tomasulo is the author of *Action Methods in Group Psychotherapy* as well as numerous articles on group psychotherapy. He maintains the research and training Web site http://TheHealingCrowd.com.